ILLEGAL IMMIGRATION

Other books in the Current Controversies Series:

ILLEGAL IMMIGRATION

David L. Bender, *Publisher*
Bruno Leone, *Executive Editor*

Bonnie Szumski, *Managing Editor*
Katie de Koster, *Senior Editor*

William Barbour, *Book Editor*

CURRENT X CONTROVERSIES

Cover photo: © David Maung/Impact Visuals

Library of Congress Cataloging-in-Publication Data

Illegal immigration / William Barbour, book editor.
   p. cm. — (Current controversies)
  Includes bibliographical references and index.
  Summary: A collection of articles debating the seriousness of illegal immigration and the adequacy of immigration laws in America.
  ISBN 1-56510-072-7 (lib. : alk. paper) : — ISBN 1-56510-071-9 (pbk. : alk. paper)
  1. Aliens, Illegal—United States.   2. United States—Emigration and immigration—Government policy.   [1. Aliens, Illegal.   2. United States—Emigration and immigration.]   I. Barbour, William, 1963- .   II. Series.
JV6493.I48   1994
353.0081'7—dc20   93-1808
                                                                            CIP
                                                                             AC

Printed on
recycled paper

© 1994 by Greenhaven Press, Inc., PO Box 289009, San Diego, CA 92198-9009
Printed in the U.S.A.

Contents

Chapter 1: How Serious a Problem Is Illegal Immigration?

Illegal Immigration Is a Serious Problem

Illegal Immigration Is Not a Serious Problem

Chapter 2: Does Illegal Immigration Harm the United States?

Yes: Illegal Immigration Harms the United States

No: Illegal Immigrants Are Not Treated Fairly

Chapter 4: How Should the Government Respond to Immigration?

The Government Should Strictly Control Immigration

The Government Should Ease Its Immigration Controls

Foreword

By definition, controversies are "discussions of questions in which opposing opinions clash" (Webster's Twentieth Century Dictionary Unabridged). Few would deny that controversies are a pervasive part of the human condition and exist on virtually every level of human enterprise. Controversies transpire between individuals and among groups, within nations and between nations. Controversies supply the grist necessary for progress by providing challenges and challengers to the status quo. They also create atmospheres where strife and warfare can flourish. A world without controversies would be a peaceful world; but it also would be, by and large, static and prosaic.

The Series' Purpose

The purpose of the Current Controversies series is to explore many of the social, political, and economic controversies dominating the national and international scenes today. Titles selected for inclusion in the series are highly focused and specific. For example, from the larger category of criminal justice, Current Controversies deals with specific topics such as police brutality, gun control, white collar crime, and others. The debates in Current Controversies also are presented in a useful, timeless fashion. Articles and book excerpts included in each title are selected if they contribute valuable, long-range ideas to the overall debate. And wherever possible, current information is enhanced with historical documents and other relevant materials. Thus, while individual titles are current in focus, every effort is made to ensure that they will not become quickly outdated. Books in the Current Controversies series will remain important resources for librarians, teachers, and students for many years.

In addition to keeping the titles focused and specific, great care is taken in the editorial format of each book in the series. Book introductions and chapter prefaces are offered to provide background material for readers. Chapters are organized around several key questions that are answered with diverse opinions representing all points on the political spectrum. Materials in each chapter include opinions in which authors clearly disagree as well as alternative opinions in which authors may agree on a broader issue but disagree on the possible solutions. In this way, the content of each volume in Current Controversies mirrors the mosaic of opinions encountered in society. Readers will quickly realize that there are many viable answers to these complex issues. By questioning each author's conclusions, students and casual readers can begin to develop the critical thinking skills so important to evaluating opinionated material.

Current Controversies is also ideal for controlled research. Each anthology in the series is composed of primary sources taken from a wide gamut of informational categories including periodicals, newspapers, books, United States and foreign government documents, and the publications of private and public organizations. Readers will find factual support for reports, debates, and research papers covering all areas of important issues. In addition, an annotated table of contents, an index, a book and periodical bibliography, and a list of organizations to contact are included in each book to expedite further research.

Perhaps more than ever before in history, people are confronted with diverse and contradictory information. During the Persian Gulf War, for example, the public was not only treated to minute-to-minute coverage of the war, it was also inundated with critiques of the coverage and countless analyses of the factors motivating U.S. involvement. Being able to sort through the plethora of opinions accompanying today's major issues, and to draw one's own conclusions, can be a complicated and frustrating struggle. It is the editors' hope that Current Controversies will help readers with this struggle.

"Contradictory assertions make it difficult to decide whether illegal immigrants are a burden or a blessing on the U.S. economy."

Introduction

The debate over illegal immigration in America often takes the form of two equally persuasive but irreconcilable assertions. The economic impact of immigrants is one area in which such views are especially entrenched. Opponents of immigration argue that large numbers of new immigrants strain the economy by competing for scarce jobs and by draining social service funds. Many immigration advocates, on the other hand, believe that immigrants stimulate the economy by providing cheap labor and by increasing the demand for goods and services. When the immigrants in question are illegal, the debate gets hotter. Undocumented immigrants are frequently accused of taking jobs from legitimate U.S. workers and of abusing the welfare system. At the same time, they are welcomed by many others as highly motivated workers who provide menial services that legal residents are unwilling to perform.

One controversial charge is that illegal immigrants adversely affect U.S. workers. Donald L. Huddle, professor of economics at Rice University in Houston, Texas, argues that illegal immigrants "provide unfair competition for natives and [legal] immigrants by working for cash off the books, either paying no taxes or underpaying taxes . . ., and by undercutting legal wage and safety standards." The result is that "for every 100 undocumented workers at least 65 U.S. workers are displaced or remain unemployed." Not only do they take jobs from U.S. workers; according to Robert N. Dunn Jr., professor of economics at George Washington University in Washington, D.C., illegal immigrants also cause a reduction in the wages of citizens who retain jobs. Dunn argues that illegal immigration has contributed to a dramatic decrease in the real wages (the value of wages in terms of goods and services) of unskilled and low-skilled U.S. workers since the 1970s.

Along with their direct adverse impact on U.S. workers, many believe that illegal immigrants also harm the taxpaying public at large because they utilize social services but pay few taxes to compensate for their costs. John Tanton and Wayne Lutton, editors of the *Social Contract*, a quarterly anti-immigration journal, argue that faulty governmental policies allow illegal immigrants to burden state education, health care, and welfare systems. For example, under the U.S. Constitution, any child born within America's borders—even a child of illegal immigrants—is automatically a U.S. citizen and is therefore eligible for welfare benefits. California governor Pete Wilson believes that "some illegals come to our country simply to have a child born on U.S. soil who can then gain American citizenship. That, of course, renders the child eligible for a host of public benefits." According to *Newsweek*'s Rich Thomas and Andrew Murr, "In California, children born to illegal parents now account for one in eight beneficiaries of one program alone, Aid to Families with Dependent Children (AFDC)."

On the other side, supporters of immigration believe that illegal immigrants stimulate economic progress by providing cheap labor and increasing the demand for goods and services. Dan Lacey, author of *The Essential Immigrant*, contends that "higher immigration results in higher consumption and consequently fuels the economy." Illegal immigrants, furthermore, "often energize the American economy even more" than legal immigrants because they are highly motivated and intrepid. Lacey and others reject the argument that illegal immigrants take jobs from U.S. workers. They contend that illegal immigrants fill a need by taking jobs U.S. workers will not accept due to low wages, harsh conditions, and lack of prestige. Moreover, in *Friends or Strangers: The Impact of Immigrants on the U.S. Economy*, George J. Borjas disputes the theory that illegal immigrants depress the wages of U.S. workers. Citing a study that compares the earnings of U.S. workers in cities with varying numbers of illegal immigrants, he concludes that "there is no evidence . . . to suggest that illegal immigration had a significant adverse impact on the earnings opportunities of any native group."

Many commentators also challenge the argument that illegal immigrants cost U.S. taxpayers more in public service dollars than they pay in taxes. Julian L. Simon, author of *The Economic Consequences of Immigration*, argues that "very small proportions of illegals receive free public services" because illegal immigrants are usually "young adults who need relatively little health care" and because they "are afraid of being apprehended if they apply at government offices." Moreover, many studies on the issue have been misleading, says Simon, because they assess the costs of illegal immigrants to individual states without acknowledging the contributions they make at the federal level. He argues that the payments illegal immigrants make at local, state, and federal levels combined far exceed the costs of benefits they receive from those three sources. Simon concludes that the U.S. citizen does not suffer from the effects of illegal immigration, but on the contrary, taxpayers "exploit illegal immigrants through the public coffers by taking much more from the illegals than is spent on them in public expenditures."

These contradictory assertions make it difficult to decide whether illegal immigrants are a burden or a blessing on the U.S. economy. This debate over the

Introduction

economic effects of illegal immigration is one of the conflicts explored in *Illegal Immigration: Current Controversies*, which contains the following chapters: How Serious a Problem Is Illegal Immigration? Does Illegal Immigration Harm the United States? Are Illegal Immigrants Treated Fairly? How Should the Government Respond to Immigration? Throughout these chapters, similarly persuasive but incompatible assertions convey the complexity and divisiveness of the debate over illegal immigration in America.

Chapter 1

How Serious a Problem Is Illegal Immigration?

CURRENT CONTROVERSIES

Chapter Preface

On June 6, 1993, the *Golden Venture*, a freighter transporting nearly three hundred Chinese immigrants to the United States illegally, hit a sandbar off the coast of New York. Its passengers abandoned ship, and several of them died as they swam toward the shores of America. The *Golden Venture*'s dramatic arrival quickly focused national attention on the growing business of immigrant smuggling from China.

In the days following the shipwreck, the national news media ran numerous stories about gangs of Chinese smugglers that charge immigrants up to thirty thousand dollars apiece for transport to America. *Newsweek*'s Melinda Liu refers to the practice as a "slave trade" because of the cramped, unsanitary conditions aboard the ships and because the immigrants, once in America, are often forced into servitude for several years in order to pay off the smugglers' fees. "Many are forced to work 18-hour days at menial jobs for substandard wages," Liu writes, "and others are forced into prostitution, gambling and crime. . . . Those who fail to pay the gangs face kidnapping, torture and death."

Others, however, applaud the pluck of the hopeful passengers. When the *Golden Venture* ran aground, *New York Times* columnist A.M. Rosenthal, while condemning the behavior of the smugglers, proposed giving the newly arrived immigrants a parade. "Let them in," he writes, "treat them with the courtesy, dignity and respect their brave hearts merit—that is what America should do." Jacob Sullum, associate editor of *Reason* magazine, echoes Rosenthal's call to "let them in." Sullum, furthermore, defends the conduct of the smugglers. Although he concedes that the passengers of the *Golden Venture* were treated poorly, Sullum contends that "it's a mistake to view immigrant smugglers as brutal criminals who exploit the hopes of poor, ignorant peasants. . . . Illegal immigrants from China seem to be getting what they bargained for: a chance to improve their lives."

Whether the business of Chinese immigrant smuggling is an exploitative scam or an arrangement mutually acceptable and beneficial to both immigrant and smuggler, it is likely to continue as long as the vision of America as a land of promise remains more powerful than the harsh realities of a grueling voyage and an uncertain future. Immigrant smuggling from China is one topic covered in the following chapter on the seriousness of the problem of illegal immigration.

Illegal Immigration Is a Serious Problem

by Lawrence E. Harrison

About the author: *Lawrence E. Harrison has directed development programs for the Agency for International Development. This viewpoint is adapted from his book,* Who Prospers? How Cultural Values Shape Economic and Political Success.

The United States is one of the few advanced countries in the world that does not effectively control immigration. Large numbers continue to enter the United States illegally each year, most of them from Latin America, and most of those from Mexico. Conservative estimates place the number of illegal immigrants residing in the United States at three to four million. Some estimates run as high as ten million. The illegal immigrant population may be increasing by as many as 300,000 people each year. The Center for Immigration Studies in Washington estimates that the pool of illegal Mexican settlers alone currently may be increasing by as many as 250,000 annually.

Melting Pot or Salad Bowl

Immigration is an important engine of growth of America's population, which has increased more rapidly since 1950 than the population of any other advanced country. Apart from the number of legal and illegal immigrants, their high fertility rates after arrival have helped drive the national fertility rate close to the 2.1 percent replacement level. Current immigration and fertility trends, if sustained, would result in a national population of 500 million, twice that of 1992, by the end of the next century. The mind boggles at the implications for the quality of life—for example, the impact on the environment—not to mention the stresses of a slow pace of acculturation that threatens to transform the assimilative "melting pot" into a multicultural "salad bowl."

We are a society inspired by the words of Emma Lazarus on the Statue of Liberty: "Give me your tired, your poor, your huddled masses yearning to breathe free." When the Statue was dedicated, 105 years ago—about the time my grandparents emigrated from Eastern Europe—some 60 million people lived in the United States, less than a quarter of today's population. An open immigration policy clearly suited its needs. Today the United States, with more than 250 million people, each year accepts over half of all the persons in the world who mi-

> *"The illegal immigrant population may be increasing by as many as 300,000 people each year."*

grate permanently across an international border. The competition of immigrants with poor citizens for jobs and social services is particularly troubling in our current economic distress. The words of Katherine Betts, in *Ideology and Immigration*, about the immigration issue in Australia are relevant to the United States: "Humanitarianism became the chief goal of immigration for some people and immigration itself came to be seen as a form of international aid . . . the relatively poor in this country pay a disproportionate share of the cost of the conscience of the rich."

Americans Opposed

Emma Lazarus notwithstanding, there is compelling evidence that most Americans are opposed to continuing high levels of immigration, legal and illegal. A 1990 Roper poll found that about three-quarters (including 74 percent of Hispanic-Americans) are opposed to proposals to increase immigration, two-thirds support reducing legal immigration, and 91 percent support an all-out program to stop illegal immigration.

They are right. We should call a moratorium on immigration while we forge a new policy that meshes the needs of our society with the educational and professional experience of immigrants, rather than one that emphasizes family relationships, as the current one does. We should also be moving more aggressively to deport those who are here illegally and have not qualified under the amnesty provisions of the 1986 act, and to devise an effective and humane border control system. We should not be deterred by fatuous comparisons with the Berlin Wall, whose role was to keep dissatisfied citizens in, not dissatisfied foreigners out. . . .

Impeding Progress

Most [new immigrants] will come [to the United States] without the skills needed to upgrade the labor force, the wage structure, and the competitiveness of our products. The availability of cheap labor skews investment decisions downward toward low-tech, low-wage, employment-intensive production. As a consequence, the skill levels of the work force, wages, and American technology do not advance as rapidly as in other advanced industrial countries, most notably Japan and Germany. As historian Otis Graham of the University of California at Santa Barbara has observed, a world-class economy "constantly moves its labor force toward higher value-added activities requiring higher skills." But George Borjas concludes that "the skill composition of the immigrant flow entering the United States has deteriorated significantly in the past two or three decades" with major implications for American global competitiveness.

Immigrants Burden the Economy

High levels of immigration have not produced the positive economic results that advocates like Ben Wattenberg, the author of an article entitled "The Case for More Immigrants," and Julian Simon, author of *The Economic Consequences of Immigration*, expected. In addition to the adverse impact on productivity and wage levels in general, researchers like Rice University's Don Huddle are finding that immigrants compete for jobs with poor citizens, particularly blacks—for example, large numbers of blacks have been displaced by Hispanics, chiefly Mexican-Americans, in building maintenance jobs in Los Angeles. To be sure, many immigrants pay taxes, but studies conclude that what they contribute does not cover the cost of services they receive, particularly when the costs of education are factored in (a Supreme Court ruling has assured the children of illegal aliens access to primary and secondary schools, and some states have granted residential tuition rates at public universities to illegal aliens). According to one study done in 1987, long before the recession, almost 40 percent of Haitians in Miami and Fort Lauderdale were receiving welfare assistance. A 1988 government report showed that 21 percent of California's adult welfare recipients were non-citizens. The extensive social services programs of Massachusetts have made that state a magnet for immigrants. From the 1980 census to the 1990 census, the Hispanic component of the state's population more than doubled, from 141,000 to 288,000. Almost half of the increase represents immigration. During the same period, the Asian population of Massachusetts almost tripled, from 49,000 to 143,000, with immigration accounting for the bulk of the increase. The imbalance between the state and local taxes immigrants pay and the social services they receive has contributed to the state's fiscal crisis. For example, Massachusetts officials, faced with an intensifying fiscal crisis, discovered that about 10 percent of the prison population consisted of illegal aliens. (It costs taxpayers about $30,000 per year per prisoner.) In April 1992, New York sued the federal government to recover the $100 million the state claims it pays out annually for some 4,000 illegal aliens in its prisons.

Immigrants of some ethnic and national groups do better than others. The

"We should ... be moving more aggressively to deport those who are here illegally."

principal explanation lies in cultural values and attitudes. There is a close correlation, for example, between the impressive economic and social development of Taiwan and South Korea since World War II, and of Japan since 1868, on the one hand, and the performance of Chinese, Korean, and Japanese immigrants in the United States, on the other. The Confucian ethos has profoundly influenced all three nations. Similarly, the poor performance of Mexican immigrants has reflected Mexico's—and Latin America's—history of slow growth, social inequality, and limited political participation, the chief consequences of the traditional, anti-progressive Iberian value system. . . .

The success of the East Asians in America is testimony to the virtues of an open political and economic system in which fair play is increasingly a reality. But it is also testimony to immigrant cultures heavily influenced by Confucianism, in which work, austerity, education, family, and community are all highly valued. Peter Rose has observed that "to most [Asians], meritocratic principles are the norms by which their lives in the United States have been organized in the past and ought to be in the future. It is this ethos—and the publicity their achievements have received—that causes many to look to them (but rarely to the Hispanics) as archetypes of acculturation."

East Asian communities are not without problems, particularly with respect to recent immigrants, many of whom have entered through the family preference emphasis of current immigration legislation. Chinese gang activity, for example, has increased notably in New York and California. But the successful adaptation of prior generations of East Asian immigrants should leave us hopeful about the acculturation of the new immigrants in the long run. . . .

Immigration from Mexico

Mexicans constitute the single largest immigrant group of recent decades, accounting for more than half the burgeoning Hispanic-American community. . . .

The principal motivator of the flow was the disparity in wages between the United States and Mexico, aggravated by high unemployment in Mexico. The World Bank estimates Mexico's 1988 per capita GNP at $1,760 and the United States' at $19,840, more than ten times larger (the disparity would be larger yet if Mexico's highly inequitable income distribution were taken into account). A powerful magnet pulls on the U.S. side of a 2,000-mile-long border, while a combination of rapid population growth, slow job creation,

"The availability of cheap labor skews investment decisions downward."

and social injustice on the Mexican side gives a powerful push. As a result, illegal immigration has become so massive that no one knows with any degree of precision how many Mexicans, or indeed other foreign nationals, are living in the U.S.

How many people of Mexican origin live in the United States? The 1990 census shows 22,354,000 Hispanics (Hispanics accounted for 6.5 percent of the total population in 1980, 8.9 percent in 1990). Of the 1990 total, 14,000,000 or 63 percent were estimated to be of Mexican antecedence. That represents about 5 percent of our total population. About 75 percent live in California and Texas. Thus, Hispanic-Americans (predominantly Mexican-Americans) accounted for 12 percent of California's population in the 1970 census, 19 percent in the 1980 census, and 26 percent in the 1990 census. Leon Bouvier and Philip Martin project that the Hispanic component may rise to 38 percent by 2030. A similar study of Texas by Bouvier and F. Ray Marshall projects an Hispanic—presumably even more predominantly Mexican—population in a range of 28 percent to 53 percent in the year 2035, depending on assumptions about the rate of immigration. Short of a concerted effort by the United States to stem the flow, we must expect a continuation of the influx, particularly into the Southwest. . . .

> *"The poor performance of Mexican immigrants has reflected Mexico's . . . anti-progressive Iberian value system."*

Hispanic Values Impede Progress

The Hispanic value system has been the principal obstacle to human progress throughout Hispanic America, and indeed in Spain itself until recent decades, and it may contribute to lagging Mexican-American performance in such indicators as education, employment mobility, income, and political participation. A principal element of Hispanic culture is familism—emphasis on the interests of the family to the exclusion of the interests of the community and country. Family is also central to East Asian culture, but in Korea and China, and above all Japan, the idea of family carries over to the community and the nation. Several other aspects of traditional Iberian culture are the major obstacles to progress in Latin America and Mexico: an excessive individualism, particularly in the upper classes, that expresses itself in authoritarianism on one hand, and social irresponsibility on the other (passivity in the lower classes is also a consequence); mistrust of, even hostility toward, those outside the family; a flexible ethical code; and negative attitudes about work, saving, and entrepreneurship, in part the consequence of a present-oriented, zero-sum world view.

Thomas Sowell observes that "the goals and values of Mexican-Americans have never centered on education." Second-generation native-born Mexican-Americans ages 25-34 in California average about 10.5 years of education. All Californians (including Hispanics and blacks) average about 12 years (the national average for native-born Chinese is 14.9 years, for native-born Japanese 13.7 years, for native-born Koreans 13.8 years). Nearly two-thirds of Mexican immigrants have had no high school education. Department of Education nation-wide data show an Hispanic high school dropout rate of 35.7 percent in 1988, three times higher than white students and more than twice that of black students.

In *Out of the Barrio*, Linda Chavez points out that this alarming dropout rate is skewed upward by the inclusion of recent immigrants from Mexico; she adduces data showing the dropout rate for second-generation Mexican-Americans to be 22 percent and *29 percent* for the third-generation compared with 10 percent for non-Hispanic whites. The overall Hispanic rate is 1.4 percent higher than it was in 1972, when dropout statistics for Hispanics were first recorded. High dropout rates suggest that many Mexican-American youngsters are not going to be qualified for the kinds of jobs the American economy is likely to generate in the future.

Mexicans Slow to Assimilate

A 1985 study by Kevin McCarthy and R. Burciaga Valdez of the RAND Corporation demonstrates that movement toward the cultural mainstream by Mexican-Americans is slower than that of most other immigrant groups, and dramatically slower than that of the Asians. Further evidence of a lag in Mexican-American acculturation is provided by the conclusions of a three-year study by David Hayes-Bautista, head of the Chicano Studies Research Center at the University of California

> *"Illegal immigration has become so massive that no one knows . . . how many Mexicans . . . are living in the U.S."*

in Los Angeles. In a June 30, 1991, article in the *New York Times*, Dr. Hayes-Bautista concluded: "We could come back in 100 years and the Latinos will not have assimilated in the classic sense." The article also stresses the ease with which that culture is maintained in places like East Los Angeles, citing the experience of Jose Hernandez, a twenty-six-year-old Mexican, who was shocked to discover that the "Mexican community in East Los Angeles is so self-contained that he could not even find anybody with whom he could practice English." Poor enclave communities not only make it easier for homeland values and language to persist, but they also possess the potential, particularly during bad economic times, for resentment-driven violence, such as the rioting in the Mount Pleasant district of Washington, DC, in the spring of 1991 or the devastating April-May 1992 Los Angeles riots. One-third of those apprehended in Los Angeles for looting were illegal Hispanic immigrants.

Spanish Language Slows Acculturation

The persistence of Spanish as the dominant language for many Hispanic-Americans virtually assures a slow pace of acculturation, since language is the conduit of culture. Strident Chicano "nationalism" and insistence on bilingual education and bilingual public services are evidence of the "salad bowl" rather than the "melting pot" view of the United States. Linda Chavez observes that bilingual education was sold to Congress and the American people principally by Hispanic activists as a means of facilitating the transition to English and improving the quality of education received by Hispanic-American youngsters. But the reality, as documented by several studies, has been very different: As Chavez says, bilingual education has proven to be "at its heart a program to help maintain the language and culture of Hispanic children," a conclusion also stressed in Rosalie Pedalino Porter's *Forked Tongue*. Isolation from the cultural mainstream is likely to have tragic consequences for human beings: a sense of alienation and resentment as well as disproportionate levels of poverty, welfare dependence, drug usage, and crime.

In addition to promoting bilingual education, Hispanic activists have also succeeded in convincing Congress that the nonavailability of electoral material, including ballots, in Spanish was the equivalent of the literacy tests that were used in the South to prevent blacks from voting. Congress ignored the fact of substantial Hispanic voting—and large numbers (relative to blacks) of elected Hispanic officials—long before the Voting Rights act of 1965 and legislated an automatic requirement for bilingual election materials where voting fell below 50 percent of the Hispanic population. This pandering to Hispanic activists reinforces the divisive bilingualism movement.

If large numbers of Mexican-Americans are acculturating very slowly, in part because of the very size of the immigration flow, then the long-term implications of the vast immigration from Mexico—along with heavy immigration from Latin America in general—are profoundly troubling. . . .

The New Asians

Immigrants from China, Japan, and Korea have brought the positive Confucian values of work, education, merit, and future orientation—similar to the Protestant ethic—to an environment that substantially unburdens them of the negative Confucian values of authoritarianism, hegemony of the bureaucrats, and disdain for economic activity. They have made a successful transition to the American cultural mainstream, notwithstanding a history of racism and persecution. Asian-Americans today inject a commitment to achievement and excellence into a society where, over recent decades, those values have eroded.

"The Hispanic value system has been the principal obstacle to human progress throughout Hispanic America."

In recent years, however, many uneducated and unskilled Asians, particularly from China and Southeast Asia, have immigrated, both legally and illegally. While their long-term prospects may be better than those of Mexican immi-

23

grants because of their value system, in the short run the benefits to the United States of their immigration are limited, and may well be exceeded by the costs, particularly at a time of slow growth, high unemployment, and fiscal distress at all levels of government.

Responding to U.S. Interests

The roots of our economic troubles are deep, and a recovery from the current recession will not produce circumstances in which the national interest will be served by the immigration of uneducated, unskilled people. . . . Although the border with Mexico is 2,000 miles long, vastly improved control *is* feasible if we have the will. Almost all of the border is forbidding desert, and surveillance and control need to be fortified significantly only for about 200 miles. The problem would, of course, be far easier with the cooperation of the Mexican government, which we should insist on in negotiating Mexico's inclusion in the U.S.-Canada Free Trade Area. . . .

It is time to work toward an immigration policy based on U.S. national interests, one that leaves the decisions about who enters the United States in the hands of the U.S. authorities rather than individual citizens of other countries, one that emphasizes our obligations to our own society and its citizens, particularly those in need. We need an immigration policy less responsive to the failures of other societies and more responsive to the needs of our own.

Illegal Immigration from Mexico Is a Serious Problem

by Daniel James

About the author: *Daniel James is the president and chief executive officer of the Mexico-United States Institute, a nonprofit organization that studies, researches, and analyzes U.S.-Mexican relations. This viewpoint is excerpted from his book* Illegal Immigration: An Unfolding Crisis.

WE WANT ORDER ON OUR BORDER

Those words, emblazoned on red bumper stickers on hundreds of cars parked along the U.S. border opposite Tijuana, bluntly express the resentment of American residents over nightly incursions into their area of swarms of illegal Mexican immigrants. . . . Passenger autos and pickups converged there at night with headlights turned on to maximum brightness, creating a blinding glare visible on the Mexican side of the narrow strip of marshland ahead. This "Light Up the Border" campaign at the Otay Mesa crossing, near San Diego, was organized by a U.S. Border Patrol agent's widow and the city's former mayor to protest rising illegal immigration. It partially achieved its objective of convincing the U.S. Government to install stadium lighting in the Tijuana River levee area, which deters illegal entries there; but they have increased in adjacent border areas.

Farther north, in Washington, D.C., a group calling itself the Coalition for Freedom organized a seminar on illegal immigration entitled "The Sinister Invasion." The speakers were highly respected academics and former officials of the Immigration and Naturalization Service [INS] and Customs Service, sophisticated professionals who would never dream of demonstrating at the border. But their message was substantially the same as that of the "Light Up the Border" people: Unremitting illegal immigration was sowing disorder along the

2,000-mile stretch separating Mexico and the United States. . . .

The illegal entry of human beings into the United States, overwhelmingly from Mexico, is an issue that is potentially as explosive as the illegal traffic in narcotics. It is a persistent irritant that could severely damage relations between the two neighbors. In fact, both problems are intertwined: the Department of Justice has reported a significant rise in both drug smuggling and illegal immigration during 1990 and into 1991. This grim dual trend may be a harbinger of what the last decade of the 20th century might bring.

The illegal movement of both drugs and human beings is frequently accompanied by violence. . . .

A "badlands atmosphere in an area overwhelmed by illegal immigration and drug trafficking," is how the Southern California border is described in a December 11, 1990, *Washington Post* account citing U.S. authorities.

"This last [agricultural] season the violence has increased a lot, and it worries us a lot," the *Post* story goes on to quote Luis Wybo Alfaro, Director General of Border Affairs in the Mexican Government's Department of Foreign Relations.

Problems Multiplied

As illegal immigration has rebounded, the problems and social tensions it brings have correspondingly multiplied. Cross-border drug violations shot up in 1990 and California National Guardsmen and U.S. Marines had to pitch in to help the INS, Customs Service, and Drug Enforcement Administration to monitor the border. Marines had traded gunfire with illegal alien drug-runners the year before.

Navy Seabees have fortified fencing along the most heavily transited segment of the border, the San Diego Sector, where smugglers of aliens and drugs have made a practice of simply driving their wards into the United States through gaps in border fences. In 1989, the INS and the International Boundary and Water Commission proposed to dig a ten-mile drainage ditch in western San Diego County that would also serve to block illegal cross-border auto and truck traffic. The proposal was shelved in the face of a chorus of protests from immigrant and civil rights advocates.

> *"Illegal immigration was sowing disorder along the 2,000-mile stretch separating Mexico and the United States."*

U.S. border communities are feeling increasingly beleaguered by the housing blight, crime, education and welfare burdens, and in general the disruption that have accompanied the resurgence of illegal immigration. Overcrowding has become the most common of many housing code violations in immigrant-impacted areas of Los Angeles. A 1987 *Los Angeles Times* survey concluded that as many as 200,000 people were living illegally in converted garages.

Illegal Immigration

All four Southwest border states, but particularly Texas, share a relatively new problem: *colonias*—shantytowns, heavily populated by illegals and possessing only minimal water and sanitary facilities. The rapid growth of the colonias, already overcrowded with a population of 400,000 which is expected to double in a few years, has sparked pressures for new outlays of Federal and state funds to ameliorate their Third World-like lot. Some opponents have cautioned that publicly financed improvements would only reward the slumlords and encourage further proliferation.

Owners of well-kept, carefully zoned housing developments in Encinitas, San Diego County, have found that increasingly their neighborhoods are invaded by illegal alien squatters who inhabit tents or caves. Other residents of once serene border neighborhoods complain of a growing procession of illegals in their streets and backyards, with acts of crime (not necessarily committed by them) following not far behind. Among other consequences, the Los Angeles Unified School District found it must plan for a 20 percent annual rise in its operating costs to educate alien children. The State of California saw the cost of Medicaid for indigent illegal aliens reach $300 million in 1990.

> *"As illegal immigration has rebounded, the problems and social tensions . . . [have] multiplied."*

Signs of serious federal action to halt rising border violations are at best uncertain. Legislation on legal-immigration reform, enacted late in 1990, made deportation easier, raised the penalties for document fraud, and provided for 1,000 more Border Patrol agents (based on assumed future appropriations). But dropped at the last moment was a proposed pilot project to curb immigration document fraud by improving the reliability of state drivers licenses. On the other hand, major Hispanic advocacies decided to make their top legislative priority for the 102nd Congress the repeal of employer sanctions, which they consider profoundly discriminatory against Hispanics.

The Soccer Field

Americans know it as the "Soccer Field," a plain covering two acres opposite Tijuana south of San Diego. For Mexicans, it is "Zapata Canyon"—an odd rubric, since Emiliano Zapata, the revolutionary peasant general after whom it might have been named, hailed from a region south of Mexico City very far away. Though it lies in U.S. territory, it is the chief staging area for prospective illegal immigrants from Mexico. When night falls, most of the Mexican men, women, and children who have congregated in Zapata Canyon head north through the mesas and ravines, hoping to rejoin loved ones in the United States, to find jobs, or both. Some bring in contraband or prey on targets of opportunity, including their fellow illegal aliens.

Chapter 1

Observing the nightly massing of humanity at the Soccer Field, a handful of U.S. Border Patrol agents will intercept some of them and, after perfunctory paperwork, send them back to Mexico. No sooner do they arrive, however, than many will head back to El Norte again. As the numbers have grown and the aliens themselves have become more assertive, so have the risks of patrolling the border. A total of 363 Border Patrol agents were the targets of assaults in 1990 with weapons varying from knives to stones to guns. Most nights, more than a thousand border crossers, some of them women with babes in arms, will elude the Border Patrol and melt into the huge illegal population of the United States.

> *"Neighborhoods are invaded by illegal alien squatters who inhabit tents or caves."*

On the Rise

Illegal immigration is on the rise again. After a period of decline, it is once more moving upward coincident with a decade of economic stagnation and rapid population growth in Mexico: 1990 showed a 20 percent jump over 1989, and arrests of illegal Mexicans broke the one million mark for the first time since 1987. All other indicators of increasing illegal immigration also leaped ahead in 1990: arrests of alien smugglers up 37 percent; seizures of smugglers' vehicles, 63.2 percent; the value of narcotics seized by the Border Patrol, 32 percent (to an incredible $1.6 billion). Best estimates are that the predominantly Mexican illegal population of the United States, despite 3 million legalizations since 1987, today totals between 3 and 5 million and is growing by about 300,000 a year.

INS apprehensions of illegal aliens, at best a crude measure of total illegal border crossings, reached an all-time high of 1.7 million in 1986. When Congress, late that year, passed the Immigration Reform and Control Act (IRCA)—which penalized employers of illegal aliens, boosted Border Patrol strength, and screened illegals from welfare rolls—apprehensions dropped 30 percent. There was hope that the new law would finally close the "back door" of illegal immigration. By 1989, arrests of illegal aliens were down 44 percent from the 1986 peak. Visa overstayers also dropped in number.

The amnesty of more than 3 million former illegal aliens accounted for much of the decrease. Aliens who were legalized could enter and leave the United States freely, and no longer appeared in INS apprehension statistics.

Most of the 1,000 new positions that Congress voted for the Border Patrol—a 28 percent increase—fell victim to budget austerity. Only 3,857 of the nation's 4,324 Border Patrol agents are now assigned to guard our long border with Mexico. Of these, only about 800 are on duty at any one time. Moreover, as Senator Dennis DeConcini (D.-AZ) has repeatedly pointed out, "the amount of time spent [by the Border Patrol] on border enforcement activities along the Southwest border has declined 11 percent."

A Proliferation of False Documents

The centerpiece of IRCA, the reform law, was supposed to be employer sanctions, a way of turning off the magnet of jobs that lure illegal aliens to the United States. But the deterrent effect of employer sanctions has withered under the proliferation of false ID documents—more bitter fruit of illegal immigration.

"We've been seeing the apprehension numbers going up, and at the same time, we've been seeing more and more people carrying fraudulent documents," was how the problem was put by Dale Musegades, Chief Border Patrol Agent in the El Paso area, as reported in the *New York Times*. He added wryly, "And the quality of the documents has been improving."

Counterfeiters apprehended in Harlingen, Texas, in late 1990, had employed a laser scanning device to produce near perfect copies of ID documents such as Social Security cards. The market for documents of that kind is enormous, as indicated by the seizure in Houston, in January 1990, of a single cache of 25,000 counterfeit ID documents. As Agent Musegades summed it up: "They have adapted to employer sanctions and found a way around it.". . .

A Human Tidal Wave

The problem will probably become acute in the remaining years of this century and first years of the next, for the trend is toward a decided increase in the flow of Mexicans into this country illegally. Three million or more illegals, the great majority of them Mexicans, are expected to enter during the 1990s—and that is a conservative estimate, since more than one million of them were apprehended in 1990 alone. A still larger number of Mexicans is likely to cross the border illegally between 2000 and 2010. The Mexican illegal movement will probably be augmented by hundreds of thousands of persons from Central America, thus swelling the grand total of illegal aliens to numbers that are impossible to project. If, for example, economic and political conditions in their countries should deteriorate further, the number of Mexicans and Central Americans compelled under those circumstances to cross into the United States illegally could reach the proportions of a human tidal wave.

The presence of swelling millions of illegal aliens in the United States who cannot be assimilated in the short run could pose, eventually, a

> *"Most nights, more than a thousand border crossers . . . will elude the Border Patrol."*

threat to its stability and security. Although this problem may well develop into the most important one Americans will have to face in the next generation, the country at large seems scarcely aware of it. The Administration, apart from those agencies directly involved such as INS, has shown little interest in it judging by its policies and statements; it is obsessed, rather, by the problems of countries far from these shores. Likewise our nation's lawmakers, excepting perhaps those from the border states, seem more concerned about other issues, whether foreign or domestic, than the illegals problem. Even when our leaders focus on such crucial matters as . . . revitalizing education, and they dwell upon how much it will cost and who will pay for it, few factor into their discussion the additional burden illegals represent for many school districts. It is as if a "conspiracy of silence" existed about the problem of illegals in our midst.

Yet they already constitute a threat to our very sovereignty. For if, by definition, the movement of people from one nation to another without the latter's consent is a violation of its fundamental laws, that constitutes a breach of its sovereignty. The 159 members of the United Nations recognize that every sovereign nation-state has the right to guard and protect its borders, and the right, above all, to determine who shall be permitted to enter and reside within its national territory.

Illegal immigration could have all sorts of social and political consequences. One of the most important is its negative impact upon the labor market in certain urban areas, where the presence of a large number of illegal aliens willing and able to work for much less than the average legal worker tends to depress wages. Even immigrants who have arrived legally can

> *"We've been seeing more and more people carrying fraudulent documents."*

be affected: A U.S. Department of Labor study finds, for example, that a 10 percent increase in the number of new immigrants willing to work decreases the average wage of foreign-born workers by between 2 and 3 percent.

A Foreign Underclass

A dangerous side effect of the illegal immigration is that it tends to create a foreign underclass. Persons who do not have proper documentation live in fear of detection by the authorities and of resultant imprisonment or deportation to their homelands. It is to protect themselves that they resort to false identification papers, including Social Security cards and drivers licenses, thus compounding their violation of the law, and worse, nurturing the vast industry in counterfeit documents of all kinds noted above. Fear of detection makes them pliable victims of unscrupulous employers as well as unscrupulous compatriots, both of whom exploit their helplessness in a variety of ways.

The underclass of illegal aliens tends to be vulnerable to serious criminal activity like drug-smuggling. Though the overwhelming majority of immigrants coming into the United States illegally are upright persons, who probably obey the law at home, some are tempted to break U.S. laws when narcotics smugglers offer them money to carry cocaine or heroin across the border. . . .

What is wrong with allowing people from other nations to migrate to the United States? Wasn't this country founded, after all, on the principle that others have a right to enjoy its fruits as long as they work hard and obey the law? The history of the United States is, essentially, the history of successive waves of immigrants landing on its shores and contributing everything they could to its growth into a great nation. As the inscription on the Statue of Liberty proclaims:

> Give me your tired, your poor,
> Your huddled masses yearning to breathe free,
> The wretched refuse of your teeming shore.
> Send these, the homeless, tempest-tossed to me,
> I lift my lamp beside the open door!

Immigrants have traditionally been accepted in America. Sooner or later, they have become assimilated into the mainstream and evolved into citizens every bit as hard-working, law-abiding, and loyal as earlier settlers. Exactly the same pattern has characterized Mexican immigrants: They, too, have taken their place in American society along with the rest of us as people who work hard and assume their share of responsibility for maintaining a stable and prosperous country. The problem, however, is not those who come here legally, in conformity with the nation's immigration laws; or who, like the ones who fled the ravages of the Mexican Revolution lasting from 1910 until the late 1920s, have received special dispensation to remain. We must and should continue to extend, as always, a cordial welcome to such persons, among them the 1 million Mexicans who are projected to enter the United States legally in the 1990s. Rather, it is those who enter the country illegally, in violation of its laws, who are the problem. It is about them we must be rightfully concerned.

The issue is clear: Immigration that is legal, hence under the control of the appropriate authorities of the host nation—in this case, the United States—is welcome. Immigration that is illegal, hence uncontrolled, can by its very nature become a menace to American institutions and must therefore be brought under control before it is too late.

Illegal Immigration Through U.S. Airports Is a Serious Problem

by Ira H. Mehlman

About the author: *Ira H. Mehlman is director of media outreach for the Federation for American Immigration Reform (FAIR), a Washington, D.C., organization that favors greater restrictions on both legal and illegal immigration.*

It's a slow day at New York's John F. Kennedy International Airport [JFK]. Mondays usually are. "You should be here on a Friday or a Saturday, that's when the action is," says one of the uniformed immigration inspectors who deal with up to 1,300 political-asylum claimants a month.

At the secondary inspection area in the East Wing of JFK's International Arrivals Building, a Liberian national is entering a claim for political asylum. He is traveling on a British passport which he purchased for $300 in Bangkok. The flight that he arrived on several hours earlier originated in Tokyo.

Well Rehearsed

The man, about 30, has his lines well rehearsed: "My uncle was killed in an attempted coup. He was a soldier in [Samuel] Doe's army."

"What would happen if you would go back?" asks a skeptical officer from the Immigration and Naturalization Service.

"I'm afraid of the situation," replies the Liberian.

"What would happen?" insists the officer, a man who has clearly heard it all before.

"My father was killed," the Liberian states emphatically.

"When?"

A long pause. "February. February '92. My mother is in Ghana."

"When did she go?"

"I don't know."

"Did she go to Ghana alone?"

"I cannot say."

The interview drags on. Both men are going through the charade. The Liberian will be out on the street in a matter of hours—he knows it and so does the officer.

The political-asylum claimant left Liberia in 1988, stowing away by ship to Thailand. Two years later he moved on to Malaysia, then back to Bangkok, followed by a stint in Japan. Frustrated by poor earnings over the past four years, he's decided to try the land of opportunity: the United States.

He has a bogus passport, he's been out of Liberia for four years, but he knows the magic words that will get him past the harried officers at JFK. Once he utters "political asylum" his chances of remaining in the United States are 93 per cent.

"We're being deluged. It's scandalous," complains the officer filling out the papers on this case. "In a matter of hours he's going to be walking out onto the street joining the ranks of the unemployed. We don't know anything about him. We don't know if he has AIDS. We don't know if he's a murderer." In most cases immigration authorities don't even find out a real name. It's a complaint heard over and over again from any of the 360 immigration officers who work America's most unguarded border—JFK.

Odds Favor Aliens

In 1992, 14,688 excludable aliens attempted to enter the United States through JFK, nearly triple the number just two years earlier. Of these, 9,194, or 63 per cent, asked for political asylum. All but 428 of them had either fraudulent documents or no documents at all.

The deck is stacked in favor of the aliens. The detention center at JFK airport has a maximum capacity of 100 beds and only 12 to 15 vacancies for some 1,300 new excludable aliens every month. For someone contemplating illegal immigration, it's difficult to find better odds. "During fiscal 1992, I detained only 1,169 of the 15,000 inadmissibles who came through JFK," says William Slattery, New York district director for the INS.

"Only about 7 per cent of the inadmissible aliens who come in at JFK can be detained."

In total, only about 7 per cent of the inadmissible aliens who come in at JFK can be detained. The rest are simply released onto the street and asked to present themselves for a hearing at a future date. "We have no good, solid data" on how many ever show up for their hearings, says Duke Austin, an INS spokesman. "I know it sounds crazy, but it's just not collected." On background, other INS people concede that probably not more than 5 per cent of the airport asylum claimants are ever heard from again.

Beginning in October 1992, the INS started keeping computerized records of asylum seekers who come through Kennedy and other major airports. INS also no longer lets a claimant leave the airport before it has scheduled him for a preliminary hearing before an asylum judge. The first hearings under the new rules had been set for mid January 1993, which means the INS will finally have some hard data about how many of these asylum seekers actually bother to show up. The new system won't make it any easier to apprehend and deport the no-shows, but at least INS will know how many people are scamming the system.

China and the Asian subcontinent are the prime sources of jet-set asylum seekers, accounting for more than two-thirds of the applicants at JFK. The remainder are from an assortment of countries in Africa, the Middle East, Eastern Europe, and the Caribbean. Though U.S. immigration authorities have moved to crack down on abuses through fines against the airlines and pre-boarding inspection of passengers in countries such as India and Pakistan, it has done little to slow down the flow.

By and large, the "jet people" phenomenon is well-orchestrated. Though some of the asylum seekers have made it to JFK on their own, most, particularly those from China, India, and Pakistan, rely on professional smugglers. For a fee, generally in the $30,000 range, the smuggler provides them with an airline ticket, a high-quality phony passport (which, if it's not destroyed en route to the United States, is often secretly turned over to the smuggler on the last leg of the voyage to be recycled for the next group of "refugees"), and a tale of persecution.

> *"China and the Asian subcontinent are the prime sources of jet-set asylum seekers."*

Veteran immigration officers at JFK say they can easily identify the smuggling rings' local agents hanging around the International Arrivals terminal, waiting for their clients to finish up their paperwork and be on their way: they're the ones with the cellular telephones.

For some arrivals, particularly among the Pakistanis, the U.S. is not even the final objective—Canada is. Being admitted to Canada for political asylum is like hitting the lottery jackpot: the benefit package there—including welfare, education, resettlement assistance, and more—is worth considerably more than a similar package here. But Canada does a much better job of overseas screening of potential asylum-seekers, weeding out the ones with bad documents before they board Canada-bound planes—so Kennedy airport, it seems, has become a back door to Canada.

A Virtual Open Door

Regardless of whether the United States is the asylum-seeker's ultimate destination, or just a stop along the way, JFK's International Arrival terminal has become a virtual open door for anyone who pushes on it. The law says that anyone who requests political asylum in the U.S., regardless of the circumstances of his arrival, must be given a hearing. The system is so backed up that it takes a minimum of four months to bring a claimant before a judge for a preliminary hearing and 14 months before the actual facts of the claim are heard in court. A particularly sore point for the INS's Slattery is the length of time it can take to resolve even the most bogus asylum claim. The judges "have no standards they are supposed to meet, no work performance plans," he complains.

> *"JFK's International Arrival terminal has become a virtual open door for anyone who pushes on it."*

There are plans in the works to quadruple the number of detention spaces available at Kennedy by October 1993, but even that, Slattery points out, will be woefully inadequate. Even assuming that there isn't an increase in asylum claimants coming through JFK, 400 beds would still accommodate only 28 per cent of the current traffic.

If anyone is less pleased about the whole situation than the INS, it is the airlines. Each time someone shows up without proper documents, it costs the carrier $3,000 and the fine may soon be raised to $5,000. The U.S. Government fined the airlines $20 million in 1992 for delivering undocumented or badly documented passengers to U.S. airports. Half of those fines were levied at JFK.

Indirect Odysseys

The West Wing of International Arrivals is a mirror image of the East Wing. In a room identical to the East Wing's inspection area sit three Indian nationals with white sheets of paper stapled to their jackets bearing their names (aliases, most likely) and the name of the airline on which they arrived. All three have arrived without passports, asking political asylum. Confident the minor inconvenience of the airport waiting room will soon be behind them, they offer no more information and claim not to speak English.

Sitting in a row in front of the Indians are five Chinese nationals who have also arrived without documents. "The Chinese don't have to claim political asylum," says a Chinese-speaking agent who is handling the paper work. "They're all protected by the executive order" issued after the Tiananmen Square massacre. Though the order technically applies only to Chinese who were present in the U.S. prior to June 4, 1989, in practice it makes it virtually impossible to deport any Chinese national.

The five in the JFK inspection room arrived after an odyssey that would make anyone looking to pad a frequent-flyer account green with envy. Hong Kong to Paris. Paris to Santo Domingo. Santo Domingo to New York. The more indirect the route, the Chinese-speaking officer relates, the less scrutiny the travelers and their documents receive. There were seven people on their flight from the Dominican Republic: none had a visa to enter the United States, but all were planning to stay.

One well-dressed thirty-year-old woman was seeking political asylum based on China's single-child-per-family rule. "I'm afraid of forced sterilization if I return to China," reads her Q&A sheet, as filled out by the immigration officer. Her first child remains behind in China with the woman's mother. Her husband has been living in the U. S. since 1989. She doesn't know his address, but has a phone number for him in New Jersey.

Toward Indentured Servitude

A younger woman, in her late teens, stares shyly at the floor as she answers the questions posed in Chinese by Officer Catherine Bryant. The younger woman does not directly request asylum. When asked why she is here, she replies, "I heard life was better in the United States." She has no documents of her own, only the tattered business card of Bing Wong, a real-estate agent in the Elmhurst section of Queens who she describes vaguely as a distant relative.

Both women claim that they paid—or have promised to pay—the smuggler $30,000. The older woman's husband may have been able to come up with the cash to smuggle his wife into the U. S. The younger one will almost assuredly be working off her passage for many years to come in the sweatshops or restaurants of Chinatown. Many of the Chinese being smuggled into the United States wind up in a state of indentured servitude or as foot soldiers in the Chinese underworld.

A Ghanian woman is sitting alone in the front row of the waiting room, sobbing uncontrollably. She has just disembarked from a KLM flight from Amsterdam. The Dutch passport she is carrying is a valid one, but it does not belong to her. The photo on the document bears a resemblance to her, but on close inspection it is clearly the photo of another woman.

The sobbing woman has been living in the Netherlands for the past two years. She has not requested political asylum there because she has an aunt in New York whom she wishes to join. Upon arrival in New York she claims political persecution, for the first time.

Political asylum was first codified into U.S. law in 1980, when Congress passed sweeping reforms of the refugee laws. At the time it was estimated that about 5,000 people a year would seek asylum in the U.S. In re-

> *"Many of the Chinese being smuggled into the United States wind up in a state of indentured servitude."*

cent years, the number of asylum requests has exploded to about 100,000 annually. Because the system was never designed to handle anything approaching that volume, and because every claim must get a hearing, it can take years for the process to play itself out.

The system's Achilles' heel is the right granted to each person who presses a claim for political asylum to have his case heard by a judge. The more people who apply, the more the system becomes bogged down. The more bogged down the system becomes, the more inviting it becomes for those filing bogus claims.

Jonathan Fuchs, who represents Iceland Air and other Europe-based carriers, would like to see summary exclusion for obvious abusers of the process, particularly aliens who flush their documents down the airplane toilet and then ask for political asylum. "Flushers should not get an automatic right to go see a judge. Just because they get their feet on the ground in the U.S. doesn't mean they're entitled to a hearing," he claims.

The airlines would much rather put these people on the next flight back to wherever it is they came from, and not have to pay the $3,000 fine for delivering an inadmissible alien to the U.S. "When someone arrives at JFK or any other international airport, they are at the functional equivalent of a border," and if they lack adequate documentation, they ought to be turned around and sent back, Fuchs contends.

> *"People sneaking past Border Patrol . . . are less irritating than people who mock our humanitarianism."*

Slattery would like to see summary exclusion for applicants who have entered by way of a third, presumably safe, country. The majority of claimants at JFK fall into this category. "If I have someone from China who has been through six or seven countries before finally asking for asylum when they hit JFK, I don't see why I should have to admit them," he says.

Serious Consequences

In striking contrast to your typical illegal alien who sneaks across the border, an asylum claimant who arrives at an airport without documents or with phony documents is almost always rewarded not only with admission to the U.S., but also with authorization to hold employment for as long as he can manage to clog the court's docket. With work authorization, the asylum abuser can obtain a Social Security card and a driver's license, the de-facto identifiers used by most Americans to prove eligibility for everything from welfare benefits to the right to vote.

Although the casual way in which we hand out these documents usually amounts to nothing more than the government aiding and abetting violation of our immigration laws, the consequences can be more serious. In the case of Mir Aimal Kansi, the man alleged to have gone on a shooting spree outside CIA headquarters in February 1993, that laxness led to two deaths and three other people being wounded.

Kansi, a Pakistani citizen, entered the United States through JFK in February

1991 using what the INS now believes was a phony business visa (which he overstayed anyway). A year later, Kansi applied for political asylum at the INS office in Arlington, Virginia. Using the work-authorization document issued to him by the INS, Kansi was able to obtain a Social Security card and a Virginia driver's license. With that license Kansi had all the documentation he needed to purchase the AK-47 rifle he allegedly used to go on his rampage. Ironically, although nearly a year had passed between the time he filed his asylum petition and the date of the shootings, his case had not been scheduled for a hearing.

> *"The ideal solution would be to screen out the abusers before they ever set foot on American soil."*

Mocking Our Humanitarianism

Even when the results are not quite so tragic, the abuse of asylum at JFK airport, though still relatively small, tends to have greater outrage value than other forms of illegal immigration. People sneaking past Border Patrol, even in much greater numbers, are less irritating than people who mock our humanitarianism. Senator Edward Kennedy, who chairs the Immigration and Refugee Affairs Subcommittee and who has traditionally worked for more liberal immigration and asylum laws, has dispatched two top aides, Jerry Tinker and Michael Meyers, to JFK to assess the situation.

After seeing the situation firsthand, Tinker, the subcommittee chief of staff, agrees that the asylum system is abused. . . . But Tinker believes the problem can be handled without requiring any new legislation. Additional detention facilities at the airport and quick hearings for asylum claimants, he believes, will deter people from abusing the system.

When Los Angeles International Airport [LAX] boosted its detention capacity to 800 beds, asylum abuse all but stopped there. The addition of the extra detention space at LAX, however, also happened to coincide with the increase of asylum abuse at JFK. It seems likely, then, that simply building more detention facilities at JFK will not solve the problem; rather, it is likely to shift it to some other airport less well-equipped to hold inadmissible aliens.

Screen Out Abusers

While Tinker opposes summary exclusion as premature and unnecessary, he does favor a quick airport hearing for applicants and the immediate return of those whose claims have no merit. This is precisely what was being done in the case of Haitian boat people until May 1992. "While we agree this is a real problem that needs to be nipped in the bud, I would like to see them have a hearing and be put back on a plane. I don't think civil libertarians could have any problem with that," says Tinker. . . .

The ideal solution would be to screen out the abusers before they ever set foot on American soil. Under the law, a person must have physically reached the United States in order to press a claim of political asylum. A mobile corps of just ten agents moving from airport to airport to keep smugglers off-guard, says Slattery, would have a greater deterrence potential than the 360 agents currently at JFK.

The Canadian Immigration Service tested a similar program for six weeks beginning in November 1992, and their preliminary findings indicate a reduction in the number of bogus asylum claimants turning up at Canadian airports. Pre-screening of passengers before they board flights to the U.S. can work, but it is a somewhat dicey proposition for the INS and the airlines.

Neither the U.S. Government nor the airlines want to appear to be hassling legitimate visitors. Adding to the problem is the matter of racial and ethnic sensitivities. Inevitably, somebody is going to raise an objection if the only passengers whose documents are closely scrutinized happen to be wearing turbans. Moreover, refugee-rights advocates have serious reservations about such screenings in countries whose human-rights records are suspect. Pulling someone with bad documents out of line in London or Paris is one thing. Pulling that person out of line in Karachi or Bombay is quite another matter, says Arthur C. Helton.

Reconsider the Rules?

The number of people seeking political asylum will continue to grow as long as the odds of beating the system remain so high. Other democratic countries have concluded that the only way of dealing with asylum abuse is through summary exclusion of people they know are abusing the process. In some European countries, people who show up without documents, with phony documents, or who have traveled through other safe countries are simply presumed to be asylum abusers and are sent packing.

In a highly mobile world filled with billions of desperately poor people, some of the rules may have to be reconsidered. Our commitment to due process is admirable, but it has clearly become a magnet for abuse. Under such circumstances, blind obeisance to the notion that every human being on planet earth is entitled to a day in an American court, no matter how frivolous the claim to asylum, can only undermine our ability to protect the truly persecuted.

"Our commitment to due process is admirable, but it has clearly become a magnet for abuse."

Applying to come to the United States as an immigrant or a refugee can entail years of waiting. Entering illegally means risking apprehension. Going the political-asylum route, however, means no waiting your turn, a set of documents entitling you to work, and a virtual assurance that you'll never be caught. The only thing that's surprising is that far more people haven't caught on.

Back in the East Wing of International Arrivals at JFK, a Dominican who has been sitting in the secondary inspection area for about 24 hours—the immigration officers suspect he is a criminal—gives up and asks to be sent home. He's destined to be one of the unlucky 7 per cent who winds up in detention. A return flight home sounds like a much better option.

A victory of sorts—at least for now. "He'll try again," says the immigration officer as he begins filling out the inevitable forms.

Illegal Immigration from China Is a Serious Problem

by Jim Mann

About the author: *Jim Mann is a staff writer for the* Los Angeles Times.

When U.S. Coast Guard officials first boarded the cargo ship *East Wood* in the middle of the Pacific in early February 1993, they found 524 Chinese hoping to come to America jammed into the hold and on the deck of a filthy, unseaworthy vessel.

After several weeks spent in limbo in the Marshall Islands, the would-be emigrants were flown back to China. And the compelling saga of the *East Wood* came to a close.

A Growing Phenomenon

But the phenomenon of which the *East Wood* was the latest and most disturbing example—the apparently organized effort to smuggle cargoes of Chinese by boat from the Asian mainland to the United States—is continuing and growing.

U.S. authorities, from the Immigration and Naturalization Service to the Coast Guard and the State Department, are becoming increasingly concerned about the recent upsurge in illegal immigration by Chinese "boat people." And they are gradually starting to devote new efforts to combat the smuggling rings.

According to U.S. officials, the passengers on the *East Wood*, virtually all of them from China's Fujian province, had paid up to $30,000 to criminal syndicates to smuggle them by boat to America. So far as is known, the Chinese on the *East Wood* were the largest shipment yet in the increasingly lucrative business of transporting human cargoes out of China.

"If this is an indication of things to come, we've got a major problem on our hands," says Rear Adm. William C. Donnell, commander of the 14th Coast Guard District in Honolulu.

In Washington, John F. Shaw, the INS's assistant commissioner for investigations, observes that when U.S. authorities first detected the oceangoing smuggling operations two years ago, each boat was relatively small, carrying fewer than 100 Chinese at a time. Now, he says, the smuggling rings "are using larger and larger boats and putting more and more people on them."

Breathtaking Voyages

The number and variety of routes the boats have taken from China to America are breathtaking.

Fishing trawlers have been found unloading their Chinese passengers not only in the coastal waters off California and Hawaii, but even at East Coast locations off the shores of North Carolina and Massachusetts.

Authorities have discovered other vessels carrying Chinese emigrants bound for the United States in Japan, Singapore, Mexico, Guatemala, El Salvador and the African countries of Mauritius and Kenya. And American officials believe there are more boats already outfitted in Asia and preparing to transport more human cargoes from China.

Generally, the smuggling boats avoid coming inside U.S. coastal waters, which extend to 200 miles beyond the shoreline. Instead, they remain on the high seas, safely outside the reach of U.S. law enforcement officials, and hire smaller boats to ferry the Chinese to American shores.

> *"Smuggling rings 'are using larger and larger boats and putting more and more people on them.'"*

"The whole object is to offload in international waters," says the INS's Shaw. "Normally, they contract with people in the United States to do the offloading. The prices are around $1,000 a head. They've used Vietnamese crews, everyone." If caught, the hired hands face penalties of up to five years in prison for illegal smuggling of foreigners.

The departures by ship from China invite comparisons with the Indochinese "boat people" who fled Vietnam and Cambodia in the years after the 1975 Communist takeovers of the two countries. But the Indochinese fled in small boats, family by family, in a mass exodus whose numbers reached the hundreds of thousands. The Chinese are leaving in smaller numbers, using larger ships.

Criminal Affairs

And in contrast with the Indochinese boat people, the Chinese smuggling operations are, Shaw and other U.S. authorities believe, highly organized criminal affairs, the work of rings whose international activities extend from China, Hong Kong, Taiwan and Singapore to the United States and other countries.

"This takes a very involved network," says Wayne R. McKenna, an INS senior special agent for investigations. "It takes recruiters in China, other people to move aliens from the Chinese interior to the coast, and others to ferry them out to vessels off the Chinese shoreline.

"It takes people to get a boat and provisions and a crew. It takes people at ports around the world to take care of things like refueling and engine problems. There have to be people to help out the Chinese when they reach the United States. And most importantly of all, the money has to be collected, and the only way to collect the money is through muscle and intimidation, both in the United States and in China."

> *"The potential profits that can be made from smuggling people are huge."*

For organized crime, the potential profits that can be made from smuggling people are huge.

The math is simple. A ship the size of the *East Wood*, carrying about 500 Chinese paying an average of $20,000 apiece to get to the United States, would take in gross revenues of $10 million.

Some of the Chinese get or borrow money from relatives in America or elsewhere overseas, authorities say. But whenever those Chinese who have been smuggled into the United States can't make their payments, they become a ready supply of labor that can be put to work in restaurants, laundries or even drug-dealing and prostitution.

"They live as indentured servants, paying off their debt," says Vern Jervis, a spokesman for the INS. " . . . We have found instances where they are virtually held as prisoners."

Some U.S. officials believe that organized crime groups that were previously involved in importing drugs have now converted to smuggling Chinese as a way of earning comparably large sums of money.

"The information strongly suggests that organizations already established for the smuggling of narcotics are now using their ships to transport human cargo," Shaw maintains.

100,000 Per Year and Growing

How many Chinese have been smuggled into the United States? The figures are sketchy.

INS officials say that they have caught only a relatively small number of Chinese, about 1,800, trying to come here by boat between 1991 and 1993. But they believe that many other boats have succeeded in landing, dropping off thousands more Chinese, without being detected.

In addition, at least another 1,000 Chinese—believed ultimately destined for the United States—have been intercepted in foreign ports.

Overall, INS and State Department officials estimate, about 100,000 Chinese are illegally entering the United States—by all means of transport—each year. And these numbers are growing.

Those figures far exceed the numbers of Chinese—approximately 28,000 to 32,000 a year—who immigrate legally into the United States. However, they are small in comparison with the levels of illegal immigration from Mexico. INS officials say they apprehend about 1 million people a year trying to cross the Mexican border into the United States, and they have no numbers for the people who cross without being caught.

The levels of illegal Chinese immigration have revived the old specter raised 14 years ago by China's paramount leader Deng Xiaoping.

While on a 1979 visit to Washington, Deng asked Jimmy Carter Administration officials to grant China most-favored-nation trade benefits. He was told that, under an American law first written with Soviet Jews in mind, China would have to guarantee freedom of emigration from its soil.

"Sure, how many Chinese do you want?" Deng replied. "One million? Two million?". . .

Hampered Efforts

The American efforts to combat the Chinese smuggling operations have been hampered by some bureaucratic wrangling. The problems have been particularly acute in the immigration service, where agents in several field offices have complained that INS headquarters in Washington isn't doing enough about the Chinese smuggling operations.

"They [the Chinese boat people] are on the upswing, and it's something that INS should start planning for and getting some operations and programs for," says David Ilchert, the INS's district director in San Francisco. "My feeling is that it's like the Haitians on the East Coat. The only difference is the expansiveness of the Pacific Ocean."

In Washington, Shaw bristles at the complaints from field offices. He says he has assigned a total of 16 new INS agents in the Los Angeles, San Francisco, New York, Honolulu and Boston district offices to investigate Chinese boat smuggling operations, and that he has allocated an additional $2 million for use by a special new Chinese boat task force within INS.

"There is a plan," Shaw says. "There is a Chinese boat task force. But the problem goes beyond the bounds of an enforcement solution."

Some of the law enforcement efforts are beginning to pay off.

In New York City in March 1993, the Justice Department for the first

> *"About 100,000 Chinese are illegally entering the United States . . . each year."*

time obtained the convictions of two boat owners for conspiring to smuggle Chinese into the United States.

The two men, George Huang and William Chen, who formerly owned restaurants in New York City, were found to have purchased a fishing boat called the

Chin Wing 18 in Taiwan. Evidence at the trial showed that last year, the *Chin Wing* picked up 151 Chinese from the mainland and, for fees of up to $30,000 apiece, promised to smuggle them into the United States.

Over a period of more than four months, the *Chin Wing* carried its 151 passengers from the waters off China to Mauritius, South Africa and Haiti before it was intercepted off the coast of North Carolina last September.

Immigration and State Department officials are also pleased with their success in having the Chinese aboard the *East Wood* flown back to China.

After the Coast Guard boarded the Panamanian-flagged *East Wood* Feb. 3, 1993, the ship was escorted to Kwajalein atoll in the Marshall Islands, where the ship's 524 passengers were held and fed on an American military base.

U.S. officials asked a number of Asian governments to take the refugees there for processing. "Basically, they all said no," admits a State Department official.

Finally, the United States worked out a deal with China to take back the people who had fled its soil. State Department officials say they got assurances that once returned, the Chinese from the *East Wood* would be treated fairly and not punished.

U.S. officials hope the return of the *East Wood* will send the message that the Chinese boat smuggling operations don't always succeed. But they acknowledge that every effort to catch a ship full of Chinese and send them home is difficult and expensive. The INS estimates that each individual anti-smuggling operation costs as much as $125,000.

Illegal Immigration Is Not a Serious Problem

by Francis Fukuyama

About the author: *Francis Fukuyama is resident consultant at the RAND Corporation, a nonprofit think tank, and the author of* The End of History and the Last Man.

At the Republican convention in Houston in August 1992, Patrick J. Buchanan announced the coming of a block-by-block war to "take back our culture." Buchanan is right that a cultural war is upon us, and that this fight will be a central American preoccupation now that the cold war is over. What he understands less well, however, is that the vast majority of the non-European immigrants who have come into this country in the past couple of decades are not the enemy. Indeed, many of them are potentially on his side.

Peculiar Bedfellows

Conservatives have for long been sharply divided on the question of immigration. Many employers and proponents of free-market economics, like Julian Simon or the editorial page of the *Wall Street Journal*, are strongly pro-immigration; they argue for open borders because immigrants are a source of cheap labor and ultimately create more wealth than they consume. Buchanan and other traditional right-wing Republicans, by contrast, represent an older nativist position. They dispute the economic benefits of immigration, but more importantly look upon immigrants as bearers of foreign and less desirable cultural values. It is this group of conservatives who forced the inclusion of a plank in the Republican platform in August 1992, calling for the creation of "structures" to maintain the integrity of America's southern border.

Indeed, hostility to immigration has made for peculiar bedfellows. The Clinton administration's difficulties in finding an attorney general who had not at some point hired an illegal-immigrant babysitter is testimony to the objective depen-

From Francis Fukuyama, "Immigrants and Family Values," *Commentary*, May 1993. Reprinted with permission.

dence of liberal yuppies on immigration to maintain their life-styles, and they by and large would support the *Wall Street Journal*'s open-borders position.

On the other hand, several parts of the liberal coalition—blacks and environmentalists—have been increasingly vocal in opposition to further immigration, particularly from Latin America. The Black Leadership Forum, headed by Coretta Scott King and Congressman Walter Fauntroy, has lobbied to maintain sanctions against employers hiring illegal immigrant labor on the

> *"The last people in the world we should be blaming are recent immigrants."*

ground that this takes away jobs from blacks and "legal" browns. Jack Miles, a former *Los Angeles Times* book-review editor with impeccable liberal credentials, has in [an] article in the *Atlantic* lined up with the Federation for American Immigration Reform (FAIR) in calling for a rethinking of open borders, while liberal activist groups like the Southern California Interfaith Task Force on Central America have supported Senator Orrin Hatch's legislation strengthening employer sanctions. Environmental groups like the Sierra Club, for their part, oppose immigration because it necessitates economic growth, use of natural resources, and therefore environmental degradation.

Conservative Arguments Confused

But if much of the liberal opposition to immigration has focused on economic issues, the conservative opposition has concentrated on the deeper cultural question; and here the arguments made by the Right are very confused. The symptoms of cultural decay are all around us, but the last people in the world we should be blaming are recent immigrants.

The most articulate and reasoned recent conservative attack on immigration came in the summer of 1992 in an article in *National Review* by Peter Brimelow. Brimelow, a senior editor at *Forbes* and himself a naturalized American of British and Canadian background, argues that immigration worked in the past in America only because earlier waves of nativist backlash succeeded in limiting it to a level that could be successfully assimilated into the dominant Anglo-Saxon American culture. Brimelow criticizes pro-immigration free-marketeers like Julian Simon for ignoring the issue of the skill levels of the immigrant labor force, and their likely impact on blacks and others at the bottom end of the economic ladder. But his basic complaint is a cultural one. Attacking the *Wall Street Journal*'s Paul Gigot for remarking that a million Zulus would probably work harder than a million Englishmen today, Brimelow notes:

> This comment reveals an utter innocence about the reality of ethnic and cultural differences, let alone little things like tradition and history—in short, the greater part of the conservative vision. Even in its own purblind terms, it is totally false. All the empirical evidence is that immigrants from developed coun-

47

tries assimilate better than those from underdeveloped countries. It is developed countries that teach the skills required for success in the United States. . . . It should not be necessary to explain that the legacy of [the Zulu kings] Shaka and Cetewayo—overthrown just over a century ago—is not that of Alfred the Great, let alone Elizabeth II or any civilized society.

Elsewhere, Brimelow suggests that culture is a key determinant of economic performance, and that people from certain cultures are therefore likely to do less well economically than others. He implies, furthermore, that some immigrants are more prone to random street crime because of their "impulsiveness and present-orientation, while others are responsible for organized crime which is, by his account, ethnically based. Finally, Brimelow argues that the arrival of diverse non-European cultures fosters the present atmosphere of multiculturalism, and is, to boot, bad for the electoral prospects of the Republican party.

American National Identity?

A similar line of thought runs through Buchanan's writings and speeches, and leads to a similar anti-immigrant posture. Buchanan has explicitly attacked the notion that democracy represents a particularly positive form of government,

> *"A million Zulus would probably work harder than a million Englishmen today."*

and hence would deny that belief in universal democratic principles ought to be at the core of the American national identity. But if one subtracts democracy from American nationality, what is left? Apparently, though Buchanan is somewhat less explicit on this point, a concept of America as a Christian, ethnically European nation with certain core cultural values that are threatened by those coming from other cultures and civilizations.

There is an easy, Civics 101-type answer to the Brimelow-Buchanan argument. In contrast to other West European democracies, or Japan, the American national identity has never been directly linked to ethnicity or religion. Nationality has been based instead on universal concepts like freedom and equality that are in theory open to all people. Our Constitution forbids the establishment of religion, and the legal system has traditionally held ethnicity at arm's length. To be an American has meant to be committed to a certain set of ideas, and not to be descended from an original tribe of *ur*-Americans. Those elements of a common American culture visible today—belief in the Constitution and the individualist-egalitarian principles underlying it, plus modern American pop and consumer culture—are universally accessible and appealing, making the United States, in Ben Wattenberg's phrase, the first "universal nation."

This argument is correct as far as it goes, but there is a serious counterargument that reaches to the core of 1992's debate over "family values." It runs as follows:

America began living up to its universalist principles only in the last half of this century. For most of the period from its revolutionary founding to its rise as a great, modern, industrial power, the nation's elites conceived of the country not just as a democracy based on universal principles, but also as a Christian, Anglo-Saxon nation.

American democracy—the counterargument continues—is, of course, embodied in the laws and institutions of the country, and will be imbibed by anyone who learns to play by its rules. But virtually every serious theorist of American democracy has noted that its success depended heavily on the presence of certain pre-democratic values or cultural characteristics that were neither officially sanctioned nor embodied in law. If the Declaration of Independence and the Constitution were the basis of America's *Gesellschaft* (society), Christian Anglo-Saxon culture constituted its *Gemeinschaft* (community).

Indeed—the counterargument goes on—the civic institutions that Tocqueville observed in the 1830's, whose strength and vitality he saw as a critical manifestation of the Americans' art of associating, were more often than not of a religious (i.e., Christian) nature, devoted to temperance, moral education of the young, or the abolition of slavery. There is nothing in the Constitution which states that parents should make large sacrifices for their children, that workers should rise early in the morning and labor long hours in order to get ahead, that people should emulate rather than undermine their neighbors' success, that they should be innovative, entrepreneurial, or open to technological change. Yet Americans, formed by a Christian culture, possessed these traits in abundance for much of their history, and the country's economic prosperity and social cohesion arguably rested on them.

The Family-Values Controversy

It is this sort of consideration that underlay the family-values controversy during 1992's election. Basic to this line of thought is that, all other things being equal, children are better off when raised in stable, two-parent, heterosexual families. Such family structures and the web of moral obligations they entail are the foundation of educational achievement, economic success, good citizenship, personal character, and a host of other social virtues.

The issue of family values was badly mishandled by the Republicans and deliberately misconstrued by the press and the Democrats (often not distinguishable), such that mere mention of the phrase provoked derisive charges of narrow-minded gay-bashing and hostility to single mothers. Yet while many Americans did not sign on to 1992's family-values theme, few would deny that the family and community are in deep crisis today. The break-

> *"The American national identity has never been directly linked to ethnicity or religion."*

49

down of the black family in inner-city neighborhoods around America in the past couple of generations shows in particularly stark form the societal consequences of a loss of certain cultural values. And what has happened among blacks is only an extreme extension of a process that has been proceeding apace among whites as well.

> *"The notion that non-European immigrants are a threat to family values . . . [is] quite puzzling."*

The issue, then, is not whether the questions of culture and cultural values are important, or whether it is legitimate to raise them, but whether immigration really threatens those values. For while the values one might deem central either to economic success or to social cohesion may have arisen out of a Christian, Anglo-Saxon culture, it is clear that they are not bound to that particular social group: some groups, like Jews and Asians, might come to possess those values in abundance, while Wasps themselves might lose them and decay. The question thus becomes: which ethnic groups in today's America are threatening, and which groups are promoting, these core cultural values.

A Puzzling Notion

The notion that non-European immigrants are a threat to family values and other core American cultural characteristics is, in a way, quite puzzling. After all, the breakdown of traditional family structures, from extended to nuclear, has long been understood to be a disease of advanced industrial countries and not of nations just emerging from their agricultural pasts.

Some conservatives tend to see the third world as a vast, global underclass, teeming with the same social pathologies as Compton in Los Angeles or Bedford-Stuyvesant in Brooklyn. But the sad fact is that the decay of basic social relationships evident in American inner cities, stretching to the most intimate moral bonds linking parents and children, may well be something with few precedents in human history. Economic conditions in most third-world countries simply would not permit a social group suffering so total a collapse of family structure to survive: with absent fathers and no source of income, or mothers addicted to drugs, children would not live to adulthood.

But it would also seem *a priori* likely that third-world immigrants should have stronger family values than white, middle-class, suburban Americans, while their work ethic and willingness to defer to traditional sources of authority should be greater as well. Few of the factors that have led to family breakdown in the American middle class over the past couple of generations—rapidly changing economic conditions, with their attendant social disruptions; the rise of feminism and the refusal of women to play traditional social roles; or the legitimization of alternative life-styles and consequent proliferation of rights and entitlements on a retail level—apply in third-world situations. Immi-

Illegal Immigration

grants coming from traditional developing societies are likely to be poorer, less educated, and in possession of fewer skills than those from Europe, but they are also likely to have stronger family structures and moral inhibitions. Moreover, despite the greater ease of moving to America today than in the last century, immigrants are likely to be a self-selecting group with a much greater than average degree of energy, ambition, toughness, and adaptability.

These intuitions are largely borne out by the available empirical data, particularly if one disaggregates the different parts of the immigrant community.

Strong Family Values

The strength of traditional family values is most evident among immigrants from East and South Asia, where mutually supportive family structures have long been credited as the basis for their economic success. According to Census Bureau statistics, 78 percent of Asian and Pacific Islander households in the United States were family households, as opposed to 70 percent for white Americans. The size of these family households is likely to be larger: 74 percent consist of three or more persons, compared to 57 percent for white families. While Asians are equally likely to be married as whites, they are only half as likely to be divorced. Though dropping off substantially in the second and third generations, concern for elderly parents is high in Chinese, Japanese, and Vietnamese households; for many, the thought of sticking a mother or father out of sight and out of mind in a nursing home continues to be anathema. More importantly, most of the major Asian immigrant groups are intent on rapid assimilation into the American mainstream, and have not been particularly vocal in pressing for particularistic cultural entitlements.

> *"Most Latin American immigrants may be a source of strength with regard to family values."*

While most white Americans are ready to recognize and celebrate the social strengths of Asians, the real fears of cultural invasion surround Latinos. Despite their fast growth, Asians still constitute less than 3 percent of the U.S. population, while the number of Hispanics increased from 14.6 to over 22 million between 1980 and 1990, or 9 percent of the population. But here as well, the evidence suggests that most Latin American immigrants may be a source of strength with regard to family values, and not a liability. . . .

The Latino Family

There are very significant differences among Latino groups. Latinos of Cuban and Mexican origin, for example, who together constitute 65 percent of the Hispanic community, have a 50-percent lower rate of female-headed households than do Puerto Ricans—18.9 and 19.6 percent versus 38.9 percent. While the

51

rate of Puerto Rican out-of-wedlock births approaches that of blacks (53.0 vs. 63.1 percent of live births), the rates for Cuban- and Mexican-origin Latinos are much lower, 16.1 and 28.9 percent, respectively, though they are still above the white rate of 13.9 percent.

When looked at in the aggregate, Latino family structure stands somewhere between that of whites and blacks. For example, the rate of female-headed families with no husband present as a proportion of total families is 13.5 percent for whites, 46.4 percent for blacks, and 24.4 percent for Hispanics. If we adjust these figures for income level, however, Hispanics turn out to be much closer to the white norm.

Poverty is hard on families regardless of race; part of the reason for the higher percentage of Latino female-headed households is simply that there are more poor Latino families. If we compare families below the poverty level, the Hispanic rate of female-headed families is very close to that of whites (45.7 vs. 43.6 percent), while the comparable rate for blacks is much higher than either (78.3 percent). Considering the substantially higher rate of family breakdown within the sizable Puerto Rican community, this suggests that the rate of single-parent families for Cuban- and Mexican-origin Latinos is actually lower than that for whites at a comparable income level.

Work Ethic and Devotion to Family

Moreover, Latinos as a group are somewhat more likely to be members of families than either whites or blacks. Another study indicates that Mexican-Americans have better family demographics than do whites, with higher birth-weight babies even among low-income mothers due to taboos on smoking, drinking, and drug use during pregnancy. Many Latinos remain devout Catholics, and the rate of church attendance is higher in the Mexican community than for the U.S. as a whole as well. But even if one does not believe that the United States is a "Christian country," the fact that so many immigrants are from Catholic Latin America should make them far easier to assimilate than, say, Muslims in Europe.

> *"Mexican-Americans have ... higher birth-weight babies [than whites] even among low-income mothers."*

These statistics are broadly in accord with the observations of anyone who has lived in Los Angeles, San Diego, or any other community in the American Southwest. Virtually every early-morning commuter in Los Angeles knows the streetcorners on which Chicano day-laborers gather at 7:00 A.M., looking for work as gardeners, busboys, or on construction sites. Many of them are illegal immigrants with families back in Mexico to whom they send their earnings. While they are poor and unskilled, they have a work ethic and devotion to family comparable to those of the South and East European immigrants who came to the U.S. at the turn of the century. It is much less common to see African-Americans doing this sort of thing.

Immigrants Not to Blame

Those who fear third-world immigration as a threat to Anglo-American cultural values do not seem to have noticed what the real sources of cultural breakdown have been. To some extent, they can be traced to broad socioeconomic factors over which none of us has control: the fluid, socially disruptive nature of capitalism: technological change; economic pressures of the contemporary workplace and urban life; and so on. But the ideological assault on traditional family values—the sexual revolution; feminism and the delegitimization of the male-dominated household; the celebration of alternative life-styles; attempts ruthlessly to secularize all aspects of American public life; the acceptance of no-fault divorce and the consequent rise of single-parent households—was not the creation of recently-arrived Chicano agricultural workers or Haitian boat people, much less of Chinese or Korean immigrants. They originated right in the heart of America's well-established white, Anglo-Saxon community. The "Hollywood elite" that created the now celebrated Murphy

> *"The real fight . . . should not be over keeping newcomers out."*

Brown, much like the establishment "media elite" that Republicans enjoy attacking, does not represent either the values or the interests of most recent third-world immigrants.

In short, though the old, traditional culture continues to exist in the United States, it is overlaid today with an elite culture that espouses very different values. The real danger is not that these elites will become corrupted by the habits and practices of third-world immigrants, but rather that the immigrants will become corrupted by them. And that is in fact what tends to happen.

While the first generation of immigrants to the United States tends to be deferential to established authority and preoccupied with the economic problems of "making it," their children and grandchildren become aware of their own entitlements and rights, more politicized, and able to exploit the political system to defend and expand those entitlements. While the first generation is willing to work quietly at minimum- or subminimum-wage jobs, the second and third generations have higher expectations as to what their labor is worth. The extension of welfare and other social benefits to noncitizens through a series of court decisions has had the perverse effect of hastening the spread of welfare dependency. Part of the reason that Puerto Ricans do less well than other Latino groups may be that they were never really immigrants at all, but U.S. citizens, and therefore eligible for social benefits at a very early stage.

Chapter 1

As Julian Simon has shown, neither the absolute nor the relative levels of immigration over the past decade have been inordinately high by historical standards. What is different and very troubling about immigration in the present period is that the ideology that existed at the turn of the century and promoted assimilation into the dominant Anglo-Saxon culture has been replaced by a multicultural one that legitimates and even promotes continuing cultural differentness. . . .

The real fight, the central fight, then, should not be over keeping newcomers out: this will be a waste of time and energy. The real fight ought to be over the question of assimilation itself: whether we believe that there is enough to our Western, rational, egalitarian, democratic civilization to force those coming to the country to absorb its language and rules, or whether we carry respect for other cultures to the point that Americans no longer have a common voice with which to speak to one another.

Objections to Illegal Immigration Are Exaggerated

by *Los Angeles Times*

About the author: *The* Los Angeles Times *is a daily newspaper in Los Angeles, California.*

Although we're proud to be a "nation of immigrants," Americans have never really been comfortable with foreign newcomers. Even in Revolutionary times, Thomas Jefferson worried that immigrants could undermine the new political culture of the nation. And Benjamin Franklin warned against letting German immigrants settle in Pennsylvania. Even great men underestimated the ability of the new nation, with the freedom it offered, to absorb people from all over the world and turn them into Americans.

Calm amid Hysteria

Remembering the history of immigration to this country—and the often generous, sometimes mean-spirited response of native-born Americans to it—helps make it easier to remain calm amid the recent near-hysteria over illegal immigration, epitomized by the overreaction to news that two women whom President Bill Clinton considered for attorney general, Zoe Baird and Kimba Wood, once employed illegal immigrants as baby-sitters. In Wood's case, she did nothing illegal, but any association with "illegal aliens" was enough to send the Clinton Administration into a dither.

Wood's case reflects the Administration's profound ignorance of the complex realities of immigration. That is not harsh criticism, however, because most Americans are in the same situation. And while no sin, this widespread ignorance has allowed myths about immigration to take hold. For many years this newspaper has tried to take a thoughtful and balanced stance on immigration issues. We remain convinced that there are humane and constructive ways to better regulate the flow of newcomers to this country. But before restating them, it is important to first refute some of the more egregious myths about immigration.

A Fact of Life

Myth: Illegal immigration is an out-of-control problem. A gross oversimplification. It is better to think of illegal immigration simply as a fact of life in Los Angeles and any other place close to the U.S.-Mexico border. To be sure, problems come along with it, like overcrowding, border crime and other forms of exploitation of illegal immigrants, but so do many benefits, such as low-cost labor that helps keep many small U.S. companies in business.

Myth: We are being silently invaded. In fact, the movement of people across our borders goes both ways—in and out. Although some foreigners come to stay, many are migrants who come to work for a time before returning home. This has especially been the case with Mexicans and other Latin Americans, many of whom live here just long enough to build nest eggs in a U.S. economy that, even in bad times, is far more robust than those of their homelands.

Myth: U.S. borders are out of control. Veteran Border Patrol agents say they have never had things under better control. Although controversial in many respects, the Immigration Reform and Control Act (IRCA) of 1986 increased the Border Patrol's size and budget. The construction of a new, sturdier border fence with surplus Navy landing-strip material has reduced illegal border crossing dramatically. In fact, the Border Patrol is actually building new border access roads for its own use because agents are confident that smugglers won't be able to use them even when border guards aren't around.

Sheer Numbers

Myth: The level of immigration today is higher than ever before in U.S. history. Though in some recent years the absolute number of immigrants to this country has reached the level of the late 19th and early 20th centuries, the last great era of U.S. immigration from Europe, the actual immigrant percentage, relative to overall U.S. population, is a quarter of what it was a century ago because the population is much larger now.

"Widespread ignorance has allowed myths about immigration to take hold."

Myth: Today's immigrants are harder to Americanize. Even if one is willing to accept the insulting premise that today's mostly Asian and Latin American immigrants are not as capable as the immigrants of our great-grandparents' day—and we are not willing to do so—sheer numbers are once again on the side of Americanization. Not only are there more native-born Americans to help the process along but the influence of U.S. mass media—movies, music, et al.—is pervasive. And

English is increasingly the world's most popular language.

Myth: Immigrants take jobs. Myth: Immigrants take welfare. The contradictory nature of these two is obvious, but that doesn't keep them from being repeated.

In fact, most foreigners do come here looking for work. But most of the jobs they take are so menial and low-paying that Americans won't take them. Raising the pay to make those jobs more attractive to Americans isn't as easy as it sounds. Research indicates, for example, that if wage scales in light manufacturing in Southern California were not kept low with immigrant labor, the jobs would be not here but in other countries where wage scales are even lower.

> *"As for illegal immigrants, they do not qualify for welfare. Period."*

The immigrants-on-welfare myth stems from confusion over the benefits extended to refugees under a separate section of U.S. immigration law. Refugees from communist nations, like Vietnam, do get education and relocation assistance, although both the federal and state governments have been reducing it in recent years. As for illegal immigrants, they do not qualify for welfare. Period. Even the otherwise generous amnesty provisions of IRCA prohibited immigrants who legalized their status from receiving public assistance for five years.

Real Challenges

All this is not to downplay in any way the real challenges posed by immigration for American society. As noted above, for all the benefits that immigrants bring, they also bring problems. And when those problems fester they contribute to xenophobia, nativism and other anti-immigrant sentiments. Among the solutions this newspaper has endorsed in the past to help this country better deal with immigration, and which we urge the Clinton Administration to consider:

• More federal financial aid to local jurisdictions heavily impacted by immigration. Immigration is a federal government responsibility, but immigrants tend to congregate in a handful of states and cities, where they add to the cost of public services such as schools, safety and public health. California, and especially cities like Los Angeles and Santa Ana, needs federal help to pay for those services. President Clinton announced in February 1993 that he would consider Gov. Pete Wilson's request for help; Clinton's words are encouraging. But the $4 billion allocated for local assistance when IRCA was enacted has never been fully paid out—and more money than that is needed.

• The Border Patrol should be separated from the U.S. Immigration and Naturalization Service and be consolidated with the Customs Service and other federal agencies into a new, more efficient border management agency. That new agency should then put all its resources at the border and ports of entry to stop illegal immigration there. Once relieved of its border patrolling duties, the INS should focus its resources on assisting immigrants, particularly encouraging them to become citizens.

Improve Enforcement, Encourage Development

• To improve the enforcement of IRCA, and to make sure it is applied in a non-discriminatory fashion, all workers in this country should be required to have counterfeit-proof Social Security cards. And the responsibility for administering IRCA should be transferred from the INS to the Department of Labor, which should combine its enforcement with other workplace laws such as wage and hour standards and worker-safety rules. The Labor Department should be given a sufficient budget to carry out these added responsibilities.

• To deal with the most fundamental cause of immigration, poverty in "sending" countries such as Mexico and Haiti, the United States should encourage development projects abroad and free trade, so that poor countries can prosper and put their people to work at home. The North American Free Trade Agreement with Mexico and Canada is only the first step in this direction. But it will be an important first step because 60% or more of the illegal immigrants to this country come from Mexico. And, as a logical follow-up to NAFTA, the United States and Mexico should negotiate a guest-worker program to allow those migrants who will inevitably keep crossing the border to look for work to at least do so legally.

The Biggest Myth of All

That's just a short list—but with some big, complicated proposals. But then the international migration of human beings is, in itself, a very big and very complex phenomenon—one that responds more to the immutable laws of economics, and the unpredictable vagaries of human behavior, than to laws passed by legislatures. As one Border Patrol veteran once told us, "It can't ever be stopped, just regulated." Like him, we long ago concluded that the biggest immigration myth of all is that this "problem" is somehow amenable to easy, or glib, "solutions."

Objections to Illegal Immigration Are Misdirected

by Stephen Chapman

About the author: *Stephen Chapman is a nationally syndicated columnist.*

Anyone giving away beer can always count on plenty of takers, and anyone denouncing immigrants can always be sure of finding lots of agreement. But just as thirsts are greater in July than in January, the resentment of newly arrived foreigners heads up whenever the economy heads down.

During hard times, Americans look for two things: a cure and a scapegoat, and if the first often escapes them, they rarely fail to find the second. . . . The animus this time is being directed at foreigners abroad (such as Japanese automakers) and foreigners here, both of whom are accused of grand theft of American jobs.

A Reawakened Issue

Only two years after Congress enacted a major immigration bill [in 1990] intended to put the issue to rest for a good long while, it suddenly awakened even more vigorous than before. Gov. Pete Wilson of California blamed immigrants for the state's large budget deficit, which he says came about because California has a growing number of "tax receivers," many of them foreigners, and a shrinking number of taxpayers. Pat Buchanan . . . calls for constructing a fence along the entire length of the U.S.-Mexico border to keep out illegal aliens.

The impulse to slam the golden door reflects not only economic anxiety, but also a fear that immigrants are polluting our culture, weakening our political system, spurning our language, breaking our laws, over-seasoning our food, drinking our whiskey and deflowering our daughters. They have been blamed for every unwelcome development except the assassination of JFK, though I

Stephen Chapman, "Americans Have Anti-Immigration Fever," *Conservative Chronicle*, January 29, 1992. Reprinted by permission of Stephen Chapman and Creators Syndicate.

shouldn't give Oliver Stone any ideas.

The resentment of immigration attests to the brief duration of memory, since most Americans wouldn't be here, and some wouldn't be alive, if not for the generous immigration policies of the past. Pat Buchanan, who claims Irish and German ancestry, is a direct political descendant of the 19th century Know-Nothings, who were organized to oppose the influx of unattractive foreigners from . . . Ireland and Germany.

American Indians may oppose admitting foreigners without being hypocrites, but the rest of us have the hard duty of explaining why, after several hundred years of accepting outsiders, the perfect time to pull up the drawbridge is after we're safely inside. An American opposing immigration is a little like an Israeli rejecting Zionism.

Opponents Wrong

Opponents of immigration also have the sad burden of being wrong on almost all the important facts, starting with the economic ones. It is not true that immigrants generally cost the government more than the government costs them. As University of Maryland economist Julian Simon documented in his definitive 1989 book, *The Economic Consequences of Immigration*, both legal and illegal immigrants consistently pay more than their own way, using fewer government services and paying more taxes than native-born Americans.

It's possible that particular cities or states (like California) come out on the short end, since their immigrants may pay more in federal taxes than

"Resentment of newly arrived foreigners heads up whenever the economy heads down."

the federal government gives back to fund services. But the simple remedy is to change how we divvy up the cash.

Common sense may say that newcomers put natives out of work, but common sense says the sun revolves around the earth. Historically, there is no connection between the level of immigration and the level of unemployment. That's because newcomers not only take jobs, they create jobs—which means that shutting them out won't do a thing to boost employment.

A Boon in the End

Americans may not like putting up with strange accents and alien habits, but Americans have always put up with them, and usually in greater profusion than today. As a share of the population, there are fewer foreign-born people here today than in the early part of this century, when my German grandfather was irritating his Texas neighbors and your ancestors were probably proving a total exasperation to real Americans.

But in the end, those foreigners turned out to be a boon, and today's immigrants can be expected to do the same. Contrary to nativist legend, the vast majority of immigrants and their children stay off welfare, obey the law, learn the language and brush between meals. Foreigners, after all, generally don't make great sacrifices to come to this country in order to destroy everything that drew them in the first place.

Look in the Mirror

If Americans think their society is going to hell or their prosperity is in serious danger, they may have a point. But if they want to find the culprits, they shouldn't round up the immigrants; they should look in the mirror.

Racism Exaggerates the Problem of Illegal Immigration

by John Anner

About the author: *John Anner is managing editor of* Third Force, *formerly the* Minority Trendsletter, *a bimonthly publication of the Center for Third World Organizing. CTWO is a nonprofit organization that promotes the interests of Asian, African-American, Latin, and native American peoples.*

What do David Duke and a gleaming metal wall along the U.S.-Mexico border in southern California have in common? More than you might think, say immigrant and refugee rights advocates.

"Who gets blamed when things start to get bad?" asks immigrant rights attorney Richard Garcia rhetorically. "It's always the low person on the totem pole, the immigrant or the poor person trying to survive any way they can.

"When you add this to the racism that's always around, well, we are seeing what can happen." Duke's repackaged, "kinder, gentler" Nazism that promised to do something about the "illegitimate welfare birthrate" is one example of what Garcia is talking about. The on-going attempt to turn the U.S.-Mexico border into a militarized no-man's land impermeable to "illegal immigration" by welding surplus military material into a solid wall is another. The wall, however, is just the tip of the iceberg.

Violence Epidemic

Violence on the border has reached epidemic proportions. People attempting the dangerous illegal crossing from Mexico into the United States, pushed by deteriorating economic conditions and attracted by the promise of higher wages, are routinely robbed, beaten and raped. . . . Bandits on both sides of the border are responsible for some of the brutality, but an increasing number of in-

From John Anner, "The Ones to Watch Out For," *Minority Trendsletter*, Winter 1991/1992. Reprinted by permission of the Center for Third World Organizing, Oakland, California.

cidents are the result of vigilante racists.

In 1990, a teenage gang calling itself the "Metal Militia" dressed in camouflage and shot people thought to be undocumented immigrants, using mock-warfare paint guns. A sniper who killed two Mexican farmworkers near the border admitted at his trial that he killed them just because they were from Mexico. Less dangerous, but still a hazard, were the "Light Up the Border" folks who came out at night to shine their car headlights across the border, hoping to scare potential immigrants and embarrass the Border Patrol into arresting more people.

> *"An increasing number of incidents are the result of vigilante racists."*

The main danger to people trying to make the crossing, however, is not from civilian racists, according to some activists. "The ones to watch out for are the Border Patrol and the INS," says Arnoldo Garcia, program director at the National Network for Immigrant and Refugee Rights. "Not only do they do most of the killings and the beatings, but they egg on and encourage the border bigots."

Between 1974 and 1991, at least 33 people were killed and another 48 wounded by the Border Patrol in the San Diego area alone. People who work with monitoring projects on the border say abuse is common; they have recorded hundreds of incidents of abuse, but point out that few undocumented immigrants are willing to report being harassed because they fear deportation. By some estimates, over 50 percent of the women picked up by Border Patrol agents have been sexually assaulted. First-timers are advised by experienced crossers to take birth control pills in case of rape; the FBI is currently investigating charges that some Border Patrol agents were among the rapists.

A War Zone?

"These guys have a cowboy mentality about what they are doing out there," says Arnoldo Garcia. "They think they are in a war zone and the immigrants are the enemy, people who don't matter. They fire on vehicles carrying people if they don't stop, they chase people across the border into Mexico, they beat people up. Random incidents are one thing. This is a systematic pattern of violence."

Roberto Martínez, who works with Immigration Law Enforcement Monitoring Project of the American Friends Service Committee (AFSC), believes that "there is a history of violence and conflict and racism on the border that has created a kind of culture of violence here in terms of how people perceive undocumented people" (quoted in the *New York Times*).

At least part of that culture of violence, says director of the AFSC project Maria Jimenez, is a result of the perception that illegal immigration has "become a national security question . . . that has to be met with military force."

She points out that although very few of the immigrants are ever apprehended with firearms, the Border Patrol is now equipped with assault rifles, automatic handguns, infra-red scopes (for night vision), helicopters and other military hardware. "I think these people believe they are fighting a foreign invasion," she said in an interview.

In fact, that perception extends far beyond the Border Patrol, into more mainstream organizations and the halls of Congress. Conferences such as the one held in San Diego the weekend of November 16, 1991, that ask "How can we maintain our quality of life with the flood of illegal immigration?" are becoming more common. The former Mayor of San Diego, Roger Hedgecock, uses his radio show to demand more official action to "secure the border."

The metal wall built to replace the sagging chain-link fence along the border is one effort to reduce the flow of immigrants, but there are many others. . . .

Taken in the context of anti-Mexican sentiments along the border, say civil rights activists, these actions reinforce the perception that so-called "illegal immigrants" are stealing American jobs, importing drugs, undermining the U.S. economy, and burdening the social welfare system. As [Rep. Bill] Lowery puts it, "The American people are demanding that we regain the integrity of our borders . . . [to stop the flow of] illegal drugs, illegal immigration and illegal goods coming across from Mexico."

More Give Than Take

Lowery and anti-immigration groups like the Federation for American Immigration Reform (FAIR) argue that high unemployment, overwhelmed social welfare systems, increasing drug use, higher crime rates and other social ills can be traced to high levels of undocumented immigration. Undocumented immigrants, says one of the "Light Up the Border" protesters, who is himself an immigrant from Canada, "get on welfare just by showing up at the office." The perception that millions of Mexicans are pouring across the border and heading straight for the welfare and food stamp offices is common along the border, although unsupported by the available evidence. Most of the studies of the economic effects of immigration conclude that immigrants—

"There is a history of violence and conflict and racism on the border."

with or without documents—add far more to the economy than they take out of it. Generally younger than the average age of the population, they pay more into the social welfare system than they receive, thereby expanding the economy. In fact, the *Wall Street Journal* has argued strenuously for years that an open immigration policy would contribute to the growth and efficiency of the U.S. economy. Border control advocates, says the *Journal*, are making a mistake by associating the crime, violence and other problems on the border "with immigration itself, instead of with the laws that drive it underground." (Of course, the *Journal* also hopes that an increase in immigration will push down wages and undermine the power of unions, to the benefit of employers.)

Mexicans Scapegoated

Immigrants rights advocates in general believe that Mexicans are being scapegoated for economic problems in the U.S., and feel that more people should be allowed to come to look for work. In any case, immigrants rights advocates argue that immigrants are protected under international law and have the right to be treated fairly by the U.S. Border Patrol or INS, even if they are arrested for breaking U.S. law. Advocates are convinced that increased surveillance and enforcement efforts are likely to lead to increasing human rights violations, without really doing anything to stop immigration. . . .

Unfortunately, as the rapid rise of ex-Ku Klux Klan leader David Duke indicated, when times are hard people are all too willing to embrace racist solutions, and there will be no shortage of politicians willing to play to those prejudices. California governor Pete Wilson, for example, announced in November 1991 that a huge projected budget deficit was due to "illegal immigrants" burdening the welfare system and the schools. In the case of the border with Mexico, the metal wall might not do much to actually stop the flow of immigrants, but it does give the impression that the official U.S. policy is that Mexicans have to be kept out, at whatever cost.

Chapter 2

Does Illegal Immigration Harm the United States?

The Effects of Illegal Immigration: An Overview

by Mark Gabrish Conlan

About the author: *Mark Gabrish Conlan is a contributor to* Uptown, *a monthly newsmagazine in San Diego, California.*

"There are too many people coming here, who just don't fit," says Ben Seeley, Southern California program director for the Federation for American Immigration Reform (FAIR). "Instead of a melting pot, we have melting pools: large segments of society that are maintaining separate cultures and Third World conditions. With this steady flow, it's not going to get upgraded. . . . Our education and health systems are breaking down."

"You always hear the negatives," says Roberto Martinez of the San Diego office of the American Friends Service Committee (AFSC). "You never hear about the positive contributions [immigrants] make: how they stimulate the economy, take low-wage jobs and thus keep the market competitive. As a human rights office, we're concerned about the way they're treated as scapegoats."

The Two Extremes

These two San Diego-based activists epitomize the extreme opinions on immigration, especially from Mexico and other Latin American countries. On one side, you have advocates organizing campaigns to discourage illegal immigration. On the other side, Latino activists say that California was historically part of Mexico, and they have a right to keep coming no matter what Anglos think—or try to do to stop them.

The Immigration and Naturalization Service (INS) estimates that 1,041,000 new immigrants arrived in 1992, and approximately 200,000 were illegal (or "undocumented," the term immigrant rights advocates prefer). Most recent immigration—520,000 people in 1992, according to INS estimates—were close relatives of people who had come here previously. Of the remainder, 140,000

From Mark Gabrish Conlan, "Immigration: Who's Paying the Price?" *Uptown*, February 1993. Reprinted with permission.

were skilled workers and their families, 40,000 were citizens of countries which had supplied relatively few immigrants and 141,000 were political refugees, many from the former Soviet Union. . . .

Seeley said he got involved in the immigration issue after Congress passed the Immigration Reform and Control Act of 1986, which attempted to control illegal immigration by penalizing employers who hired people without proper documentation. The 1986 bill also offered amnesty and permanent-resident status to illegal immigrants who had entered the country in 1981 or earlier. While immigrant-rights advocates like Martinez didn't think the bill went far enough, to Seeley, the 1986 bill paved the way for a permanent population of unassimilated Latinos in the U.S.

Are "They" Costing Us Tax Money?

One common argument for further restrictions on immigration, and for more border enforcement, is the alleged tax burden of immigration. A series of federal and state court decisions at both levels have certified that immigrants—legal or illegal—are entitled to most services on the same basis as American citizens. They have access to education and publicly funded health care and welfare. Control advocates also cite criminal justice system costs related to immigrants who commit crimes.

Immigrant-rights supporters argue that those immigrants who are working earn income and, unless they are employed "under the table," pay taxes. Much of the debate over immigration policy is centered on whether immigrants bring in more in taxes than they cost in services, or is it the other way around? Unfortunately, the attempts to answer that question statistically have been inconclusive.

San Diego State University professor Richard Parker's study of illegal immigrants attempted to estimate both the costs of services to immigrants and the local taxes they pay. He left out both costs and revenues to the feds. "We identified a net cost in the range of $150 million, in terms of criminal justice, public health, social services and education within San Diego County," Parker told *Uptown*.

"We found that undocumented immigrants represented about 9 percent of the county population," Parker explained, "[and] 12.5 percent of the crime. They consumed 9.1 percent of

> *"The INS estimates that 1,041,000 new immigrants arrived in 1992, and approximately 200,000 were illegal."*

all health services to the county, directly proportional to their share of the population, but since they were less likely to be employed in jobs that carried private health insurance, they consumed 18.3 percent of all *public* health and community clinic services." Parker's research did not identify what share of the county's expenditures on welfare and other social services are attributable to illegal immigrants.

Martinez disagreed with Parker's methodology and suggested the study might have been skewed to support the anti-immigrant political agenda of its sponsor,

> *"We just don't need any more people."*

Senator Craven. He said the main problem with the study was an unrealistically large estimate of the total number of illegal immigrants in the county. "How did they base that 9 percent?" He pointed to the U.S. Census data on San Diego County which says only 20 percent of the county's *entire* population is Latino—illegals, legal immigrants and citizens combined. "What did they use as criteria? According to our sources, if everybody in a family spoke nothing but Spanish, they listed them as illegal immigrants."

Are "They" Taking Our Jobs?

No argument for immigration control seems as emotional as the assertion that immigrants are taking jobs away from U.S. citizens. *Business Week* reporters Michael J. Mandel and Christopher Farrell, in a July 13, 1992, story acknowledged, "The million or so immigrants—including 200,000 illegals—that will arrive in the U.S. this year are coming at a time when unemployment is high and social services strained. Hungry for work, the newcomers compete for jobs with Americans, particularly with the less skilled."

FAIR's Seeley is blunt. "We just don't need any more people," he says. "We're at 30 million Californians already, and we're doing a horrible job. We have high rates of unemployment and all these people are competing for fewer and fewer opportunities. . . . I have nothing against immigration," Seeley said, "but we need to have a national policy and national goals to meet the needs of the people who are already here. Natural resources are limited, job resources are limited, and we're letting in 800,000 more *legal* immigrants into the U.S. each year than we're creating jobs for."

Immigration opponents have argued that the influx of low-skilled Latino immigrants is hurting U.S.-born African-Americans most by taking low-skilled service jobs which U.S. blacks have traditionally held. Jack Miles stated in the October 1992 *Atlantic*, "The almost total absence of black gardeners, busboys, chambermaids, nannies, janitors and construction workers in a city with a notoriously large pool of unemployed, unskilled black people leaps to the eye." Miles argued, "If the Latinos were not around to do that work, non-black employers would be forced to hire blacks—but they'd rather not. They trust Latinos. They fear or disdain blacks. The result is unofficial but widespread preferential hiring of Latinos—the largest affirmative-action program in the nation, and one paid for, in effect, by blacks."

"I seriously doubt that," replies Adolfo Guzman of *Voz Fronteriza*, a

Chicano/Latino publication at the University of California at San Diego. "I've heard rumors about [immigrants displacing African-American workers], but I've yet to see facts or hear actual complaints." Guzman and AFSC's Martinez see the argument as a typical divide-and-conquer strategy on the part of the *real* beneficiaries of cheap immigrant labor: white employers seeking to cut their labor costs.

"You know who's really taking jobs away from American workers?" Guzman says. "American companies who move their production out of the

> *"I'd like to see more workers allowed to come through."*

U.S., to *maquiladoras* in Mexico and factories in Asia, . . . not undocumented workers. Nobody ever mentions that more jobs are leaving the country than there are undocumented workers coming in."

According to Martinez, many of the jobs traditionally filled by low-skilled Latino immigrants are jobs that cannot be filled through the U.S.-born labor pool, either because American workers don't have the skills or won't work for the low wages these employers can offer. "People still want to buy lettuce at 30 cents a head, and they don't realize they can only do that because the people who pick it are working for such low wages," Martinez explains.

"Employers continue to solicit cheap labor from across the border, but I have yet to see one American worker who has been replaced," says Guzman. "A few years ago, they had a program called 'Operation Jobs' to replace immigrant workers on farms and racetracks with Americans. The longest anyone lasted was one week. The employers had to make a deal with the INS to get [the immigrants] back."

An Ongoing Debate

The two sides usually can't even agree on how to define the problem, much less agree on a solution. Immigration-control advocates argue that "the U.S. has lost control of its borders," and strict new controls must be instituted to regain that "control."

FAIR's demands include restricting *legal* immigration to the pre-1965 average of 300,000 per year; encouraging immigration of highly skilled workers while closing the door to current immigrants' relatives; developing "a secure work authorization system"; further tightening the regulations on political asylum claims and ending "the employment and welfare magnets" allegedly attracting illegal immigrants to the U.S. "We have to stop the flow of *all* immigration, legal as well as illegal," FAIR's Seeley explains. "Immigration has to be based on a need and a plan."

AFSC's Martinez advocates policies in just the opposite direction. "I'd like to see more workers allowed to come through," he says. He'd like Border Patrol enforcement equalized between America's two borders. Right now, Martinez claims, 3,500 Border Patrol agents are stationed on the border with Mexico, while there are only 300 on the U.S.-Canadian border, "which allows hundreds of thousands of Irish, Canadians and other Europeans to come here and take jobs from Americans."

Martinez would also like to see an end to alleged abuses by the Border Patrol. "A Border Patrol agent was acquitted after having shot an unarmed Mexican undocumented worker in the back," Martinez explained. "He was acquitted on all charges, even though he tried to hide the body and didn't report it for 15½ hours. This is one of many cases in which workers—not criminals, drug traffickers or whatever—have been shot and killed at our borders."

"As long as the situation of poverty and economic weakness exists in Mexico, you're going to have immigration, no matter how many walls you put up or how many Border Patrol or Army Reserves or National Guardsmen you put on the border to reinforce the fences," Guzman warned. "If you really want to go after this so-called 'problem,' you need to address it at the source by helping to build up the economy of Mexico so it can put its own people to work."

It's axiomatic that a problem which cannot readily be defined is a problem which cannot readily be solved. But, with increasing numbers of Americans favoring immigration control—and increasing militancy on the part of those Americans who disagree—it's clear that the immigration issue is one which will be argued, debated, discussed, acted upon and *not* resolved for a long time to come.

Illegal Immigration Threatens American Society

by Humphrey Dalton

About the author: *Humphrey Dalton is the pseudonym of an individual in Washington, D.C., who wishes to remain anonymous.*

America is in trouble. The budget is out of control, the nation has become the world's largest debtor. Real wages have fallen, unemployment is high in the inner cities. Educational levels have fallen. Crime and drug consumption are rising. Large sections of our major cities, once envied by much of the world, have degenerated into forlorn wastelands which most of us fear to enter. . . .

Immigration may not be the sole reason for America's sickness. But America will never recover unless it can control the immigrant flood. America is being overwhelmed by immigrants who are destroying the very structure of our society.

They are drawn into America by what the Governor of California called "the Welfare Magnet." The U.S. welfare system was designed to take care of America's own poor; the U.S. is quite incapable of taking care of the surplus population of the world.

Waves of Third World Immigrants

The Third World is undergoing a population explosion which is creating mounting waves of migrants who by their very numbers threaten eventually to destroy the resources of the world like locusts.

Many Third World women average six or even seven live births, and Paul E. Ehrlich of Stanford University has noted that the population of many Third World countries is doubling every 24 or 25 years.

World population has risen from 2.5 billion to around 5.5 billion in the past thirty years. It is expected to double again within the next thirty years!

From Humphrey Dalton, "Help Save America," *Conservative Review*, December 1992. Reprinted with permission.

Illegal Immigration

Each hour the Third World produces 11,000 more mouths to be fed. In one week, births in the Third World equal the entire population of North Carolina, and in 15 months equal the number of Americans living west of the Mississippi.

> **"America is being overwhelmed by immigrants who are destroying the very structure of our society."**

As the Third World countries reach bursting point their populations start moving outward, invading any country that will let them in. Their numbers are sufficient to ensure that they will produce desolation wherever they go.

To quote Paul Ehrlich again, "the world has hundreds of billions fewer tons of topsoil and hundreds of trillions fewer gallons of groundwater than it had in 1968." This mass of humanity brings with it "a desolation of society as we know it," he warns.

Professor Edward O. Wilson of Harvard confirms this dismal vision of the future: "Paul Ehrlich was right."

Professor Antonia Golini of Rome's Institute of Population Research estimates that every decade the world population increases by close to a billion people. This figure is also confirmed by America's respected Population Reference Bureau.

America is a golden country which has not yet been depleted in the way that the masses of the Third World have depleted their own countries. But as the Third World population skyrockets, the surplus people seek to flood into America.

During the past ten years America accepted over 10 million legal immigrants, and the number of *illegal* immigrants is unknown. The lowest estimate exceeds 4 million. Illegal immigrants could exceed 8 million, since the last census missed illegals who had fraudulent papers or just preferred not to be identified. . . .

Land, Sea, and Air

U.S. border patrols currently apprehend more than 3,000 illegal immigrants every day, only to have them re-enter after they have been turned back.

Boatloads of illegal immigrants land on our coasts after dark.

Airport authorities are unable to control the huge numbers of illegal immigrants who arrive in the States with visitor's visas but never leave.

It is questionable whether the government even knows how many illegal aliens enter on visas and just don't leave—the INS is so overburdened. . . .

Numbers of Chinese are already beginning to enter the U.S. as illegal immigrants, travelling across the Pacific Ocean in packed freighters, and being smuggled ashore on the American Pacific coast at nighttime in overloaded yachts and motorboats.

Those U.S. employers who seek cheap manual labor often claim that "immigration is good for America." In the past, when America was undeveloped, and

73

before the development of modern technology, America did need more people. But today it does not. Today America needs skilled labor, and large areas of America are already suffering from lowered water tables, accumulating human waste and garbage due to overpopulation.

Areas which are receiving the main impact of the immigrants are going bankrupt; crime is rising in those areas, as also are taxes. Businesses are actually fleeing California's rising taxes.

Twenty-five percent of California's budget for social services goes to illegal immigrants, who by law receive all social and medical benefits, including free education for their children.

Ironically, because of affirmative action legislation, the children of illegal Third World immigrants receive preferential admission to universities over the children of legitimate white American citizens.

In 1992 California has been reduced to paying its debt by I.O.U.s. The fearsome deficits in the U.S. Federal budget, the escalating U.S. national debt and the huge U.S. trade imbalance are well known.

Professor Seymour Itzkoff of Smith College has pointed out that in this modern world America needs an intelligent, highly educated work force if it is not itself to become a Third World country.

> *"The number of illegal immigrants . . . could exceed eight million."*

Professor Richard Herrnstein of Harvard has shown how modern science is making the less educated and less intelligent workers unemployable.

Guggenheim scholar Professor J. Philippe Rushton of Canada has documented scientific research which reveals that not all peoples of all countries are equally intelligent. The Third World countries that are sending most immigrants to America can be shown to be less intelligent than Europeans and Orientals.

Professor Otis L. Graham of the University of California at Santa Barbara has said that: "America can either evolve toward a high technology economy with a labor force of constantly advancing productivity, wage levels, and skills, or it can drift towards a low technology, low skill, and low wage economy. . . . Immigration policy will be important to the outcome."

Professor Graham adds that immigration is transforming America and disrupting its economy by supplying chiefly low-skilled labor.

Fewer Jobs and More Spending

Already immigration is causing unemployment in America, and those who suffer most from the surplus labor are America's own lower income minorities.

According to the *New York Times*, between January 1989 and June 1991, an additional 820,000 jobs were created in America, but the number of unemployed instead of falling actually increased by 4.1 million—roughly the same number as the illegal immigrants that had entered during the past few years!

Today the cost of providing immigrants with the welfare benefits designed originally for America's own population has brought California into economic disaster.

Most of America's major cities face the same problem, massive immigration of lowly skilled immigrants who need assistance but cannot contribute to the cost of running the cities.

Los Angeles had 27.1% foreign born residents in 1990, and more now. Miami had 33.6% foreign born, New York had 20%, and even Washington D.C. had over 12%.

Immigration involves more than welfare costs. It means that vast capital spending is needed to enlarge the infrastructure to provide for the needs of the immigrants in roads, hospitals, water and even waste disposal.

It is calculated that the cost/value of the infrastructure of America, provided by Americans living and dead, amounts to $40,000 per individual. With low-producing or non-producing immigrants, American workers have to find the additional money to enlarge this infrastructure to meet the added burden of the new immigrants.

People who join a club are usually asked to pay an entrance fee to cover the infrastructure costs of what is already there and that may have to be extended. Immigrants pay nothing to enter America.

Los Angeles is so short of water that additional money has to be spent to bring more water from northern California, where agriculturalists have to make do with less water in order to supply the immigrants packing into the south.

Pollution and waste disposal problems in Southern California have reached hitherto unimagined limits.

Illegal Immigrants and Crime

In the Los Angeles riots, illegal immigrants played as large a role as the American blacks—who got most of the blame! Attorney General William Barre stated at a White House press conference that of the first 6,000 arrested for rioting in Los Angeles, about a third were illegal aliens.

Illegal alien criminals cost Los Angeles County over $75 million annually, when one adds the expense of trials to incarceration. This does not

"U.S. border patrols currently apprehend more than 3,000 illegal immigrants every day."

include the cost of the additional law enforcement work that their presence in America necessitates.

The Director of the INS told a meeting in Washington D.C. last August that no less than 25% of the inmates of the already overcrowded and highly costly federal prisons were illegal immigrants. This does not include the illegal alien criminals incarcerated in state prisons.

Congressman Tom Lewis (Florida) has stated that "Local, state and federal governments throughout America spend *half a billion dollars each year* to incarcerate criminal aliens."

> *"Twenty-five percent of California's budget for social services goes to illegal immigrants."*

Alien crime is not limited to petty offenses. The lax immigration laws have helped international organized crime to invade America. Colombians have a stranglehold on South Florida; California is the playground of Hispanic and Asian gangs. In New York, organized crime has been reinforced by immigrants from South America, Russia and possibly as many as 20,000 Sicilian mafia.

The Toll on Education

The quality of U.S. education is falling. Analysts rarely link this to the vast influx of immigrants or the fact that the immigrants produce far more children than the existing U.S. population.

New York schools now use 86 different languages as their media of education. History books and social science books throughout America are being rewritten to accommodate the new "multicultural" U.S.A.

In 1990 the U.S. Department of Education estimated that the number of public school children with limited English proficiency grew at a 14.3% *annual rate* nationally. In Florida the growth rate of pupils with "limited English proficiency" was 35% per annum.

Teaching Third World children English is costly and takes time away from the real objects of education—to prepare our children to compete with other advanced nations in the world.

The U.S. educational system is slowly being pulled downward in the direction of Third World schools.

A standard excuse for lax immigration laws is that the U.S. will benefit from being more "multicultural." As Professor Tomislav Sunic has said, no nation benefits from being culturally divided—witness Yugoslavia.

Professor Dwight D. Murphey warns that those who press for "multiculturalism are indifferent to traditional American values," and in fact reveal a "strident cultural alienation. No longer is there to be pride in our pioneer ancestors who crossed America in covered wagons and tamed the wilderness."

Pride in America's traditions is being replaced, Professor Murphey says, by a "negative critique of everything that is 'Eurocentric.'"

Immigration is supported by lobbies that are well funded. It is supported by numbers of employers who choose to seek cheap labor today without looking to what it implies for the future. It is aided by lawyers who make profits out of helping immigrants obtain permits, or evade repatriation. It is helped by "rights"-oriented groups such as the National Lawyers Guild, the Lawyers for Human Rights and the so-called Center for Constitutional Rights.

Under the pressure of pro-immigrant lawsuits, the U.S. Dept. of Justice backed down on a five year dispute and allowed tens of thousands of illegal immigrants from democratic Salvador and Guatemala to remain in the U.S. although they could not prove their claim to be "political refugees."

Nothing will change unless the people demand that excessive immigration be halted.

Pro-immigrant lobbies attempt to argue that the American people favor high rates of immigration. The exact reverse is the truth. A 1992 Roper Poll showed that 69% wanted immigration reduced, and 72% said that sound national leadership on the immigration issue was needed.

But the American people have failed to make it clear that they will not elect Congressmen who permit excessive immigration. It is Congress and the President who permit this irrational level of immigration.

To Control Immigration

The Administration and Congress need to be forcibly persuaded, those who fear uncontrolled immigration say, that the people of America do *not* intend to lose their country. They argue that:

• Uncontrolled immigration is invasion without weapons, and theft of other peoples' property.

• Stricter quotas must be placed on immigrants, and only well-educated and law-abiding, culturally-compatible immigrants should be accepted.

• The laws concerning "political refugees" and immigration need to be changed, and the INS needs to be given the financial resources to stop illegal immigration.

• This could be done by an increase of border patrol personnel to defend the land, sea and air, and to ensure that those entering legally on visitors' permits do not illegally take up permanent residence.

• New fences in the more vulnerable land areas are needed, as well as high technology to detect border crossers. The army exists to protect our borders, and could be used to do just this.

> *"Immigration is transforming America and disrupting its economy by supplying chiefly low-skilled labor."*

• Tight immigration control would assist in the war on drugs. It could be paid for by a small INS fee of only a few dollars charged to all persons entering the country.

• The Administration must clamp down on welfare abuse, making sure that social security cards are only issued to legal residents.

• Social security cards should be forgery proof, and should be given the same level of security that private corporations extend to credit cards.

• The law should be changed so that visitors' children are not automatically American citizens because of having been born here.

> *"Illegal alien criminals cost Los Angeles County over $75 million annually."*

Congressman Elton Gallegly of California has introduced legislation into Congress to create tamper-resistant social security cards and resident alien "green cards."

If social security cards were protected in the same way that credit cards are protected, social welfare officials and employers could check into a central computer to find out whether individuals were truly entitled to be in America. Illegal aliens could be prevented from fraudulently obtaining welfare benefits at the taxpayer's expense—and from taking jobs away from the large numbers of unemployed Americans.

The saving on welfare fraud alone would amount to billions and would repay the cost many times over. Fraud-resistant social security cards would also reduce the "welfare magnet" attraction that pulls illegal immigrants into the country through every available chink in the INS defenses.

The American welfare system was designed to support America's own poor. Neither it nor the nation can support the surplus children being produced in the Third World at the rate of 11,000 per hour.

What Americans Are Doing

Many [Americans] are calling and demanding to know where their elected representatives stand on immigration. This is felt to be especially necessary where Congress is concerned. If House and Senate members are not willing to take a strong stand on this vital issue, they need to know how the electorate feels.

Activists talk to their friends and neighbors about immigration and get them involved in the political process. There are well-funded pro-immigration groups lobbying constantly to increase immigration, and those who want immigration to be controlled feel that *if YOU don't get involved they will win*.

They urge that Americans should make sure their money isn't being used to fund immigrant and refugee "rights" groups (which mostly bring lawsuits against, in effect, the taxpayer), or "ethnic diversity" programs.

Those who belong to churches are urged to find out how the churches use their congregations' donations. Many churches quietly fund pro-immigration lobbies and even law-breaking activities such as hiding illegal immigrants. Opponents of free immigration work to keep their church free from such activities.

Illegal Immigration

Immigrants, often aided by illegal immigrants who vote without authorization, have already taken over political control of numerous cities in Texas, California and Florida.

As more aliens come in, politicians are beginning to regard them as a potential "swing" vote in national politics. Alien political organizations such as *La Raza* ("the race") are already actively working toward this.

Anti-immigration activists urge that you remember that Americans need to fight for a stricter immigration policy for the sake of your children and your children's children. It is their future that is at stake.

Illegal Immigrants Drain U.S. Social Services

by Daniel James

About the author: *Daniel James is the president and chief executive officer of the Mexico-United States Institute, a nonprofit organization which studies, researches, and analyzes U.S.-Mexican relations. This viewpoint is excerpted from his book,* Illegal Immigration: An Unfolding Crisis.

Almost hidden away in its Metro section, the *Washington Post* published a poignant story headlined:

SCORES OF ARLANDRIA HISPANICS, FAR FROM HOME, NOW HOMELESS

After Losing Their Jobs, Men Are Begging, Sleeping on the Street

The story, appearing on March 16, 1991, reported that 50 to 100 Hispanic males between the ages of 18 and 40 had been thrown out of work and were living on the streets of Arlandria, an Alexandria, Virginia, community. Civic leaders, it went on, "are seeking expanded services to cope with what they describe as a growing problem that surfaced about six months ago," involving widespread unemployment in Northern Virginia due to the general recession. But unfortunately, Alexandria "is strapped for cash."

Avoiding Help

The *Post* reporter, Pierre Thomas, added that "matters are further complicated by cultural and language barriers," then explained:

> Some men in this group are not American citizens and do not have legal resident status, making them ineligible for many federal welfare programs. Many want help, but are wary of seeking government assistance because they fear it may lead to deportation, city officials say.

How many of Arlandria's 2,325 Hispanics, out of a total population of 5,335, were illegals, the story did not venture to calculate. It broadly hinted at their status, however, that "some of these [homeless] people are in almost chronic underground status."

Consequently, they avoid city shelters and must rely on support networks, often "staying with family members in overcrowded apartments." During the day they beg on the streets, creating an image of harsh poverty in a city generally considered affluent and attractive to tourists and other outsiders because of its considerable beauty and historical importance.

> *"As they [illegal immigrants] acquire 'street smarts,'. . . they grow more confident in applying for aid."*

This vignette of social blight associated with illegal immigration may be relatively minor compared with what is happening in the Southwest and some major northern cities, but it reflects a persistent penetration of traditional American communities.

Beyond the Fear of Discovery

Typically, Arlandria's homeless Hispanics avoided seeking official relief for as illegals they belonged, as we have noted, to a growing underclass which generally shuns contact with officialdom. Studies bear out the fact that they make little use of income transfer programs such as Aid to Families with Dependent Children (AFDC), and food stamps, simply because they fear discovery of their illegal status. But as they acquire "street smarts," and learn to use the resources of networks and advocacy groups, they grow more confident in applying for aid.

As early as 1979, a survey of illegal aliens who had been living in Los Angeles for a long time and among whom there was a heavier presence of spouses and children, confirmed this trend. It showed an 8.9 percent participation rate in welfare programs, with 18.5 percent of the women reporting receipt of welfare payments, according to a study by M. D. Van Arsdol and others. Professor David Heer, in a study of illegal aliens who gave birth in Los Angeles County hospitals, found that 19 percent were current recipients of food stamps. George J. Borjas, in an article in the *Wall Street Journal*, reported:

> Although the conventional wisdom is that immigrants shy away from welfare, the facts are quite different. Both immigrants and natives became more prone to take welfare in the 1970s, but the rate of increase was much faster for immigrants than for natives. . . . By 1980, immigrants were more likely than natives to take welfare: 8.8 percent of immigrant households as against 7.9 percent of native.

Legal and regulatory bars to illegal aliens' use of welfare have been inconsistent, shifting, and riddled with exceptions, and are frequently reshaped by court decisions. Thus:

• Illegal aliens are denied AFDC and food stamps, but pro-rata amounts of such aid can be allocated for use by their U.S. citizen children living among them.

• Congress forbade public housing assistance to illegal aliens in 1981, but because of litigation and Congressional second thoughts the implementing regulations were not initiated until 1988. The Housing and Community Development Act passed in 1987 gave local housing authorities the option of allowing illegal aliens to remain in public housing, to avoid dividing families, or to allow them an extensive period to seek alternative, affordable housing.

• Medicaid, the nation's $80-billion-a-year medical welfare program, is open to illegal aliens who are pregnant, disabled, or require emergency care. In a 1986 decision (*Lewis v. Gross*), the Federal District Court of New York held that illegal aliens are entitled to Medicaid because the federal Medicaid statute did not explicitly exclude them.

• The judicial concept of "Permanent Resident Alien under Color of Law," or "PRUCOL," has expanded the access of illegal aliens to welfare and public services. This doctrine holds that an illegal immigrant is *lawfully* present and is therefore entitled to public assistance unless the INS is actively seeking to deport him. Hundreds of thousands of aliens who remain under "deferred voluntary departure," or whose deportations are stayed while they legitimize their immigration status, are covered under "PRUCOL," report Daniel Stein and Steven Zanowic.

> *"Legal and regulatory bars to illegal aliens' use of welfare have been inconsistent, shifting, and riddled with exceptions."*

• Illegal alien workers in such industries as California's perishable crop agriculture have been heavy users of unemployment compensation because of the inherent instability of seasonal farmwork, according to a report by David North. New legislation and regulations now bar illegals from receiving unemployment payments. But in 1989, the California legislature passed a law excusing formerly illegal aliens who had received amnesty from repaying unemployment compensation received while in illegal status.

Educating Illegal Immigrants

Probably the biggest single public assistance cost for illegal aliens is primary and secondary schooling. A watershed in the ongoing debate over the entitlements of illegal aliens was reached in the 1982 Supreme Court decision, *Doe v. Plyler*, which overturned a Texas law barring illegal immigrant children from free public education.

It is estimated that 3 to 5 million persons have remained in the United States illegally since the 1986 amnesty. Family data on legalized aliens show that about 14 percent of that population would be of school age (5 to 19 years), or 560,000 to 700,000 public school users. Using an average annual per pupil cost for U.S. public schools of $4,800, the total cost to taxpayers would be $2.7 billion to $3.4 billion. School nutrition programs and bilingual education add further costs whose totals are impossible to estimate but would clearly run high.

Confused policies, inconsistent laws, and generous court decisions on the rights of illegals have added up to a major burden on state and local public services and assistance budgets, particularly in low-income areas of the Southwest:

• In Los Angeles County "the costs of services provided to undocumented aliens continue to escalate," according to an official report by the County's Chief Administrative Officer, Richard B. Dixon. "The estimated net cost to the County grew . . . from 207.2 million in 1989-90 to $276.2 million in 1990-91," it calculated. A second report by Dixon, on the Federal Government's share of the cost, noted that it had "increased from $57.7 million in 1989-90 to $140.5 million in 1990-91, and could reach $533 million by the year 2000."

• Educating illegal alien children in the Los Angeles Unified School District costs $500 million a year, and is increasing by an estimated 20 percent annually.

• Nearly 5,000 students in the Brownsville, Texas, independent school district are illegal aliens, many of whom commute illegally from Matamoros, directly across the border. Enrollment in the impoverished district is increasing by about 1,000 a year.

• A neighboring Texas community, Hidalgo County, reported even more rapid growth of enrollments by illegal aliens from Mexico—a doubling of them in the first half of the 1980s.

• In a Brooklyn school district known as the "United Nations of Immigrants," just one bilingual class serves 2,400 non-English speaking children.

Stress on Health Care

• Public hospitals in the Southwest have felt intense stress. Between 1983 and 1989, unreimbursed health care to illegal aliens cost Los Angeles County $778.8 million. In 1986, it cost much smaller El Paso $10 million for the care of indigent illegals at its Thomason General Hospital; it billed the Federal government but could not collect.

• California Medicaid administrators are struggling with the problem of "illegal" illegal aliens. They are residents of Mexico who cross the border to receive subsidized medical assistance, show false documents proving that they are illegal alien "residents" of California, then become eligible for Medicaid. Providing Medicaid coverage to illegal aliens cost California $300 million in 1989.

> *"Probably the biggest single public assistance cost for illegal aliens is primary and secondary schooling."*

• In 1990, the welfare rolls in 49 states increased, due to the recession and the efforts of state governments to supply the needy with food, cash, and medical care. One reason for the welfare increase was, "changes in the immigration law [which] allowed more non-citizens onto the welfare rolls, an especially important factor in California and the Southwest."

Confirming these experiences, Lief Jensen found in 1988 that the foreign born, according to U.S. Census data, were 56 percent more likely than natives to be in poverty, 25 percent more likely to receive public assistance and to have an average per capita income from public assistance 13.6 percent higher than natives.

Do Taxes Compensate?

Why shouldn't federal, state, and local agencies foot the bill for the health, education, and welfare of illegals, as long as they pay their taxes? The question is, do they pay taxes as a rule? If so, do they pay *all* the taxes that would normally fall upon citizens or legal alien residents of the communities in which they live? . . .

> *"Educating illegal alien children in the Los Angeles Unified School District costs $500 million a year."*

It is argued, by those who believe that illegal immigration carries little or no cost to the U.S. taxpayer, that illegals pay the taxes that fund the costs of public services to them. A major study in 1985 of Mexican aliens in Southern California, many of them illegal, analyzed extensively their contributions in state and local taxes and compared them to the total costs of state and local services they obtained. The study, done by Thomas Muller and Thomas J. Espenshade, found that Mexican immigrant households received $2,200 more in state and local services, including education, than they paid in taxes.

Given the poor economic circumstances of illegal aliens generally, it is hard to see how their taxpaying ability could match, much less exceed, the costs of services rendered to them. A person's capacity to pay taxes depends ultimately on his earnings ability. Illegal aliens are concentrated in low-wage, unstable occupations and tend to work fewer hours a year than the population as a whole. Obviously, low wages mean a low state and local income tax liability.

Although illegals often pay Social Security (FICA) taxes, those with children who are at or near the poverty level have their contributions rebated through earned income tax credits. Further, the indications are that tax compliance among illegals is lower than for the general population. North and Houston's 1976 survey of illegal alien workers shows that 22.7 percent of them did not have Social Security taxes withheld, 26.8 percent did not have federal income tax withheld, and 68.5 percent did not file federal income tax returns. Subsequently, in a 1989 study of GAO [Government Accounting Office] data on noncompliance of the foreign born with labor and tax laws, immigration researcher David North found that 44 percent of illegal aliens had received wage payments in cash, indicating the likelihood of non-payment of income tax and Social Security contributions.

According to George J. Borjas:

> National income and tax revenues are substantially lower than they would
> have been if the U.S. had attracted more skilled immigrants. If the people who
> immigrated in the late 1970s had been as skilled as those who came in the
> early 1960s, national income would be at least $6 billion higher and tax rev-
> enues would have increased by $1.5 billion per year.

The classic argument in favor of unrestricted immigration into the United
States, whether legal or illegal, is that the country needs workers able and willing to perform tasks that American citizens are unwilling to perform and at
lower wages but the same level of efficiency.

That is not necessarily true. Various observers have noted that Americans and
legal aliens will accept a variety of low-paying jobs. In Houston, for example,
former INS District Director Paul B. O'Neill, related during an interview:
"There are thousands and thousands of jobs American citizens would take [if illegal aliens did not compete for them]." So would legal aliens.

As a concrete instance, in 1986 O'Neill's staff investigators apprehended 69
illegals working for a janitorial service which was contracted to clean prestigious office buildings in downtown Houston. Within three days, he reported,
130 U.S. citizens and legal aliens applied for the vacated janitorial jobs.

In any event, immigration scholars
who have examined data on the foreign-born over the last two decades
have found evidence of a significant
decline in the labor-market performance, competitiveness, and educational achievements of immigrants,

> *"It is hard to see how [illegal
> immigrants'] taxpaying ability
> could match ... services
> rendered to them."*

along with a rising incidence of poverty and greater use of income transfer and
public assistance programs. Borjas found, upon examining 1970 and 1980 census data, that immigrants are 15.2 percent more likely to be in poverty, 6.1 percent to suffer unemployment, and 13.8 percent to be on welfare.

The Unskilled and Uneducated

In his latest book, *A Marriage of Convenience: Relations Between Mexico
and the United States*, Sidney Weintraub corroborated the findings of Borjas
and others who hold that today's immigrants, particularly Mexicans, are relatively unskilled and have little education. He writes:

> Recent immigrants tend to come with fewer skills and fewer years schooling
> than did earlier ones, and their economic progress may not prove to be compa-
> rable. This is particularly true of Mexican immigrants, who have an average of
> 7.5 years of schooling, compared with more than 11 years for other Hispanics
> and whites.

Weintraub adds that "the illegality of undocumented immigrant settlers makes their economic progress problematic," but qualifies his statement with the caution that "precise time-series data are not readily available as a consequence of the illegality."

The trends contrast starkly with the popular view of the immigrant as an energetic self-starter who displays a high degree of upward mobility after resettlement in his new land. That appears no longer to be true, except where some recent Asian and Soviet Jewish arrivals are concerned.

> *"There are thousands and thousands of jobs American citizens would take [if illegal aliens did not compete for them]."*

Borjas and University of Chicago social scientist Barry Chiswick attribute the declining quality of immigrants to a weakening of the process for selecting immigrants. In the 1960s, 1970s, and 1980s, ever larger proportions of new arrivals in this country were refugees or illegal aliens who are not subject to the immigration law's requirements for screening for labor market adaptability or likelihood of becoming a public charge.

The illegal immigrant stream into the United States, which adds about 250,000 to 300,000 new permanent settlers each year, is predominantly Mexican, disproportionately undereducated and unskilled, and almost totally non-English speaking. These disabilities are major handicaps in securing steady, well-paid jobs. In many instances, they are a virtual prescription for poverty.

The make-up of the Mexican illegal alien influx has changed over time; a tendency to require public assistance, for example, is on the rise. Earlier waves were composed largely of young male workers under thirty years of age. In later waves, they were joined by spouses and children and even aged parents, a population with far greater need for services such as health care, schools and food stamps, as North showed in his study on the *Impact of Legal, Illegal and Refugee Migrations on U.S. Social Service Programs*.

Outsiders Threaten Community

The U.S. Government has constructed an extensive and costly social and economic safety net, over the past half-century, for the less fortunate members of the national community whose interests it exists to serve. Illegal immigration may threaten the viability and solvency of that safety net and the concept of community underlying it. The primary obligation of the nation-state is to its legitimate citizens and legal residents. The concept of community becomes hollow if outsiders can enter it in defiance of its laws and regulations, and swiftly gain entitlements to its benefits. The very viability of the U.S. welfare system is threatened when resources for the neediest are diluted by the claims of outsiders, and taxpayers conclude that the number of potential claimants is not limited by national boundaries.

Illegal Immigration Harms U.S. Workers

by Robert N. Dunn Jr.

About the author: *Robert N. Dunn Jr. is a professor of economics at the George Washington University in Washington, D.C.*

The United States in general, and the Democratic Party in particular, face a direct conflict between two historic goals: increasing real incomes for working-class Americans and the maintenance of a relatively open and compassionate immigration policy. Real incomes of low-wage American workers have been falling for almost two decades, and there is strong reason to suspect that the arrival of large numbers of unskilled people from abroad, many of whom are illegal immigrants, has been an important reason for that decline. It is unlikely that real wages of U.S. unskilled and semi-skilled workers will recover unless the flow of undocumented workers into the country is sharply reduced.

Despite debates over magnitudes, the evidence is now overwhelming that real wages for U.S. non-supervisory production workers have declined in recent years. U.S. government data show that such hourly wages rose steadily from World War II to a peak in 1973 and then declined by about 13 percent by 1991. Real weekly wages of U.S. production workers fell by about 19 percent, the difference representing the growing role of part-time workers. This decline occurred during the Ford, Carter, Reagan and Bush administrations, so it is the result of basic trends in the economy rather than the policies of a particular president.

Income Distribution More Unequal

During the same 1973-1991 period, average real per capita disposable income in the United States rose by 27 percent. If real per capita incomes rose by more than a quarter in a period during which low-wage Americans saw their real weekly wages fall by about one-fifth, the distribution of U.S. incomes must have become far more unequal.

Robert N. Dunn Jr., "Higher Pay for Low-Wage Earners?" *The Washington Post*, August 25, 1992. Reprinted with permission.

U.S. government data show that the real incomes of families in the bottom fifth of the population rose steadily from the 1930s until the early 1970s, were relatively constant until 1978 and then fell by about 15 percent to a trough in 1984. A modest recovery in the next five years still left such incomes about 8 percent below the 1970s peak in 1989. A Department of Commerce study indicates that the share of total incomes received by the top fifth of U.S. families increased sharply between 1970 and 1990, while the shares going to the bottom groups declined.

> *"Real weekly wages of U.S. production workers fell by about 19 percent."*

There are a number of causes of this decline in real incomes of less-skilled U.S. workers, including rapid growth of imports of labor-intensive manufactured goods from low-wage developing countries, which has helped to reduce manufacturing jobs from 31 percent of U.S. employment in 1960 to only 16 percent in 1991. In addition, U.S. labor demand has shifted toward higher professional skill categories, which tends to reduce the relative incomes of less-well-educated Americans. Undocumented immigration, however, may be a larger factor.

An Inundation of Low-Wage Labor

There is no way to know how many illegal immigrants are here, but when such people were offered an opportunity to regularize their status a few years ago, 2.3 million people from Mexico alone tried to do so. Press reports suggest that Southern California is particularly inundated, and it is obvious that an increasing share of construction and restaurant jobs in Washington are held by recent arrivals from Latin America and the Caribbean.

If the United States faces an unlimited supply of labor from the south at a wage of about $5 per hour, incomes of less-skilled Americans will not increase even if economic growth in this country accelerates. If real wages of poorer Americans are to increase and the inequality of incomes is to be reduced, there must be some restriction on the foreign supply of low-wage labor, and that means both stricter immigration policies and tougher enforcement measures.

High-Skill vs. Unskilled Labor

Immigration of high-skill, professional and technical labor has an effect on the distribution of income that is the opposite of the immigration of unskilled people. Adding to the supply of highly educated labor reduces income of high-income Americans and makes the distribution of income more equal. It is not a pleasant conclusion, but it is inescapable. If Washington wants to increase incomes of low-wage Americans and reduce the growing inequality of U.S. incomes, it must severely restrict the inflow of unskilled workers from abroad and allocate the available immigration quotas to highly educated foreigners.

Illegal Immigration

When supply-siders and other "free market" economists argue for open immigration policies, it ought to be remembered that they usually reflect the views of owners of business, who benefit from the abundance of low-wage labor that immigrants provide.

It is Bill Clinton and the Democratic Party who face a nasty conflict over this issue. Low-wage Americans are part of the core constituency of the Democrats, and such people would clearly gain from policies that restrict the immigration of unskilled people from Latin America and the Caribbean. But the Democrats also represent black and Latin voters who have personal and political reasons to oppose policies that would restrict entry of more black and Spanish-speaking people. Clinton has begun to face this issue, saying that our "first obligation" is "to ensure that immigration laws do not displace American workers." But it is going to be a tough issue for Democrats.

Illegal Immigration Threatens U.S. Security

by Allan C. Brownfeld

About the author: *Allan C. Brownfeld is a syndicated columnist. His editorials appear in the* Washington Inquirer *and* Human Events, *conservative weekly newspapers in Washington, D.C.*

The lethal bombing at the World Trade Center in New York on February 26, 1993, is stirring widespread concern about the ability of the American society to prevent terrorist attacks.

In the five years from 1987 to 1991, the FBI thwarted 24 terrorist attempts in the U.S., according to FBI records. Even so, officials noted, the country's very strengths, particularly its tolerance of extremist views and its embrace of immigrants, will continue to make America vulnerable to terrorism.

"This is a democratic country and one that is not all that difficult to get into," a senior counterterrorism official said. "We try to be open to the various and sundry oppressed peoples of the world. Obviously we want to keep out the bad guys, but you have to have a reason to do it. And absent some pretty good reasons, there's little you can do to stop the flow."

U.S. Lets Them In

The U.S. government, however, is not doing a very good job of keeping out even clearly identified "bad guys."

Much, of course, remains to be learned about the World Trade Center bombing. The man who has been arrested in the terrorist attack, Mohammed Salameh, is a fundamentalist Muslim affiliated with the As Salam Mosque in Jersey City, which has been the pulpit of an angry, blind sheik who has been preaching holy war against the "Great Satan," the United States, and has been investigated by the FBI in connection with three killings.

Sheik Omar Abdel Rahman is the man who issued the "fatwa," or Islamic

Allan C. Brownfeld, "One Answer to Terrorism: Control Entry of Illegal Aliens," *Human Events*, March 20, 1993. Reprinted with permission.

sanction, for the assassination of Egypt's President Anwar Sadat, according to Egyptian authorities. Why was he permitted into the United States in the first place? Why is he still here now, using the U.S. as his base for fund-raising to foment terrorism?

When he entered the U.S. in 1990 on a tourist visa, he was on the official U.S. terrorist list. The State Department, in the wake of the World Trade Center bombing, now acknowledges that U.S. government officials twice acted in error in giving Abdel Rahman permission to enter and remain in the U.S.

> *"This is a democratic country and one that is not all that difficult to get into."*

In first granting him a visa in 1990, the U.S. Embassy in Khartoum, Sudan, apparently overlooked the fact that he had already been placed on a lookout list because of his role in fomenting violence in Egypt. Even after that visa was revoked, said State Department spokesman Richard Boucher, the Immigration and Naturalization Office in Newark, N.J., mistakenly granted Abdel Rahman permanent resident status in April 1991.

The government rescinded that status in February 1992. Sheik Rahman, however, did not leave the United States after that decision. Instead, he applied for political asylum, a request that was made during a January 20, 1993, hearing in Newark. The asylum process and its various levels of appeal can take years.

Behind the Bombing?

And what has Sheik Rahman been doing here during this time? He has been investigated in connection with three killings in the U.S., including the 1990 slaying of the radical Rabbi Meir Kahane. In none of these cases is the sheik suspected of killing anyone. But FBI agents have been looking into whether he gave religious approval for the bloodshed, and probably will examine whether a similar decree was made before the World Trade Center bombing.

Sheik Rahman is using the U.S. as a base to raise funds and to foment violence and terrorism in Egypt. In taped broadcasts sent back to Cairo from Jersey City, Rahman urged fundamentalists to kill Western tourists in Egypt in order to weaken the government and replace it with fundamentalist Muslims.

Egyptian authorities said that they believe the followers of Rahman are responsible for at least two recent assassinations in Egypt: that of Parliament speaker Rifaat Mahgoub and secularist author Forag Foda. They also accuse him of sanctioning the recent wave of Islamic militant attacks against foreign tourists in Egypt, the most recent of which was the February 26, 1993, bombing of a downtown Cairo cafe.

Sheik Rahman, however, is symbolic of a much larger problem. This is the ability of illegal aliens, many from the Third World, to enter the U.S. and bring their violent politics to our shores. During the recent murders in front of the CIA in suburban Virginia, for example, the suspected killer turned out to be Mir Aimai Kansi, a Pakistani who was in the country illegally, and has now vanished.

The ability of Pakistanis and others from troubled Third World countries to easily enter the United States illustrates what many are describing as an immigration "crisis" that has reached "out of control" levels.

Benedict Ferro, Immigration and Naturalization Service district director in Rome, recently sent a cable to Washington stating that "alien smuggling" through New York's John F. Kennedy Airport "has passed the crisis level, with hundreds of aliens with bogus documents or no documents at all arriving and claiming asylum."

Particularly worrisome, according to one immigration official, is that "a disturbingly high percentage of people arriving by air with no legitimate documentation are people from areas where there is a terrorist environment. The chances of stopping any terrorist from entering the U.S. right now are nearly zero."

One immigration official said, "In Pakistan, the corruption level is so high it is unlikely that anyone would be stopped for long who wanted to enter with phony documents. The U.S. immigration officials are not allowed to make checks at the airport in Karachi."

The Asylum Floodgates

In March 1980, President Carter signed a law allowing persons from any nation to declare themselves political refugees and get a hearing. "That opened the floodgates," said one official. In 1992 alone, 103,000 claimed political asylum in the U.S.

The illegal Pakistani immigrant wanted for the CIA killings had claims for asylum which, one INS official declared, "are pathetically transparent. He had no real grounds to claim political asylum. But it takes us at least a year to schedule a hearing." Kansi had been in the U.S. 11 months before the murders he is alleged to have committed.

> *"Illegal aliens . . . enter the U.S. and bring their violent politics to our shores."*

It is high time to change the law concerning political asylum—and to remove illegal aliens from "protected" legal status. Rep. Lamar Smith (R.-Tex.) reports that 20 per cent of the federal prison population now consists of such aliens.

The purpose of our government and law enforcement agencies should be to protect the citizens of the United States. Our willingness to permit the growth of a huge and potentially dangerous population of illegal aliens has made our society increasingly vulnerable to terrorism—as recent events have dramatically shown us.

Illegal Immigrants Burden the U.S. Education System

by Center for Immigration Studies

About the author: *The Center for Immigration Studies is a nonprofit institute that researches and analyzes the social, economic, environmental, and demographic effects of immigration on American society.*

The year 1992 marks the tenth anniversary of *Plyler v. Doe*, the Supreme Court decision granting undocumented alien children the right to free elementary and secondary public education. This decision has had a monumental effect on a number of state school systems and state and local budgets. Over the last ten years, many areas of the country, most notably southern California, have learned that the costs of educating these children are significant. In the 1990s, severe deficits and budget cuts are stretching our already overburdened and often inadequate public education system to its limits. At the same time federal and state governments are drastically reducing spending on education, the school-age population is growing dramatically, especially in many immigrant-receiving states such as California, New York, Texas and Florida. This combination of forces is resulting in overcrowded classrooms, overworked and underpaid teachers, and curricula that are not preparing students adequately for the challenges of a high-technology job market. With the national unemployment rate soaring and the number of low-skill jobs falling, America cannot afford to forsake the one factor that can ensure long-term, international economic competitiveness: education.

The Right to Free Education

In the mid-1970s, the Texas Education Code prohibited the use of state funds to educate children who were not U.S. citizens or "legally admitted aliens," and it permitted local school districts to deny such children enrollment in public schools. Thus, most local school districts either barred undocumented children

Center for Immigration Studies, "The Costly Education of Undocumented Aliens," *Scope*, Fall 1992. Reprinted with permission.

or imposed a tuition fee. The Tyler County Independent School District began charging these children $1,000 per year for tuition in 1977. In 1978 and 1979, seven complaints were filed by undocumented school-age children contending that the statute was unconstitutional since it denied their Fourteenth Amendment right to equal protection of the law. They also claimed they were a "politically powerless minority, forced to suffer [deprivation of education] because of the misdeeds of parents over whom they have no control." The State of Texas responded that undocumented aliens were not protected by the Fourteenth Amendment and that the special educational needs of these children imposed severe hardships upon an already overburdened school system with limited public funding.

> *"The costs of educating these [undocumented alien] children are significant."*

The United States District Court for the Southern District of Texas found for the plaintiffs. The court held that immigration status has no bearing on Constitutional rights and that concern for fiscal integrity is not a compelling state interest. The Court of Appeals for the Fifth Circuit upheld this decision. In the meantime, a number of other complaints had been filed by undocumented children and consolidated in *In Re Alien Children Education Litigation*. Again, the District Court found for the plaintiffs and the decision was upheld by the Circuit Court.

Plyler v. Doe and *In Re Alien Children Education Litigation* were consolidated for appeal to the Supreme Court. The Supreme Court, in 1982, ruled that all persons present in the United States, whether legally or illegally, are protected by the Fourteenth Amendment. In a 5-4 decision, the majority found that the denial of a free public education was not justifiable by any substantial state interest.

Effects on the Schools

Since undocumented alien children are, by definition, unable legally to obtain Social Security numbers, U.S. passports and other forms of identification, the *Plyler* decision has major implications for school registration requirements. In guaranteeing free access to public schools, *Plyler* also protects illegal aliens from possible deportation by forbidding schools to require any information that reveals residence status and would, in effect, limit free access to those with illegal status. Schools are not permitted to require either students or their parents to show identification documents for which illegal aliens are ineligible, since this would potentially expose their illegal status. School officials may only require proof that a child resides within the attendance zone of the school. They must accept rent receipts or utility bills showing the home address as adequate proof. School officials may not, at any time, ask students or their parents about their immigration status, or any other question that may possibly expose illegal status. Under very carefully monitored circumstances, students may be asked about their country of origin, but only if it is to be used solely for pedagogical purposes.

Plyler has also affected the ways in which schools may verify eligibility for immigrant children receiving educational services funded by federal programs including the Emergency Immigrant Education Program, SLIAG (a provision of the 1986 Immigration Reform and Control Act granting federal funds to state and local governments to alleviate the financial burden of the legalization program), and the Transitional Program for Refugee Children. To determine which students are eligible for these programs, schools have been directed to solicit *voluntary* information from students and parents or to use information from students' previous school records. They may not ask for alien registration numbers or documentation of immigration status. The Emergency Immigrant Education Program requires documentation of students' country of origin and their first entry into public school. The Transitional Program for Refugee Children requires documentation of refugee status, country of origin and the date of arrival. All this information must be obtained on a voluntary basis, unless it is included in previous school records. Voluntary information must be sought on a general, not individual, basis from parents or students, and the request must be in writing and not oral.

> *"The Center for Immigration Studies estimates an illegal population of some 4.8 million."*

All applicants, including immigrants, for the Free School Lunch program are required either to provide the Social Security numbers of all adults in the household or to indicate that they do not possess Social Security numbers. However, federal regulations say the application must include a statement that Social Security numbers are used *only* to verify income and other information on the application.

Plyler also mandates that if a student or parent voluntarily offers any immigration-related document for identification purposes, school officials may not record any immigration-related information, the type of document submitted, whether it was an INS [Immigration and Naturalization Services] document, or any other information except that "personal identification was presented."

The Cost to Taxpayers

The most tangible and easily documented implication of *Plyler v. Doe* is the monetary cost. The U.S. Department of Education estimates that public education (K-12) costs American taxpayers some $5,000 per student, whether legal or illegal, annually. The Center for Immigration Studies estimates an illegal population of some 4.8 million nationwide in 1992. About 12 percent of this population is school-age and about 11 percent (528,000) is enrolled in public school, taking into account those who either do not attend or who attend private and parochial schools. This results in a national cost of *$2.64 billion in 1992 alone*. And this price tag is a conservative estimate. It does not, for example, account for capital costs (e.g., new schools and equipment) or for all the additional costs associated with the special educational needs, especially English-language training, of many undocumented children.

According to the *Washington Times* (August 6, 1992), the national Limited English Proficiency (LEP) population grew by 14.3 percent between 1990 and 1991. About one in every 20 students in the United States can be classified as an LEP student. Since illegal immigrants tend to concentrate in certain states, this ratio is much higher in some areas. California, Texas, New York, Florida and Illinois are home to 73 percent of all LEP students. Another 12 percent live in New Mexico, Arizona, New Jersey, Massachusetts and Michigan.

Public education is by far the most expensive public service provided to illegal aliens. This is especially troubling for school districts in areas of high illegal settlement and with a high concentration of LEP students. Los Angeles County, the top choice of residence for both legal and illegal immigrants, released a report called the "Impact of Undocumented Persons and Other Immigrants on County Costs and Services (L.A. County)." This report, drafted by the L.A. County Internal Services Department, found that county school districts spend almost $380 million on educational services for illegal alien children each year.

A related study on San Diego County was released by the Auditor General's office in August 1992. This study, entitled "A Fiscal Impact Analysis of Undocumented Immigrants Residing in San Diego County," found that the county spends more than $60 million per year on educational services for illegal alien children. It also found that illegals represent about 3 percent of the school-age population and almost 20 percent of LEP students.

Similar studies in New York City, Dallas, El Paso, San Antonio, Miami, Chicago and countless other cities would likely draw similar conclusions: educating illegal aliens costs American taxpayers a *large* fortune every year. Can we continue to foot this enormous bill when 7.6 percent of our labor force is unemployed and 58 percent of the population feels the economy is still getting worse? Can our children afford for us to sacrifice the quality of their education so teachers can concentrate on teaching English to undocumented aliens? What are the effects of overcrowded classrooms, overworked teachers and a focus on multilingual teaching on the quality of education? These are just a few of the crucial questions this country must come to terms with in coming years. Education is the backbone of economic success, so if that is indeed America's goal, we cannot afford to put off these tough decisions any longer.

Illegal Immigrants Are Unfairly Blamed for U.S. Problems

by Sara Diamond

About the author: Sara Diamond, who holds a doctorate degree in sociology from the University of California at Berkeley, is the author of Spiritual Warfare: The Politics of the Christian Right, *and a regular contributor to* Z, *a liberal monthly magazine.*

Late in 1991 California Governor Pete Wilson made headlines when he publicly blamed immigrants and poor people for the state's financial crisis. In a November 18, 1991, interview with *Time* magazine, Wilson answered questions about California's strained budget by naming "illegal workers" and "their children" as key culprits. For this and similar immigrant-blaming statements, Wilson took a fair amount of criticism, not only from human rights groups but also from liberal political opponents and from the *Los Angeles Times*. Wilson backpedaled and refocused the blame on the federal government, which collects about two-thirds of the taxes immigrant workers pay, but then doesn't redistribute that revenue to state-level social service agencies. By March 1992 Wilson publicly assailed presidential candidate Patrick Buchanan as a "racist," in an apparent effort to shore up his own image as a "moderate."

Dueling Statistics

Meanwhile, the mainstream press presented dueling sets of statistics on the net societal impact of immigrant workers and their families. One study cited showed that the numbers of immigrant recipients of Aid to Families with Dependent Children was proportional to their numbers in the state's population. Analysts from two right-wing think tanks, the RAND Corporation and the Cato Institute, were quoted to the effect that immigrants not only pull their weight

From Sara Diamond, "Blaming the Newcomers," *Z Magazine*, July/August 1992. Reprinted with permission.

economically but that they subsidize the Social Security system and, especially in the case of undocumented workers, pay more into the system than they take out. Less altruistic than coldly calculating, some conservative economists favor increased rates of immigration as a means of keeping businesses "competitive." In other words, the more available workers, the lower the wages they'll accept.

Breeding Bigotry

Directly anti-immigrant arguments referred predictably to the issue of new-comers' school-aged children. Through no fault of their own, these kids burden a system unwilling to prioritize public education. This line of argument panders to the stereotype that people of color produce "too many" children. In reality, it is bigotry that has been breeding out of control for a long time.

Anti-immigrant sentiment is as old as the land grabbers who first followed Columbus. Governmental policies toward immigrants, and socio-cultural toler-ance for these policies, have shifted with the economic winds. During the labor shortage of World War II, the United States welcomed Mexican migrant work-ers, and called them "braceros" (helping hands). But once the braceros were no longer needed, during the 1950s, the Immigration and Naturalization Ser-vice (INS) launched "Operation Wet-back," and deported hundreds of thousands of Mexicanos and U.S.-born Mexican-American citizens.

"Anti-immigrant violence has escalated in recent years, as part of a larger category of hate crimes."

It's not surprising that anti-immigrant violence has escalated in recent years, as part of a larger category of hate crimes. . . . In February 1992, the Klanwatch Project of the Southern Poverty Law Center in Alabama announced a 25 percent increase in the numbers of Ku Klux Klan, neo-Nazi, and skinhead groups active from 1990 to 1991.

These groups attract the kind of individuals who've been victimizing people of color at increasing rates. In February 1992 the Federal Civil Rights Commis-sion released a report documenting the relationship between politicians' Japan-bashing and increased harassment of Asian-Americans. Also in February 1992 the American-Arab Anti-Discrimination Committee released its findings on hate crimes (assaults, bombings, arson, destruction of property) against Arab-Americans, up from 39 cases reported in 1990 to 119 in 1991. Not surprisingly, the increase correlated with the anti-Arab media campaign led by war-mongering elected officials. In late April 1992, a 19-year-old white San Diego man got in his car and chased five Mexican migrant workers through a border area neighborhood, fired a pistol several times and killed 23-year-old Humberto Reyes Miranda.

The lion's share of the violence against undocumented immigrants is perpe-trated by U.S. police agencies. The American Friends Service Committee sponsors a Mexico-U.S. Border Program that compiles data gathered by dozens of human rights groups working together on the Immigration Law Enforcement Monitoring Project. The Project focuses on the five key areas of the country in which 70 percent of all Border Patrol detentions take place: San Diego, southern Arizona, El Paso, the Lower Rio Grande Valley and South Florida. In its latest report, "Sealing Our Borders: the Human Toll," as of February 1992, the AFSC reports ongoing patterns of "law enforcement" agency

> *"The lion's share of the violence against undocumented immigrants is perpetrated by U.S. police agencies."*

abuse against immigrants and also against U.S. citizens crossing the border. Of the 1,274 cases of abuse AFSC documented during a two-year period, about 28 percent involved verbal threats, insults, and psychological harassment; about 22 percent involved physical abuse, including beatings, sexual assaults, and shootings. Smaller numbers of cases included illegal searches, due process violations, and detentions of U.S. citizens. Between May 1989 and May 1991, AFSC reports seven cases in which Border Patrol agents killed Mexican citizens.

In the aftermath of the Los Angeles rebellion against police brutality and systemic deprivations, the Border Patrol was among the police agencies dispatched to arrest people. Los Angeles Police Chief Daryl Gates blamed the riots largely on Latino immigrants. The INS kicked into high gear with sweeps of workplaces and residential areas.

In a cheap bid for votes during a tough Congressional race, Orange County Rep. Dana Rohrabacher sent a telegram to President Bush demanding that the INS deport "illegal aliens"—and he didn't mean the extra-terrestrial kind. According to the *Los Angeles Times*, in the first week after the Rodney King verdict, about 1,000 of those arrested in connection with riots were "illegal" Latino immigrants who were systematically turned over to the INS to be deported.

Green Light to Racists

Official acts of violence and disdain toward immigrants, "illegal" or otherwise, send a green light to the free-lance racists whose actions get too little attention. Several years ago, white supremacists organized a "Light Up the Border" campaign in which they repeatedly parked and directed their headlights toward Mexico, presumably to make nighttime border crossings more intimidating than they already are. Tom Metzger of the San Diego-area White Aryan Resistance (WAR) announced an anti-immigrant demonstration at the border on June 7, 1992. One organizing leaflet for this "American Spring" action advertised: "Free soft drinks and hot dogs for all . . . four live bands to entertain you. . . . Photograph thousands of future illegal aliens lining up on the border. . . . They are coming by the millions and they are all pregnant!"

Among the numerous anti-immigrant activists in southern California, not all have connections to Klan-type groups, but some do. In a lengthy telephone interview from her home office in Long Beach, Ruth Coffey of Stop Immigration Now! kept reminding me in raspy tones: "I'm no skinhead. I'm 67 years old." In the fall of 1991, Coffey addressed a meeting of the Los Angeles chapter of the Populist Party, an off-shoot of the pro-Nazi Liberty Lobby. The L.A. Populist Party is headed by neo-Nazi activist Joe Fields, who [ran] for a California State Assembly seat from the Long Beach-San Pedro area. (Fields has been a major subject of investigation by the progressive group People Against Racist Terror, which monitors neo-Nazi activity.) Coffey is an inveterate writer of anti-immigrant guest columns and letters-to-the-editor, which she manages to have published in newspapers across the country. Most of Coffey's verbal venom spews toward Mexicanos and Latinos. "Your country is on the verge of becoming a minority dictatorship," she warns.

The Anti-Immigrant Theme

Coffey is busy photocopying and circulating petitions urging members of Congress to support five anti-immigrant bills drafted by Rep. Elton Gallegly, a Republican from Ventura County's Simi Valley. The proposed bills include two that would require tamper proof Social Security and identity cards for legal residents; one that would increase the number of Border Patrol agents; and one that would more severely punish drivers who transport undocumented immigrants across the border. The most politically dangerous of Gallegly's bills, however, is House Joint Resolution 357, a proposal to amend the Constitution so that U.S.-born children of "illegal" and "legal" immigrants are not "natural" citizens entitled to the same rights of other children born here. One of the southern California Congress members already on board this draconian bandwagon is Rep. Anthony Beilenson, a Democrat representing the Beverly Hills area.

Even if Gallegly's bill dies on the legislative vine, it's a useful anti-immigrant rallying theme for groups like the Stamp Out Crime Council (SOCC) in San Diego. The Council plays a limited lobbying role because of its "educational" tax-exempt status, but some of its members have recently formed a separate Coalition for Immigration Law Enforcement (C-FILE), which does lobby and endorse candidates. SOCC holds monthly dinner and lunch meetings with local politicians, sheriffs, and police chiefs and serves as a networking mechanism for cops and

> *"Official acts of violence and disdain toward immigrants . . . send a green light to . . . free-lance racists."*

their friendly citizen-helpers who see crime everywhere. Mostly the Stamp Out Crime Council circulates literature on the supposedly related problems of "illegal aliens," drugs, pornography, welfare and declining educational standards.

Barbara McCarthy, editor of the Stamp Out Crime Council's monthly "Eleven Ninety-Nine" newsletter (11-99 is a police radio code for emergencies), had one of her anti-"illegal alien" articles published in the "paleo-conservative" Rockford Institute's *Chronicles* magazine.

Though the anti-immigrant theme has been a mainstay of the Right's alternative press, the number of articles linking "illegal aliens" to welfare crises has increased slightly, and the attack has come from "paleo-conservative" allies of Patrick Buchanan. The weekly *Human Events*, which absorbed the mailing list of Buchanan's biweekly newsletter

> *"Nativist bigotry toward immigrants . . . is politically useful to the Right."*

once he entered the primary elections, regularly attacks immigrant rights. One of Buchanan's advisors, Llewellyn Rockwell of the Ludwig von Mises Institute in Alabama, called for the restriction of immigrant citizenship rights in *Conservative Review*, Roger Pearson's latest publishing venture. (Pearson, who once headed the World Anti-Communist League, is a veteran white supremacist and long-time publisher of racialist and eugenicist "intellectual" journals.) Two staples of anti-immigrant literature are the obligatory photos of Mexican "illegal aliens" running perilously from INS agents across traffic on San Diego freeways, and the requisite folklore about "legions" of pregnant Mexican women arriving in Texas just in time to suck up free childbirth services and "instant citizenship" for their newborns.

Sources of Ammunition

Two national organizations provide much of the "research" ammunition for the grassroots anti-immigrant groups. The American Immigration Control Foundation, based in Monterey, Virginia, includes among its board of advisors Jerry Woodruff, a Buchanan campaign consultant. AICF president John Vinson was an editorial writer for the Savannah (Georgia) *Morning News* before, he says, he read Jean Raspali's *Camp of the Saints* and became an anti-immigration activist. When I asked Vinson why he thinks immigration is such an important issue, his first response was that the United States faces the potential for regional or civil war, and—several days before Rodney King's police attackers were acquitted in Los Angeles—he predicted urban riots, driven by the "explosive mixture" of unskilled ethnic minorities. Vinson thinks the answer is to patrol the southern border with federal troops. But he thinks that won't happen because "there are powerful groups in this country that profit a great deal from out-of-control borders and massive immigration." The leading conspirators, according to Vinson, are the large corporations that want "free markets" and cheap labor. "The country is being flooded and even colonized by outsiders," says Vinson. AICF sustains itself by purchasing right-wing mailing lists and sending out about one million pieces of direct mail each year. Through direct mail, AICF has amassed 100,000 subscribers to its monthly *Border Watch* newsletter, which alerts readers to anti-immigrant legislation and gives contact information for local anti-immigrant groups.

More slick than AICF, but still transparent, is the Federation for American Immigration Reform (FAIR), a $2 million a year operation that emphasizes the "ecological" rather than "cultural" dangers of U.S. immigration policy. FAIR's national board of advisors includes a few "population control" liberals like former Senator Eugene McCarthy, Anne Ehrlich, and Paul Ehrlich. FAIR takes money from the notorious Pioneer Fund, which sponsors "academic" studies of black genetic inferiority. In a 1986 memo, John Tanton, founder of FAIR, U.S. English and several related groups, asked supporters rhetorically: "Will the present majority peaceably hand over its political power to a group that is simply more fertile? . . . Can *homo contraceptivus* compete with *homo progenitiva* if borders aren't controlled?"

With headquarters in Washington, D.C., since 1979, FAIR only recently opened branch offices in Sacramento and San Diego. At the helm of the Sacramento office is Alan C. Nelson, the former INS Commissioner for the Reagan administration.

Immigration Surveys

Timed to impact public debate shortly before California's June 1992 primary, on May 19 FAIR released to the press the results of a Roper poll it commissioned. FAIR spent $45,000 to conduct a detailed survey, with both national and California-specific samples. Questions were carefully worded so as to elicit high rates of responses to the effect that current immigration rates are too high and are impacting society negatively; that political leaders have been ineffective on the immigration issue; and that tougher laws against "illegal aliens" are in order.

"Anti-immigrant activism perpetuates the most retrograde aspects of our popular culture."

Most questions produced anti-immigrant responses in the 70 to 90 percent range, lending the impression of a national consensus. In fact, in the current political climate, when people are asked questions like: "do you think the laws need revising," most may answer affirmatively without knowing anything about existing laws.

A bare majority of 55 percent polled positively toward the idea of a temporary moratorium on all immigration into the United States. FAIR is now calling for a three-year moratorium, and will use the poll results to lobby policy makers. "We would like to see politicians vying for people's votes take a position on this issue," said FAIR spokesperson Ira Mehlman at a San Francisco press conference announcing the poll results.

Illegal Immigration

To maximize the media punch of the Roper poll, FAIR held simultaneous press conferences in Sacramento, San Francisco, Los Angeles, San Diego, and Washington, D.C. In all of these cities, progressive civil rights groups found out about the FAIR poll ahead of time and were able to prepare their own press packets for interested reporters. At the San Francisco conference, for example, the Coalition for Immigrant and Refugee Rights and Services distributed background information about FAIR and factual refutations of common anti-immigrant myths. Also at the San Francisco press conference Ira Mehlman answered a question about FAIR's view that "illegal aliens" provoked the April 1992 L.A. riots by claiming that a "wave" of increased immigration from Mexico has caused massive unemployment among African-Americans.

Only by uniting the causes of immigrant rights, civil rights, and organized labor can we combat this effort to blame one group's economic struggle for the plight of another.

Nativist Bigotry

Nativist bigotry toward immigrants, especially those who can be defined as "illegal," is politically useful to the Right on two scores. First, anti-immigrant activism perpetuates the most retrograde aspects of our popular culture and, specifically, fuels the ranks of racialist and neo-Nazi hate groups. At a time when some traditional Klan-style recruiting tactics have become passe, the relative acceptability of anti-immigrant violence extends the life span of the white supremacist movement.

Secondly, elected officials who can't solve real social problems, but want to stay in office, can displace public discontent by picking on the most vulnerable members of, for example, the Chicano-Latino community. Civil rights organizations, then, must continue to protect people from the most brutal physical attacks and economic deprivations, instead of progressing toward the necessary goal: mobilizing disenfranchised peoples' voting potential. As the United States moves toward a North American "free trade" agreement that will allow money and jobs—but not human beings—to move "freely" across borders, elites would just as soon do without more pesky voters demanding things like better wages, environmental protections, and respect for the sovereignty of all Americans.

> *"Elites would just as soon do without more pesky voters demanding things like better wages, environmental protections, and respect for the sovereignty of all Americans."*

Illegal Immigrants Do Not Hurt the U.S. Economy

by Sergio Muñoz

About the author: *Sergio Muñoz is an editorial writer for the* Los Angeles Times *and senior fellow for the Center for the New West, a think tank specializing in issues that affect the Southwest United States.*

There they go again!

This week, November 9, 1992, it was Supervisor Mike Antonovich's turn to unveil a new report blaming undocumented workers for the financial crisis we are experiencing in Los Angeles County.

Antonovich hailed the report, ordered by the Board of Supervisors and paid for by the taxpayers, as proving that undocumented people have a negative impact on costs, revenues and services in Los Angeles County. Yet the report was not confined to undocumented residents; it included recent legal immigrants, legal residents who were granted amnesty through the Immigration Reform and Control Act of 1986 (IRCA) and U.S.-born "children of undocumented persons," who, of course, are citizens.

Antonovich and company argue that the costs of these four groups of "immigrants" on social services is exorbitant—close to $1 billion. They fail to acknowledge that the same study shows the "immigrants" paying $4.3 billion in taxes, mostly to federal and state government. The fact that Washington and Sacramento didn't share the revenue to compensate for the county's services is hardly the people's fault.

Perception of Latino Community Harmed

Reports like this one presented by Antonovich, with their combination of half-truths, hidden facts and exaggerated claims, are directly responsible for the climate of intolerance against Latinos prevalent in these hard financial times.

Although the focus of the report is the use of educational, health and social

Sergio Muñoz, "The Divisiveness of Half-Truths," *Los Angeles Times*, November 12, 1992. Reprinted with permission.

services by immigrants of all national origins, the true context of this issue is not educational, medical, scientific or sociological. The real context is political, and its implication, true or false, good or bad, accurate or distorted, have an impact on the public perception of the Latino community.

For many years we Hispanics/Latinos complained that our portrait as executed by some sectors of the Establishment has been unfair, incomplete, sometimes mean and usually distorted. As a community we have passed from being invisible into being problem-people.

While it is true that we have a lot of problems, and it is also true that we create some problems, that is not all we do; we are not the only ones with problems, and we are not the only ones who create problems.

It all began when Gov. Pete Wilson blamed welfare spending for the state's financial troubles. Unwilling to confront the realities of a new post-Cold War economy in a state so dependent upon a war economy, and ignoring the decline in productivity of some manufacturing sectors in a new and more competitive global environment, Wilson had the audacity to maintain that it was the heavy reliance on welfare of people coming from out of state that was responsible for California's economic crisis.

Latinos as Scapegoats

Immediately, the debate centered on the foreigners, and mostly on people who did not look European. Latinos, many people said, are abusing our system, and reports began surfacing that purportedly proved this—first, the San Diego County report, now the Los Angeles County report and soon the Orange County report.

As if all this negative reporting was not enough, the public image of Latinos suffered even more with the ads of desperate politicians seeking votes. I still feel anger remembering that ad from our since-defeated Sen. John Seymour, where he tried to look tall and tough, demanding the deportation of all jailed criminals who had entered the country illegally. The way he presented the problem was faultless, and no one could disagree with him. In fact, the government already does deport undocumented persons who have completed jail sentences.

> *"Undocumented workers fill jobs that local workers will not accept."*

What subliminal message was Seymour sending? I cannot help but feel that he was nurturing xenophobia in the minds of white suburban voters who, unable to understand why the American way of life is deteriorating, fear for their future and have to place the blame on someone. Seymour delivered the scapegoat: the undocumented worker who cannot defend himself.

What bothers me is that playing to fear puts the human rights of all undocumented persons in jeopardy. What worries me is that when these messages arrive at small border communities, they are heard as permission for lynching raids on camps where weary human beings are only trying to rest after a long, hard day. What troubles me is that the association between criminality and immigrants will remain in the minds of people who will discriminate against anyone who "looks Mexican," even fellow American citizens.

> *"We must put an end to this nonsense about the negative effects of immigration."*

This misperception of the foreigner as a predator is a direct result of our politicians' failure to solve the problems they promised us they would solve if only we would vote for them.

Productive and Strong

Elected officials shouldn't be allowed to get away with distortions that encourage prejudice. Here are some facts,

• About 80% of all Latino males in California are permanently in the labor force; only 6% of all Latinos are on welfare.

• Latinos live an average of four years longer than whites and 11 years longer than blacks, according to David Hayes Bautista of UCLA [University of California at Los Angeles]; Latinos have lower rates of infant mortality, the lowest incidence of strokes, heart attacks and cancer, as well as alcohol and drug abuse.

• Undocumented workers fill jobs that local workers will not accept; they stimulate the local economy by expanding the overall level of employment and lower the cost of locally produced goods and services.

We must put an end to this nonsense about the negative effects of immigration and embark upon a more constructive route that considers how we should meet the needs and improve this labor force that our economy demands. If we do not meet their needs, there will be consequences that will affect us all. The state's non-minority population is aging and its fertility rate is dropping. By the year 2000, the U.S. labor force growth will be primarily among minorities, immigrants and white women.

Faced with these demographic realities, it is to our benefit to ensure excellence in our labor force. But this won't happen unless our elected officials understand that either they change their attitude or we will have to change them.

Illegal Immigration Does Not Harm U.S. Workers

by George J. Borjas

About the author: *George J. Borjas is a professor of economics at the University of California at San Diego and the author of* Friends or Strangers: The Impact of Immigrants on the U.S. Economy, *from which this viewpoint is excerpted.*

The debate over immigration policy in the past decade has been dominated by questions about the size, composition, and economic impact of the illegal-alien population. The realization that the United States had lost control over its southern border led to the enactment of the Immigration Reform and Control Act of 1986 (IRCA). The main objective of this legislation is to stop the flow of illegal aliens. . . .

The fear that "immigrant hordes" displace natives from their jobs and reduce the earnings of those lucky enough still to have jobs has a long (and not so honorable) history in the policy debate. The presumption that immigrants have an adverse impact on the labor market continues to be the main justification for policies designed to restrict the size and composition of immigrant flows into the United States.

In addition, it is often argued that the labor market competition between immigrants and natives, particularly minorities, increases the likelihood of conflict among the groups and exacerbates the serious social problems afflicting many American cities. . . .

Lack of Data

Remarkably, until recently little was known about the impact that immigrants have on the native labor market. When economists Michael Greenwood and John McDowell surveyed the literature in 1986 they concluded, "substantive empirical evidence regarding the effects of immigration is generally scarce. . . . Little direct evidence is available on immigration's impact on the employment opportunities and wages of domestic workers." Put bluntly, measurements of the presumed effect that immigrants have on the U.S. labor market simply did not exist. Discussions of whether immigrants reduced the earnings and employment opportunities of natives were typically conducted in a factual vacuum, without any supporting evidence to buttress the arguments.

"Such assertions [that immigrants take jobs from natives] are . . . not based on any empirical evidence."

The absence of systematic empirical analysis did not reflect a consensus that the issues were uninteresting or unimportant. After all, the question of how immigrants and natives interact in the labor market is fundamental to any assessment of the benefits and costs of immigration. Instead, it reflected the unavailability of the data required to analyze this problem and the fact that, even if data existed, social scientists did not know how to go about measuring the labor market impact of an increase in the number of immigrants. This situation has changed rapidly in the past few years, as a number of data sets became available to researchers and econometric methodologies were developed that allow a straightforward analysis of this important question.

Remarkably, economists have quickly reached a consensus on the direction and magnitude of the labor market impacts of immigration. The conclusion suggested by the empirical evidence is likely to be controversial: the methodological arsenal of modern econometrics cannot detect a single shred of evidence that immigrants have a sizable adverse impact on the earnings and employment opportunities of natives in the United States.

Do Immigrants Displace Native Workers?

There are two opposing views about the ways that immigrants affect the native labor market. Some observers assert that immigrants take jobs away from natives: as immigrants enter the labor market, natives are displaced from their jobs. . . . At its most extreme, this hypothesis suggests that immigrants displace natives on a one-to-one basis. For every immigrant admitted into the United States, an American native worker inevitably loses his job.

Such assertions are typically not based on any empirical evidence. Instead, they follow from a set of assumptions about the way the U.S. labor market works and the types of immigrants allocated to the United States by the immigration market. Three assumptions are required to assert that immigrants displace natives on a one-to-one basis.

The first is that the number of jobs in the American economy is fixed. New labor market entrants compete with current workers for the limited number of jobs. Because no economic growth takes place as immigrants (or any other new workers) enter the labor market, this view of the labor market implies that for every person taking a job, some other worker must be displaced.

The second assumption is that the persons allocated into the immigrant flow by the immigration market arc perfectly interchangeable with natives in the production process. After all, in order for an immigrant to be able to take over a job that was formerly held by a native, the immigrant must be qualified to take on that job. In the jargon of economics, immigrants and natives must be "perfect substitutes" in production.

It is still unclear why employers, when they could hire equally skilled immigrants or natives, prefer to hire immigrants. Why is it that immigrants displace natives, and why do employers not choose to keep the natives in their jobs and leave the immigrants unemployed? After all, firing old workers and hiring new workers is costly. Hence, a third assumption is required: immigrants are willing to work for lower wages than equally productive natives. Because immigrants offer cost-conscious employers a certain set of skills at a lower price, it necessarily follows that immigrants take jobs away from natives.

False Assertions

Viewed in terms of these three restrictive conjectures about the way the immigration and labor markets work, the proposition that immigrants displace native workers becomes less plausible. Obviously, the assertion that the U.S. economy has a fixed number of jobs is false. Increases in population, whether they occur through immigration or through natural fertility, boost the demand for goods and services. Employers will typically expand their workplaces to satisfy the additional demand, and more people will be employed.

> *"There is no evidence suggesting that immigrant labor is cheaper than equally skilled native labor."*

Similarly, it is difficult to take seriously the conjecture that the typical Mexican illegal alien is perfectly interchangeable with the typical native in the labor force, or even with an unskilled young black residing in Watts or Harlem. After all, immigrants and natives differ in terms of their proficiency with the English language, their educational background, and their familiarity and experience with the American labor market. It is very unlikely that, on average, immigrants and natives are perfect substitutes in production.

Finally, there is no evidence suggesting that immigrant labor is cheaper than equally skilled native labor. Such a wage differential could arise if there were systematic labor market discrimination against foreign-born persons in the United States. The available evidence, however, does not support the assertion that immigrants are systematically discriminated against. Alternatively, it could be argued that illegal aliens, who are afraid of being reported to the immigration officials, are easy prey for exploitation and are paid less than the going wage by employers. However, illegal aliens have the same wage as legal immigrants once differences in observable demographic characteristics are taken into account. Thus, there is no reason to believe that employers would prefer to hire immigrants over equally qualified natives. In sum, the presumption that immigrants must displace natives rests on a rather peculiar, and erroneous, view of how the immigration and labor markets operate.

A Two-Sector Market?

Other observers of the immigrant experience in the U.S. labor market assert the opposite, that immigrants have no impact on the labor market opportunities of natives. Economist Michael Piore, for instance, believes that immigrants cause very little displacement of natives because immigrants "take on a distinct set of jobs, jobs that the native labor force refuses to accept."

In this view of the world, the labor market is segmented into two sectors: a primary sector, which contains the "good" jobs, and a secondary sector, where the "bad" jobs are. Natives obviously prefer the better jobs available in the primary sector. Because of labor market discrimination against immigrants, or because some immigrant groups tend to be unskilled and have little knowledge of the English language or the way the U.S. labor market works, immigrants are crowded into the secondary sector and will hold jobs that natives refuse to take.

This approach to the labor market is flawed because it too depends on assumptions that are arbitrary, logically inconsistent, and without empirical support. First, the segmentation of the economy into two sectors, though appealing to people who prefer a "black-and-white" approach to the labor market, is an extremely simplistic view of the way labor markets operate and has been difficult to establish as empirically relevant.

After all, if natives do not wish to work in secondary-sector jobs, it seems natural that a labor shortage for these jobs would quickly develop. Farmers would find their crops unpicked; consumers would find grocery shelves emptied of fresh fruits and vegetables; and householders would find their houses uncleaned and their lawns unmowed. In a market economy, the labor shortage in the secondary sector would increase competition for the workers willing to provide these services and lead to a bidding war among employers for the few persons willing to work in that sector. This would tend to equalize the rewards between the primary and secondary sectors. As wages rose in the secondary sector, even natives would be willing to work in the bad jobs.

> *"Illegal aliens have the same wage as legal immigrants."*

There is, therefore, no compelling theoretical rationale to support the assertion that natives refuse to work in certain types of jobs, and that immigrants are somehow crowded into these jobs. The conjecture that natives and immigrants do not interact in the labor market, like the one that immigrants displace natives from their jobs on a one-to-one basis, depends on arbitrary assumptions about the operations of the labor and immigration markets. Moreover, neither of these propositions is supported by any empirical evidence. . . .

The Impact of Illegal Aliens on Native Earnings

It is often argued that illegal aliens, particularly those from Mexico, have a major adverse impact on the earnings and employment opportunities of natives, particularly those of unskilled natives and minorities. This concern was perhaps the main impetus behind the enactment of IRCA. For example, during the congressional debate, Congressman E. Clay Shaw Jr. (D.-Fla.) claimed that "American workers . . . are being discriminated against, because they are losing jobs to illegal aliens who are coming to this country and working for less," while Congressman Dan Burton (R.-Ind.) stated, "Part of the unemployment problem is that . . . illegal workers take jobs from Americans. There are nine million Americans looking for work. There are five to twenty million illegal aliens. These numbers suggest a solution to the unemployment problem." Because the

studies discussed [so far] do not distinguish between the labor market impacts of legal immigrants and illegal aliens, they may be ignoring what many consider to be the most important aspect of the problem.

> *"There is . . . no . . . rationale to support the assertion that natives refuse to work in certain types of jobs."*

The 1980 Census enumerated more than one million illegal aliens of Mexican origin. Using INS administrative data on the number of Mexican-born citizens and legal immigrants, it is possible to estimate how many illegal aliens resided in each of a large number of labor markets. These data then allow the comparison of the earnings of natives who reside in labor markets with relatively few illegal aliens to the earnings of natives who reside amidst large illegal populations. This methodological approach was used in a study by sociologists Frank Bean, Lindsay Lowell, and Lowell Taylor. They contrast the earnings of natives among forty-seven cities in the southwestern United States and determine how these earnings are affected by the presence of Mexican illegal aliens in the locality.

The main lesson provided by these comparisons is that the entry of Mexican-born illegal aliens barely affects the earnings of natives. A 10-percent increase in the size of the Mexican illegal-alien population reduces the earnings of Mexican-American men by .1 percent; does not change the earnings of black men; reduces the earnings of other men by .1 percent; and increases the earnings of women by .2 percent. There is no evidence, therefore, to suggest that illegal immigration had a significant adverse impact on the earnings opportunities of any native group, including blacks. It seems that much of the political debate over the enactment of IRCA was based on conjectures that had little basis in fact. . . .

The methodology used to estimate the employment effects of immigration is the same as that used for measuring the wage effects. The employment outcomes experienced by natives are compared among different labor markets. If immigrants have a major displacement effect on native employment opportunities, natives should have lower labor force participation rates, higher unemployment rates, and work fewer hours in those areas of the country in which immigrants concentrate.

However, immigrants have a negligible impact on native employment opportunities. A 10-percent increase in the number of immigrants reduces the labor force participation rate of white natives by only .1 percentage point; reduces the number of weeks worked by .3 percent; and does not affect the native unemployment rate. The data also indicate that immigrants have little impact on the labor force participation rates or weeks worked of black native men.

The weight of the empirical evidence, therefore, indicates that immigration has practically no impact on the earnings and employment opportunities of natives. Although the conjecture that immigrants take jobs away from natives has been a prime force behind efforts to make immigration policy more restrictive throughout American history, there is no empirical evidence documenting that the displacement effect is numerically important.

Illegal Immigrants Do Not Drain U.S. Social Services

by Julian L. Simon

About the author: *Julian L. Simon teaches business administration at the University of Maryland, College Park. The following viewpoint is excerpted from his book* The Economic Consequences of Immigration.

The number of aliens illegally residing and working in the US is an issue that enters into the discussion [of immigration] in many ways. It is the focus of the writings of those who oppose immigration, and it is used to generate strong feelings on the grounds that it causes a breakdown in law and order in the country, and corrupts attitudes toward the law. Huge numbers are thrown around to suggest that the US is vulnerable to invasion or other unnamed dangers because Americans have "lost control of our borders.". . .

The view of many Americans [is] that illegals are a drain upon the taxpayer by way of the use of welfare services. Or as FAIR's [Federation for American Immigration Reform] Roger Conner puts it, "Taxpayers are hurt by having to pay more for social services." Nothing could be further from the truth. By now a considerable number of studies have been done, using a variety of unrelated techniques such as interviewing illegals who are being sent back home, and studying persons in their home villages who had at one time been in the US illegally. These studies may be discussed in two groups: those that provide data on whether immigrants do or do not use services and pay taxes—that is, yes-or-no data—and studies that calculate the net dollar effect of what immigrants take from, and give to, the public coffers. I shall discuss the two groups of studies in that order.

Few Services, Many Taxes

There is general agreement among studies of the proportions of illegals using services and paying taxes, as conveniently summarized by the Select Commis-

From Julian L. Simon, *The Economic Consequences of Immigration*, published by Basil Blackwell, in association with the Cato Institute, 1988. Reprinted with permission.

sion (1981, Staff Report, pp. 549-51): very small proportions of illegals receive free public services. The data collected by David S. North and Marian F. Houstoun may be considered as representative.

There are two persuasive explanations of the observed low use of public facilities. First, the immigrants typically are young adults who need relatively little health care. Second, illegals are afraid of being apprehended if they apply at government offices. The other studies cited by the Select Commission also corroborate the previous findings of North and Houstoun about the proportions of illegals that pay taxes: 77 percent of illegal workers in their sample paid Social Security taxes, and 73 percent had federal income tax withheld. The proportions are likely to have risen since then as a smaller proportion of illegals have worked in agriculture. . . .

Use of Welfare Services by Illegal Immigrants

Service	Percentage using service
Used free public hospital or clinic service	5.0
Collected 1 or more weeks of unemployment insurance	3.9
Have children in US schools	3.7
Participated in US-funded job training programs	1.4
Secured food stamps	1.3
Secured welfare payments	0.5

Source: North and Houstoun, 1976, p. 142

Before beginning to consider the balance of illegals' taxes and costs, I refer to the analysis of (mostly legal) immigrants using Census Bureau data. In brief, those data show that, *aside from* Social Security and Medicare, immigrant families average about the same level of welfare services as do citizens. When programs for the elderly are included, immigrant families use far *less* public services than do natives. Immigrants also pay more than their share of taxes.

Within three to five years, immigrant-family earnings reach and pass those of the average American family. The tax and welfare data together indicate that, on balance, immigrants contribute to the public coffers an average of $1300 or more per year *each year*. And what is true for legal immigrants necessarily is even more true for illegals, who are not in a position to use most welfare services and who are more likely to be in the US without wives and

> *"Very small proportions of illegals receive free public services."*

children who are heavier users of welfare services. That is, the main reason that immigrants make net contributions to the public coffers is that they tend to come when they are young and strong, and this is even more true of illegals as a group than of legals.

It is regrettable that research which has not the slightest claim to scientific re-liability is often presented in public discussion of these issues, and mud-dies the waters; it therefore must be discussed here. For example, a memo by the Western Regional Of-fice of the INS [Immigration and Naturalization Services] ("Illegal Immigration Costs to US Taxpayers," 1983) is cited by FAIR as a "study" done by "The Immigration Service" which suppos-edly indicates a "net cost to the taxpayers for every million illegals in the coun-try in excess of $900 million." However, this estimate is mainly driven not by the costs of welfare services used by illegal aliens, but by an estimated cost of supposed "job displacement"; of the $2.2 billion gross cost estimated for a mil-lion illegals, $1.5 billion is attributed to displacement, and only $700 million to welfare services, which is less than the $995 million that the same document estimates the illegals pay in taxes.

> *"Illegals . . . are not in a position to use most welfare services."*

Clearing Up Confusion

Let us begin our quantitative assessment by clearing up a frequent confusion. Though with respect to all the public coffers *taken together* the balance of illegal immigrants is positive, the picture may well be different with respect to a *partic-ular local or state jurisdiction*. For example, the Urban Institute's study of fami-lies that the Census managed to interview in California found that the costs to the State of California are greater than the state's tax revenues. Mexican immi-grants (both legal and illegal) "contribute less to the state [of California] than is spent on public services for their use." This is due partly to their average income being lower than the average of all households, and partly to their larger-than-av-erage number of children in public schools (1.09, somewhat more than twice the household average for Los Angeles County). However, the Urban Institute's sample excluded immigrants not counted by the Census, and about that group Thomas Muller says, "those immigrants probably pay more in taxes and com-pulsory public program contributions than they receive in benefits." It is reason-able to speculate that the immigrants who were easy for the Census to find, and hence were overrepresented in the sample, were those immigrants with families, whereas those without families use much less services but may pay almost as much in taxes.

Muller and Thomas J. Espenshade also estimated state and local revenues from, and expenditures for, Mexican immigrant families by carefully pulling together a wide variety of pertinent data, though the authors are candid about the difficulties of the method and the consequent uncertainty of the estimates. Their estimates generally confirm the aforementioned findings, and indicate a state-and-local shortfall of $2245 per Mexican immigrant household, in comparison to a state-and-local shortfall of $139 for all households in Los Angeles County. The immigrants' relatively large number of children in school, and relatively low earnings, mainly account for the shortfall.

Though illegal and legal immigrants may cost a state or city more than they pay in taxes, the same is *not* true for the community at large when federal taxes and Social Security contributions (as well as federal services) are included; federal levies dwarf state and local levies. These results may be interpreted as suggesting that states and cities with heavy immigration should receive additional aid from the federal government to spread the burden more evenly. But this is not grounds for concluding that illegals are a net cost to the US *as a whole*; just the opposite is true.

Taxes Exceed Costs

Sidney Weintraub and Gilberto Cardenas deal explicitly with these two issues. They provide reliable evidence that the taxes paid by the immigrants considerably exceed the cost of the services they use. "Despite our biasing the costs upward and the revenues downward, tax revenues from undocumented aliens clearly exceed costs to provide public services to them." For the sum of the impacts upon the *state-and-local* coffers, their estimates are as follows: *cost*—high estimate: $132 million, low estimate: $63 million; *revenue*—high estimate: $286 million, low estimate: $162. But even these figures greatly understate the overall positive effect of these illegal immigrants upon natives because they completely omit the Social Security taxes paid to the federal government by them, and omit 32 percent of the federal income tax paid by them. (The authors assume that 68 percent of federal income tax returns to the state. And these omitted quantities are large relative to the quantities included in their calculation; including them makes

> *"Unauthorized aliens contribute to the US economy on balance."*

the low and high estimates of revenues $359 million and $580 million, that is, more than twice the state revenues alone. And the federal costs left out of their state calculations cannot be large; food stamps is the only major federal program used by individuals as individuals. So the overall excess of government revenues over government cost caused by the illegal aliens is very great, absolutely as well as relatively; the magnitude of the effect in dollars may be roughly assessed by observing that the average undocumented worker has more than $1000 withheld each year in income and Social Security taxes this is after allowing for the roughly one-third of workers who do not pay such taxes); all other taxes are about the same amount as the cost of all state services; hence the federal taxes are pure gain to natives, figuring roughly. On a household basis the contributions to the public coffers are even greater, because there are two workers in a large proportion of households.

It may also be relevant that Weintraub and Cardenas find that an overwhelmingly large proportion of the costs for services used by the illegals—somewhere between 85 percent and 93 percent—goes for education. This should effectively demolish the myth that illegals come to the US and immediately become leeches on the public by living on welfare and unemployment compensation. Even more direct evidence on this point is the low rate of unemployment among the illegals (1.5 percent); the high rate of labor-force participation among all adults, male and female (76 percent); and the high rate (over 6 percent) of all respondents holding two or more jobs.

> *"Illegals are . . . net contributors to the public coffers on a staggering scale."*

Estimate, Not Fact

The Congressional Budget Office was asked the cost of services used by illegals, and the widely publicized response seemed to suggest that illegals are a net cost. In fact, all that the CBO study did (because of the way the question from Congress to CBO was framed) was to estimate how much more *services* the illegals would use if their status were made legal. As Rudolph Penner, CBO's director wrote:

> CBO's estimated cost for the [Simpson-Mazzoli] bill in no way implies that aliens use more in services than they pay in taxes. Nor does it account for secondary effects on the economy, but only on direct effects on federal and state and local government budgets. Precisely because *unauthorized aliens contribute to the US economy on balance*, [italics added] the bill's costs might be even higher if secondary effects were considered; the employer sanction provisions of the bill, if effective, would reduce numbers of unauthorized aliens in the US, possibly reducing GNP [gross national product] and government revenues . . . the immigration estimate in no way implies that aliens do not make a net contribution to the economy.

The anti-immigration organization FAIR has tried to negate the findings of the various studies of the use of welfare and payment of taxes by illegals in two ways. First, it has adduced a study by North of the receipt of unemployment compensation by a group of illegals who gave Social Security numbers when they were apprehended. Indeed, that group shows a raw figure for unemployment insurance use far higher than the previous studies, though probably lower than native Americans. There are two key points about that study that FAIR does not mention, however. First, when one considers dollars—which are the "bottom line"—rather than proportions of users, even in this group the illegals are seen to be net contributors to the public coffers on a staggering scale. North's own calculations suggest that the estimated tax contributions on their account *for unemployment insurance alone* exceed the cost of that program. And contributions to the state for unemployment insurance are only a drop in the bucket compared to the contributions for Social Security and income tax, which are not counterbalanced by any use of services. North estimates that the contributions for Social Security alone were twelve times the unemployment benefits obtained, and this group of people "drew no [other] benefits."

Even if North's study had shown that this group was on a balance a net cost to the public coffers—which it certainly does not show—these data would not be relevant evidence, however, because they are startlingly unrepresentative. Recall that the group was selected by choosing *only those who gave Social Security numbers at apprehension.* It is reasonable that on average these are persons far more integrated into American society over a long period of time than most illegals, especially those from Mexico. Indeed, North's data show that more than 40 percent of this group were paying Social Security for at least six years at the time the study was conducted. Just how unrepresentive they are is shown by one of North's footnotes: "a recent review of more than 500 I-213s of illegal immigrants apprehended by the Livermore (CA) detachment of the INS Border Patrol hundreds of miles north of the border during 1977 turned up exactly two SSNs." And North does not indicate how many forms he searched through to obtain his sample of 580.

The True Bottom Line

A second way that FAIR has tried to argue away the body of evidence on the low use of welfare services by illegals has been to say that recent studies show a higher rate of use than did the earlier studies. "In this monograph, FAIR reports upon recent studies of welfare use by illegals. These force a blunt conclusion: later and sounder examination reveals high and increasing levels of welfare utilization by illegal immigrants." This line of argument is seen to be wrong on several grounds. First, the recent studies by Weintraub and Cardenas, and by Muller, which are better methodologically than are most of the earlier studies, show *low* levels of usage. Second, the earlier studies are not, as FAIR tries to say, less representative than

> *"Natives exploit illegal immigrants . . . by taking much more from the illegals in taxes than is spent on them."*

are the studies that FAIR relies on—North, Maurice D. Van Arsdol et al. and David M. Heer and Dee Falasco. Rather, it seems to me that these latter three studies deal with far less representative populations—North's as discussed above, Van Arsdol's with a group of "covered aliens who sought to regularize their civil status in the US at the offices of One-Stop Immigration, a legal assistance agency in Los Angeles" and Heer-Falasco's with a group of "women of Mexican descent who had live births in Los Angeles County hospitals." Third, and the most compelling reason why FAIR's argument that new studies show a new picture is not persuasive: the percentage rates of use are only imperfect proxies for the total dollar effect upon the public coffers. And every study that provides dollar estimates shows that when the sum of the tax contributions to city, state and federal government are allowed for, those tax payments vastly exceed the cost of the services used, by a factor of perhaps five, ten, or more. This is the true "bottom line," and it is found in the studies that FAIR relies on such as North's as well as Weintraub and Cardenas', and Muller's. This argument takes precedence over all the others, and should end the discussion—though it surely will not.

On balance, then, the conclusion is quite the opposite of what is commonly supposed: natives exploit illegal immigrants through the public coffers by taking much more from the illegals in taxes than is spent on them in public expenditures.

Chapter 3

Are Illegal Immigrants Treated Fairly?

Chapter Preface

The American Friends Service Committee (AFSC) describes the border between the United States and Mexico as "a wound that divides two countries of immensely unequal power." In 1992, the human rights organization issued a report detailing 1,274 cases of human rights violations—including verbal abuse, physical assaults, and deaths—allegedly committed by U.S. law enforcement agents policing the border during a two-year period. Most abuses were attributed to the Immigration and Naturalization Service (INS) and its enforcement agency, the Border Patrol. Indeed, the Border Patrol has received scathing criticism in recent years. Since 1990, according to journalists Patrick J. McDonnell and Sebastian Rotella, agents have been charged with "unjustified shootings, sexual misconduct, beatings, stealing money from prisoners, drug trafficking, embezzlement, perjury and indecent exposure." Furthermore, some charge that the INS often tacitly encourages misconduct by withholding the names of accused agents while summarily clearing them of dereliction of duty. Because Border Patrol agents are not held accountable for their actions, says commentator Zita Arocha, the public perceives them as "a bunch of gunslingers."

This image of the Border Patrol as a mob of renegades is wrong, says senior INS spokesman Duke Austin. He believes that many accusations made against the Border Patrol by human rights groups are "motivated by a political agenda: to perpetuate illegal migration." In order to further their own interests and hamper border enforcement efforts, says Austin, the groups label any attempt to control illegal immigration as abuse. According to Austin, the more than one million arrests made by the Border Patrol each year result in relatively few complaints. In San Diego, the patrol's busiest sector, only one accusation is made for every sixteen thousand arrests. Austin stresses that these are *accusations*, many of which are unsubstantiated. He contends that no other law enforcement agency in the world, confronted with his agency's difficulties—massive numbers of immigrants, dilapidated equipment, little public support—could police the border more humanely than the Border Patrol.

At the border between the United States and Mexico, the line between perpetrator and victim, fairness and injustice, may often blur. The viewpoints in this chapter consider whether American government, business, and the criminal justice system treat illegal immigrants fairly.

Illegal Immigrant Workers Are Not Exploited

by George J. Borjas

About the author: *George J. Borjas is a professor of economics at the University of California in San Diego and the author of* Friends or Strangers: The Impact of Immigrants on the U.S. Economy, *from which this viewpoint is excerpted.*

How many illegal aliens are there, who are they, and what role do they play in the U.S. economy? The very nature of the illegal-alien population implies that the answers to all of these questions are elusive. Nevertheless, existing data portray a picture of the illegal-alien population quite different from the stereotype. The typical illegal alien is not a young, single Mexican man easily exploited by his agricultural employer. Instead, the typical illegal alien is about as likely to be non-Mexican as Mexican; about as likely to be a woman as a man. Most are permanently settled in the United States and reside with immediate family members; most are not employed in agriculture; and most face the same labor market opportunities as demographically comparable legal immigrants.

The Black Market

Whenever government regulations prevent individuals from voluntarily exchanging goods and services, incentives arise to create black markets for these goods and services. For instance, although the purchase of controlled substances or sex is illegal, consumer demand for these goods and services does not disappear simply because the government disapproves of such consumption activities. The demand persists and, if someone is willing to provide the goods and services at the right price, exchanges continue to take place in the black market.

Of course, governments often attempt to prevent such transactions, usually by punishing individuals caught conducting them. Such penalties as fines and incarceration increase the costs associated with black-market transactions for both buyers and sellers. As long as the costs associated with unlawful behavior are not prohibitively high, however, many individuals on both sides of the market find it worthwhile to incur the risk of detection, so they participate in the black market for the illegal goods and services.

The immigration market is no different. Immigration policy prohibits the entry of some classes of persons. Despite these restrictions, many persons in the affected groups still wish to migrate to the United States.

> *"Legal or not, some potential migrants are still willing to offer their services . . . and exchanges are made."*

Clearly, the entry restrictions increase immigration costs. Individuals may get caught crossing the border, or, even if they make it through, they may have to live like fugitives. There is always a possibility that the INS will catch up with them, disrupt their lives, make them lose their jobs, and deport them and their families. These costs clearly reduce the incentives of individuals to migrate illegally. But immigration will still occur as long as the economic benefits outweigh the costs. Legal or not, some potential migrants are still willing to offer their services, some employers are willing to hire these individuals, and exchanges are made.

Beneficial Transactions

The existence of a black market for immigrants and the size of this marketplace thus depend on the costs and benefits associated with unlawful behavior. For instance, if economic opportunities are much better in the United States than in Mexico, many Mexicans perceive that there are substantial gains to be made by becoming illegal aliens and entering the black market. In 1984, the per capita gross national product in the United States was eight times greater than per capita GNP in Mexico. In fact, even after netting out the costs associated with illegal immigration, such as transportation costs to the U.S. border and payments to "coyotes" (experienced guides who assist the illegal aliens across the border and lower the probability of detection), the wage differential between the two countries remains very high. It has been estimated that a person originating in a rural Mexican town can increase his income by 300 percent even after accounting for immigration costs.

These significant economic incentives are reinforced by the relatively trivial penalties associated with illegal behavior both for illegal aliens and for firms hiring them. Until IRCA [the Immigration Reform and Control Act of 1986], firms participating in the black market for immigrants were not subject to penalties for their actions. Even though it was illegal for some persons to be in the United States and for these persons to work, firms were free to hire illegal aliens. Furthermore, deportation is the only penalty imposed on aliens caught participating in the black market, both before and after IRCA. The immigrant, of course, can attempt to reenter the United States whenever it is convenient

Chapter 3

and, if caught once more, try yet another time.

The existence and persistence of a black market for immigrants implies that *all* parties participating in these exchanges benefit from these voluntary transactions. Ineffective regulations, weak enforcement of existing laws, and sizable differentials in economic opportunities are all that is required for a black market to flourish. . . .

Who Hires Illegal Aliens?

The other major players in the black market for immigrants [besides illegal aliens] are the firms that hire illegal aliens. If penalties are absent (which was the case prior to IRCA), firms have no incentive to differentiate by legal status in their hiring decision. As long as workers are equally productive and are willing to work for the going wage (or lower), firms will hire whoever applies for a job. Which firms hire illegal aliens? What kinds of products do they produce? What kinds of services do they perform?

Every time an illegal alien is apprehended, the INS fills out a Record of Deportable Alien form. This form contains demographic characteristics of the alien (such as age, sex, and national origin), as well as the name and address of the alien's employer. This information was used by economist Barry Chiswick to conduct a survey of employers known to hire illegal aliens in the Chicago area (as these firms had been identified by the apprehended illegals). He then contrasted the characteristics of these employers to those of a randomly chosen sample of Chicago firms.

> "All *parties participating in these exchanges benefit from these voluntary transactions.*"

Chiswick's analysis indicates that firms hiring illegal aliens tend to be larger, are more likely to be in the restaurant industry, and are more likely to be in industries with patterns of seasonal employment. It seems that certain types of employers demand the kinds of skills that illegal aliens have and are willing to offer. Hence a good match between illegal aliens looking for work and employers willing to hire them is struck in the black market. All of the participants in the transactions gain from participating in this marketplace. . . .

Do American Employers Exploit Illegal Aliens?

There are many reasons why the illegal flow is considered to be a bad thing for the United States. One is the often heard claim that American employers exploit illegal aliens. Because undocumented workers are obviously concerned about being detected, they lack access to the regulatory institutions that protect the rights of workers. Firms take advantage of this situation and pay illegal aliens lower wages than they would pay equally qualified workers with legal work permits. The point is forcefully made by economist Vernon Briggs:

The alien workers are also frequently victimised by employers who know of their vulnerability to detection. Accounts of alien workers receiving less than the federal minimum wage; not having their social security deductions reported; being turned-in to the authorities by employers just prior to pay day; not receiving overtime premiums; and being personally abused are legion. For as one government official who decried the exploitation of alien workers exclaimed, "Nobody gives a damn, since aliens are nobody's constituents."

In view of the scarcity of data on the number of illegal aliens, let alone on their employment opportunities, it is difficult to know exactly what evidence leads to these sweeping conclusions. In addition, the economic and social implications of the alleged exploitation of illegal aliens are unclear. After all, these persons are in the United States voluntarily. They willingly entered the black market for immigrants, and they obviously benefit from being in the United States, for otherwise they would simply return to their country of origin where they could avoid the exploitation and stigma attached to illegal status.

Legal Status Irrelevant

Moreover, the empirical evidence, limited as it is, provides little support to the proposition that American employers take advantage of illegal aliens. A study by Douglas Massey compares the earnings of legal and illegal aliens and reports that, on average, illegal aliens have about 37 percent lower earnings than legal immigrants. But illegal aliens are also younger, less proficient in English, and more likely to work on a farm, and they have much less experience with their American employers than do their legal counterparts. All of these factors imply that, even apart from legal status, illegal aliens will earn somewhat less than legal immigrants.

In fact, after controlling for these differences in observed demographic characteristics, illegal aliens have essentially the same wage rate as legal immigrants. In other words, if one compares two persons who are demographically similar (in terms of education, age, English proficiency, years on the job, and so on), legal status has no direct impact on the wage rate.

Therefore, despite the frequent claims of exploitation, the available (though limited) evidence suggests that the U.S. labor market prior to IRCA operated in a way that did not penalize illegal aliens. Generally, the same factors that determine the legal immigrant's wage also determine the illegal alien's wage. Persons with higher education, persons who are older, and persons who have been on the job longer earn more, regardless of whether they are legal. Illegal aliens in the United States have lower wages than legal immigrants not because they are illegal, but

> *"Certain types of employers demand the kinds of skills that illegal aliens . . . are willing to offer."*

because they are less skilled.

The Immigration Reform and Control Act did not change any of the statutes regulating the legal immigration process. . . . Its goal, instead, was to get control of the problem of illegal immigration, particularly that from Mexico. . . .

Beginning in 1988, it is unlawful for employers knowingly to hire an illegal alien. New employees must provide proof that they are either U.S. citizens, or permanent legal residents, or have visas permitting them to work in the United States. Employers must then complete forms for each new employee hired certifying that the relevant documents establishing legal status were reviewed. Employers who disobey the law are liable for fines that, for first-time offenders, range from $250 to $2,000 per illegal alien hired. Criminal penalties can be imposed on repeated violators. These penalties include a fine of $3,000 per illegal alien and up to six months in prison. . . .

The early impact of IRCA on the number of illegal aliens apprehended is mixed. Even though the number of apprehensions dropped from the record high of 1.8 million in 1986 to

> *"Illegal aliens have essentially the same wage rate as legal immigrants."*

about 1 million in both 1987 and 1988, it is already clear that the legislation did not stop the flow of illegal aliens into the United States. . . . Although no one knows what will eventually happen to the size of the illegal-alien flow as a result of IRCA, there are good reasons to be skeptical about the law's long-run effectiveness.

Difficult to Enforce

For instance, the only penalty imposed on apprehended illegal aliens is deportation. . . . Once an alien is apprehended and deported he is free to attempt to reenter the United States whenever it is convenient. As deportation is unlikely to be a strong deterrent, a persistent illegal alien is likely to make it through after a number of tries. Therefore, employer sanctions may be the only provision in the law that could significantly raise the costs of participating in the black market. Through its fines and criminal penalties on employers, IRCA raises the cost of hiring illegal aliens. As a result, employers' demand for this type of labor will decrease, which reduces the attractiveness of the U.S. offer to potential illegal aliens. Effective employer sanctions could significantly shrink the size of the black market for immigrants.

But this provision of the law will be difficult to enforce. The INS and the Department of Labor's wages and hours division (which is already in charge of enforcing the Federal Labor Standards Act, including the minimum-wage and the overtime-pay provisions) are jointly responsible for enforcing the employer-sanctions provisions. As of January 31, 1989, only 16,000 employers (or .2 percent of the nation's 7 million employers) had been visited by the INS to inspect the forms that employers are now required to fill out when hiring new employees, and 12,000 of these visits were made as the result of tips.

Moreover, a major loophole in the legislation is that employers need only certify that they reviewed the documents verifying the legal status of job applicants. The employer is not required to keep copies of these documents for inspection. Thus, the probability of detecting employers who decide to hire illegal aliens after "verifying" the documents provided by willing conspirators is small.

Black Market Likely to Remain

In the end, the Immigration Reform and Control Act is unlikely to stop the flow of illegal aliens simply because the legislation did not alter some fundamental facts about the immigration market: the economic benefits associated with immigration to the United States remain sufficiently great to encourage the illegal migration of large flows of persons. Similarly, for some employers, the economic benefits associated with hiring illegal aliens may be substantial and provide incentives to continue the practice. A minor detail such as the legality of entry or of hiring will not deter the immigration of many individuals in the source countries or of employers hiring illegal aliens, as long as the costs associated with entering the black market are small relative to the benefits. In view of the difficulty of enforcing the employer-sanctions provisions in the legislation and of the absence of effective penalties on apprehended illegal aliens, it seems that America's offer in the black market for immigrants remains almost as attractive today as it was before IRCA.

Employer Sanctions Are Fair

by Gene McNary

About the author: *Gene McNary was the commissioner of the U.S. Immigration and Naturalization Service in Washington, D.C., from October 1989 to January 1993.*

When President Bush signed the Immigration Act of 1990, he endorsed a sweeping reform that opened this nation's doors to many more people from foreign lands—with substantial increases in categories based on skills needed in the U.S. economy. This measure authorizing additional workers from other nations in no way has reduced America's commitment to strong enforcement of the employer sanctions provisions of the Immigration Reform and Control Act (IRCA) of 1986. Rather than a conflict of purposes, this different treatment of legal and illegal immigration profoundly reflects the responsibility to administer laws fairly and from the largest possible perspective. Employer sanctions are critical to the U.S.'s efforts to maintain a viable immigration system.

Immigration laws balance a series of national interests. IRCA did much more than impose sanctions on employers who hire or continue to employ aliens whom they know are not authorized legally to work in the U.S. It provided a generous amnesty that enabled nearly 3,000,000 people to legalize their status—with the eventual possibility of becoming citizens. IRCA also reflected a national commitment to reduce the flow of aliens who enter the country illegally through more effective enforcement of America's land borders.

A Complex Balance

Within IRCA's provisions authorizing employer sanctions, Congress combined several social objectives, as it simultaneously prohibited illegal employment, guarded against excessive paperwork, and barred discrimination. Employer sanctions, then, must be viewed as a complex balance of national policies addressing ways of protecting all people under law.

American immigration regulations treat generously those who enter legally. To the extent that illegal employment enables some people to gain access to the U.S. market faster than those who follow proper procedures, it jeopardizes the principle of equal treatment for all applicants.

Accordingly, the Immigration and Naturalization Service (INS) has maintained a delicate balance of policy objectives in implementing employer sanctions. Initially, the INS devoted a great deal of attention to educating companies about their responsibilities under the law. It sought to minimize the paperwork necessary to document the employment eligibility of people who are hired, and the General Accounting Office (GAO) concluded that such sanctions did not result in unnecessary paperwork for employers.

All employers (even those with only a single employee) are required by law to verify that the people they hire (whether citizens or aliens with proper employment authorization) are eligible to work in the U.S. At the time of hiring, every employer must request that each employee demonstrate both identity and authorization to work. Employers can satisfy these requirements by reviewing a variety of documents, but can not make different document requests of people who look or sound foreign. The law expects good faith compliance with these verification requirements for all persons hired, since this is essential to ensure that people authorized to work in the U.S. are not deprived of employment because unauthorized individuals are hired.

A Real Problem

Too many observers—among them some free-market proponents—dismiss the details of immigration enforcement. Such critics believe that the jobs illegal aliens take are often those that most legally authorized employees would not want. Moreover, they assert, even at sub-minimum U.S. wages, illegal aliens earn much more than they would in their native lands. Despite the recession, this nation has a much stronger economy than nearly all others around the globe—a reality that is dramatized by the efforts of those attempting to enter the U.S. from the many less successful nations. Per capita annual earnings in Mexico are approximately $1,900, compared to nearly 10 times that level in the U.S. Since 1986, the exchange rate for Mexican pesos has shifted from 637 pesos to the dollar to more than 2,880. Other economies are even less prosperous than Mexico's, and some are plummeting even lower than their current low bases.

"Employer sanctions are critical to the U.S.'s efforts to maintain a viable immigration system."

Employer sanctions also have been attacked by observers asserting that they have resulted in discrimination against people who lawfully are entitled to work in the U.S., especially citizens who look or sound foreign. These critics are supported by a 1990 GAO report maintaining that employer sanctions had resulted in discrimination against some authorized workers, attributing much of it to con-

> *"Verification requirements . . . ensure that people authorized to work in the U.S. are not deprived of employment."*

fusion over document requirements and other procedures associated with this complex legislation. Some of the confusion undoubtedly derives from INS policy allowing employees to present a variety of proofs to establish both identification and work authorization. This policy was adopted to minimize the burden of compliance on people providing documentation to verify their employment status.

Discrimination Can Be Alleviated

Regardless of any source of confusion, the INS fully is committed to the principle that all discrimination is intolerable. It also believes that any discriminatory side effects of the law can be alleviated without jeopardizing its proper purposes—reducing any incentives toward illegal immigration provided by prospects of U.S. employment.

Some members of Congress have advocated repeal of these employer sanctions provisions. Although the alleged discriminatory effects are the most public argument proponents of repeal use, they are joined by a faction opposed to the documentation requirements on free market grounds. As in any case wherein strange political bedfellows apparently desire a common goal for widely varied reasons, by attempting to unravel the complex social fabric of our immigration laws, both sides could learn that they are jeopardizing the public good achieved through that legislation.

Simplifying the Process

As Commissioner, I have directed INS efforts to minimize, if not eliminate, any harmful side effects of the law. In 1990, INS issued an Employment Authorization Document intended to replace a myriad of papers with a standardized and more secure card. It is becoming the primary source used to indicate employment authorization for temporary residents. The objective is to issue work authorization to aliens on just two cards—one for permanent residents, the other for temporary residents.

We are continuing the process of simplifying requirements and educating employers about their responsibilities to achieve compliance. On Aug. 23, 1991, INS published a regulation governing employment eligibility and explaining legal standards for compliance, then distributed new forms and handbooks incorporating changes made in these regulations. To combat the traffic in fraudulent documentation, we are developing a telephone verification system that, when implemented, will enable employers to ensure that the documents presented by foreign-born new employees are genuine. In short, we have a full range of programs to address the multiple dimensions of national policy concerns about the employment of aliens. . . .

Enforcement Efforts

The INS consistently has emphasized that voluntary compliance with the law is our first goal in implementing employer sanctions. In a report to the Congress signed by President George Bush on July 11, 1991, the Administration confirmed that we have gained cooperation from an estimated 81% of the nation's employers. Improvements in that rate are essential to sustain appropriate respect for this nation's immigration laws, so we are intensifying enforcement activities directed at violators.

On April 5, 1991, I initiated a pilot program to strengthen INS's employer sanctions enforcement program. Each of our district offices was directed to devote 30% of its investigative time to such cases and another 30% to fraud involved in support of illegal employment schemes. We are intensifying our efforts in the sanctions program while maintaining a concerted program to address the challenges presented to immigration enforcement by criminal aliens.

Our balanced enforcement effort includes investigations of employers selected at random to ensure that no sector of the economy feels isolated from its responsibilities under the law. We will give appropriate publicity where we discover violations, both to maintain public awareness that the law is being enforced, and so that any employers who might be tempted to violate it are deterred. We have instituted a new set of fine guidelines to ensure systematic treatment of those who violate the law, as well as stiff penalties for repeated or aggravated offenders.

Experience in Europe indicates that employer sanctions programs can take as long as 10 years to achieve their desired effects. The goals are not merely punitive, but include bet-

> *"I have directed INS efforts to minimize . . . any harmful side effects of the law."*

ter controls on immigration so that decisions about who enters the U.S. and when are consistent with law and national policies. These, in turn, require effective enforcement and compliance as essential elements.

The Border Patrol Is Usually Fair

by Sebastian Rotella and Patrick J. McDonnell

About the authors: *Sebastian Rotella and Patrick J. McDonnell are staff writers for the* Los Angeles Times, *a daily newspaper in Los Angeles, California.*

Afternoon roll call at Imperial Beach, Calif., the nation's busiest and most besieged Border Patrol station.

Two dozen men in green uniforms and close-cropped hair assemble at rows of tables, cracking jokes, adjusting sunglasses, girding for the night ahead. Theirs is a youthful gung-ho fraternity forged in the chaos at The Line where First and Third worlds collide.

Imperial Beach agents often quit after a few years, burned out by the chase: sprinting through treacherous canyons, four-wheeling down hillsides, single-handedly nabbing dozens of illegal immigrants.

An Insular and Violent Culture

Roland Gonzalez, a mustachioed Border Patrol supervisor sporting a baseball-style cap, fires up the troops.

"Catch as many tonks as you guys can," Gonzalez says, exhorting the agents to make arrests. "Safely. An alien is not worth busting a leg."

Tonks.

The expression, used matter-of-factly around the station, hints at the insular and sometimes violent culture of the Border Patrol. The onomatopoeic slang refers to the sound of an agent's flashlight striking an immigrant's head.

In the frenzied world of The Line, a code of the shadows places fraternal loyalty above the law and sometimes condones dangerous tactics and abuse of border crossers, say critics and agents.

Feeling abandoned and under siege, some agents close ranks, regarding the mostly nonviolent migrants, the public and their supervisors as adversaries in a thankless, futile battle. The job breeds a frazzled mentality—an explosive fusion of frustration, callousness and tension.

"Ninety percent of the 'thump' [abuse] cases come from agents who are fried," said Tim Still, a 12-year veteran in El Centro, Calif. "They are just not going to take any more that day. And the first person that mouths off at them—*smack*."

A Complex Reality

At the same time, the caricature of a thuggish "Green Gestapo"—an image burnished by the Mexican media and immigrant advocates—obscures a complex reality.

The patrol's task is fraught with risks. Armed criminals and drunken troublemakers frequent the border, and in the most recent fiscal year [ending 1992], authorities recorded 167 alleged assaults on agents—about one per 13,000 arrests—injuring 49 agents, four seriously. Of 11 agents killed since 1980, 10 died in vehicle and aircraft accidents and one was gunned down by a suspected smuggler in Fresno, Calif.

Barraged by faces of Third World despair, agents are moved to acts of compassion and heroism. Pursuers turn rescuers: They deliver babies in the brush, thwart robbers and rapists who prey on migrants, and on rare occasions even let the saddest cases go free.

> *"In the most recent fiscal year [ending 1992], authorities recorded 167 alleged assaults on agents."*

"Hey, we are human beings," said former Agent Ralph Hunt, a burly, well-spoken six-year veteran. "We are not brutes. We are not racists. . . . A lot of people in the Border Patrol have a lot of integrity. They are hard-working."

Slang such as *tonk* and *wet*—short for the slur *wetback*—is not malicious, agents say, although such language is officially forbidden. "It's crude, it's demeaning and it's dehumanizing," said William Thomas Veal, deputy Border Patrol chief in San Diego.

Officers defend the towering statue outside the Imperial Beach station that depicts an agent clutching a net and a chicken, the latter representing border slang for migrant: *pollo*. Agents say the sculpture, a gift from an admirer, merely embodies the twisted sense of reality found at the international boundary.

"I used to know agents whose idea of fun at night was to go across the border and drink beers and sing songs with the same people they'd be deporting the next day," said former immigration Commissioner Leonel Castillo, who served during the Jimmy Carter Administration. Agents gave Castillo, the first Latino commissioner, a nickname: "Chief Tonk.". . .

In the field, agents share a shadowy nether world with the migrants who daily stream north, often to be arrested and sent back to try again. The largely nocturnal ritual reaches peak intensity in San Diego, where agents—using horses, helicopters, all-terrain vehicles and mountain bikes—defend the most-overrun, most-fortified 15 miles on The Line.

Crowds mass at such busy crossings as the Tijuana River, a gritty arena of confrontation illuminated by stadium lights designed to reduce robberies and rock-throwing by street toughs. Regulars call the hazardous strip *el Bordo:* the Edge.

Agents generally number fewer than a hundred, their adversaries several thousand as the nightly tableau unfolds where the river curls north into San Diego.

In the dust and haze of the river levee, migrants and smugglers huddle at bonfires and perch atop a 10-foot steel border fence, waiting patiently as pale green Border Patrol vehicles rumble back and forth.

"Normally, [Border Patrol agents] behave well," said Fernando Vásquez, 30, a restaurant worker interviewed one night on the levee who said *la migra* has arrested him four times. Then Vásquez added: "Usually they only hit you if you keep running."

Agents Face Special Pressures

Violence cannot be explained solely as the product of brutal officers, say agents who cite extreme working conditions: the sheer volume of arrests, the language and cultural barriers, the youth and inexperience of many officers, the dangers of operating alone at night.

Although law enforcement can be inherently frustrating, the Border Patrol faces special pressures. Agents must confront dozens, sometimes hundreds, of suspects in a volatile milieu that has little in common with the controlled crime scene of traditional police work.

"I think, without doubt, that the Border Patrol agent's job is much more stressful than the metropolitan police officer's job," said Kevin M. Gilmartin, an Arizona psychologist who has counseled federal and local authorities.

Moreover, the Border Patrol enjoys less public empathy than other law enforcement officers. Fed-up agents leave regularly for better-paying federal agencies or local police forces, stoking one of the highest attrition rates in the U.S. bureaucracy.

"There's almost an air of hopelessness," said Gilmartin, who noted that alcoholism appears more frequent among Border Patrol agents. "They become cynical, burned out."

> *"Barraged by faces of Third World despair, agents are moved to acts of compassion and heroism."*

Overwhelmed and outnumbered, border guards deployed in dark canyons and isolated fields often come on strong, spewing profanities in crude Spanish, bluffing about nearby reinforcements. On occasion they resort to force.

"Sometimes there's one person in a group who wants to mouth off or cause problems, and you have to take him down a little harder," Agent G.W. Knight Jr. said one night, hiking through a marsh to set an ambush along paths leading out of the Tijuana hills.

"It's your judgment what the minimum amount of force is," said Knight, a chatty ex-Marine who once arrested a group of 30 people—solo. "Everyone perceives that differently."

Some managers perpetuate an abusive climate, veteran agents said.

"We have supervisors who don't know how to be supervisors," said

> *"They deliver babies in the brush [and] thwart robbers and rapists who prey on migrants."*

Agent Mike Hance. "They turn into bullies, thinking they can intimidate the aliens. Agents see them doing that and do the same thing."

Exasperated agents improvise hazardous tactics, crossing the line literally as well as figuratively.

A veteran described how he has risked triggering international incidents by charging into Mexico on foot pursuits as far as the median of Calle Internacional, a main Tijuana highway paralleling the border.

"I was mainly worried about getting caught by a *judicial* [Mexican policeman]," said the agent, who requested anonymity. "If the guy draws down on me, I'm not going to give up. . . . These people taunt you, they spit at you and throw rocks at you. Then, if you cross the line, it's like you violate their national honor.". . .

Poor Morale, Dilapidated Equipment

Compounding the hazards are a sense of futility and an us-versus-them mindset, which extends from San Diego to small, predominantly Latino border towns where agents feel marooned and sometimes reviled. Gilbert Estrada, a supervisor in Douglas, Ariz., said, "Agents aren't necessarily the most popular people around here."

Internal conflict flares as well, reflected in scathing station house graffiti, biting cartoons and accusatory memoranda. An underground newsletter penned by agents who dubbed themselves "The Phantom" mercilessly lampooned Laredo, Tex., commanders for months.

"Read all about it!" proclaimed a headline. "Management screws up again!" Chiefs brought in handwriting experts to track down the authors, who were eventually fired.

Another source of tension: the dilapidated state of vehicles, radios and other equipment, despite an expanding array of high-tech gadgetry that includes electronic sensors, aircraft and night-vision devices. A federal audit found that as many as half of agency vehicles were down for repair at any given time in 1991, leaving some areas unpatrolled during shift changes.

Chapter 3

In July 1992, a Temecula, Calif., agent charged that supervisors ignored his written warning that a sedan should not be driven. The rear axle failed the next day—not, fortuitously, during a chase. "The results could have been devastating," the agent complained in a memo.

Anti-Agency Sentiment

This incident occurred shortly after a stolen Chevrolet Suburban fleeing a patrol sedan crashed in front of a Temecula high school, killing six people and unleashing a torrent of community criticism of patrol chase tactics. The patrol said its agents did nothing wrong but acknowledged confusion with radio communications and a breakdown of emergency sirens and overhead lights in the pursuing sedan.

Condemnation after the Temecula crash reinforced a perception among agents that the government, public and press either ignore or impede the Border Patrol's mission—especially in California, seen as a bastion of anti-agency sentiment.

"Most of the country doesn't have a clue," said former agent Hunt, lamenting the cumulative social impact of illegal immigration. "The Border Patrol is a Band-Aid on a hemorrhage."

Many agents joined up to staunch the flow, drawn by the allure of secure federal employment and working outdoors in a unique brand of law enforcement. Agents come mostly from working-class backgrounds and border states, often with past experience in the military or small police departments. They take pride in enduring the onslaught, especially nabbing the minority of hardened lawbreakers.

"I like to catch the gangbangers, the little thugs sitting on the fence just waiting to steal your car," said Matt Madore, a young agent from upstate New York with a degree in criminal justice.

A Curious Bond

On patrol, however, Madore banters with prisoners who climb obediently into his caged Bronco. He once bought lunch for a Salvadoran who rode with him for several hours and helped the agent prepare for a Spanish exam.

> *"The Border Patrol agent's job is much more stressful than the metropolitan police officer's."*

This curious bond between hunter and hunted revealed itself after a large group trampled Agent Rudy Diaz under the Interstate 5 freeway in San Diego, breaking his foot. The last four stopped, however, and helped the fallen agent, who gratefully ordered them transported to McDonald's.

"I gave them $30 and told them to eat as much as they wanted," Diaz recalled.

Haunting Art Apac are the faces of two dazed children whom he arrested on a

136

bus near Laredo. They were traveling unaccompanied to their parents' home in Miami. A smuggler had robbed them and had tried to molest the 5-year-old girl, but her 8-year-old brother fought off the attack.

"I was heartbroken," said Apac. "And that's only two aliens out of the 100 you'll see in a day."

A few agents even admit to having risked their jobs by letting illegal immigrants go free. Explaining why he released a man headed to visit a hospitalized relative, a veteran concluded: "One alien isn't going to change the immigration problem."

Illegal Immigrants Are Treated Unfairly

by Cathi Tactaquin

About the author: *Cathi Tactaquin is director of the National Network for Immigrant and Refugee Rights in Oakland, California.*

Undocumented immigrants are perhaps the most powerless of any group of workers in this country—a permanent feature of the much talked about "underclass" of U.S. society. Over the last 15 years, their rights have been under constant assault. Anti-immigrant hype, restrictive immigration legislation, broad attacks on civil rights, and the worsening conditions of the poor have all served to further isolate the undocumented.

The Battle for Rights

At the same time, the undocumented have become increasingly adept at defending their rights both in the workplace and in the community at large. Numerous legal and political campaigns—waged by community groups, labor unions, immigrant and refugee rights advocates, civil rights and religious organizations, and even local governments—have managed to ameliorate some of the more repressive aspects of laws and policies pertaining to people without legal status. Occasionally, these battles have even resulted in an expansion of the limited rights of the undocumented.

Most current assessments place the number of undocumented in the United States at somewhere between 2.5 and 4 million. The number has always been hard to gauge, because this is a "shadow" population, often without the "official" recognition other residents take for granted. A great many undocumented are seasonal workers, here for a few months at a time; some come and go at the beginning and end of the workweek. While those wanting to restrict immigration often quote much higher figures, a number of experts agree that the undocumented population grows between 200,000 and 300,000 a year, about 40% of

From Cathi Tactaquin, "What Rights for the Undocumented?" *Report on the Americas*, July 1992. Reprinted with permission.

whom enter legally and overstay their visas. Among these are refugees from turbulent political situations and civil war who have not been granted official refugee status.

Current public concern over the influx of undocumented immigrants dates from the post-Vietnam war recession of the 1970s, when politicians launched appeals to save U.S. jobs for "Americans." The Immigration and Naturalization Service (INS) obligingly initiated massive raids on immigrant communities, deporting hundreds of thousands of undocumented Mexicans and provoking a heated response from immigrants and their advocates. In 1978, pledging to make a serious study of the immigration debate, President Carter created the Select Commission on Immigration and Refugee Policy.

The commission's report, "Immigration Policy and the National Interest," was released in 1981, after President Reagan had made his own appointments to the commission. The report recommended a token amnesty program for long-residing undocumented immigrants, employer sanctions, and major funding increases for border enforcement and for the creation of immigrant detention centers. These elements formed the basis of sweeping immigration legislation introduced the following year by Republican Sen. Alan Simpson and Democratic Rep. Romano Mazzoli.

The fundamental premise that the undocumented were taking jobs away from U.S. workers continued to frame the immigration debate. An aggressive campaign by the Reagan Administration painted pictures of a "border out of control" and an invasion by "hordes of feet people" to prompt audiences once more to scapegoat "foreigners" for an unstable U.S. economy.

IRCA: A Major Blow

The Immigration Reform and Control Act (IRCA) became law in November 1986. Although it sparked a fairly wide-ranging movement for immigrant and refugee rights, IRCA's passage was widely recognized as a major blow not only to the immigrant communities, but also to labor and civil rights.

Many studies since have found that large numbers of employers fearing the "employer sanctions" provision of IRCA, which imposes civil and criminal penalties on those who continuously hire undocumented workers, will discriminate against those who appear or sound "foreign" to them—namely, racial minorities and the foreign born.

> *"Undocumented immigrants are perhaps the most powerless of any group of workers in this country."*

The impact of sanctions on the undocumented is even more severe. Prior to the passage of IRCA, entering or remaining in the United States without immigration papers was illegal, but working without papers was not a crime. Undocumented workers were considered employees with the same rights as other non-immigrant workers, a definition which was upheld in court. The introduction of employer sanctions essentially redefined the labor rights of the undocumented, "criminalizing" workers without papers. A number of cases have been brought in which an employer challenged a worker's right to even file a claim because the worker was undocumented. While the courts seem to agree that claims may be filed, there is still considerable disagreement about whether reinstatement and/or back pay should be allowed as remedies in the case of an undocumented worker. . . .

The attacks on workplace rights due to IRCA have created an increased awareness in some parts of the labor movement about the importance and complexity of organizing immigrant workers. The California Immigrant Workers' Association (CIWA), launched as an associate member organization of the AFL-CIO in Los Angeles/Orange County, seeks to organize immigrant workers, many of whom are undocumented. With the assistance of CIWA, the International Association of Machinists persuaded workers to unionize at an auto-racing equipment factory in Los Angeles last year—the biggest manufacturing election victory since 1964. The workers at the plant were almost all Mexican and Salvadoran immigrants.

Day Labor

Many undocumented do not, however, have regular work, and are not affiliated with unions. "Street-corner" labor, in which immigrants and non-immigrants alike are hired by the day, is now commonplace in cities and towns across the United States. Particularly with the rise in unemployment, more and more citizens have joined the undocumented in search of any kind of work that offers a day's wage.

The passage of IRCA significantly increased the number of undocumented workers forced to stand on street corners advertising their services for the cheapest wage. In many cases, workers report that they are paid below the agreed-upon wage, or not at all. They are also often exposed to poor or hazardous working conditions. Because work-permit verification (required by IRCA of all employees hired after November 6, 1986) is not required for people who work "irregularly," "sporadically" or on an "intermittent basis," employers of day labor are generally not targets of employer-sanctions enforcement.

> *"Large numbers of employers . . . discriminate against those who appear or sound 'foreign' to them."*

The response to the growing phenomenon of day labor has been mixed—in a number of cities, residents have organized to "get them out of the neighborhood," claiming the workers are a public nuisance. Others have responded more sympathetically, working with unions and cities to create day-labor hiring halls and programs that provide language training and "know-your-rights" outreach.

In San Francisco, the city-sponsored Day Labor Program has yielded another important outgrowth: the Asociación de Trabajadores Latinos—the Latino Workers Association. The member-run organization provides mutual assistance, organizes know-your-rights presentations, and has even agreed to seek a minimum wage of $6.25 an hour.

> *"In many cases, workers report that they are paid below the agreed-upon wage, or not at all."*

Another form of "organized" casual labor is the "cooperative," in which members are essentially independent contractors, and do not have an employer/employee relationship with the person for whom they provide services. In the San Francisco Bay Area, there are a number of immigrant-based cooperatives, including "Heaven Sent," a housecleaning cooperative in East Palo Alto. Heaven Sent provides training and job referrals, and participants pay monthly dues.

Manos, in Alameda and Contra Costa counties, provides job placement for Latino immigrants. Initially organized through the Diocese of Oakland in the mid-1980s, it has helped to launch similar projects in other areas and has grown to include two job-referral collectives, and home-care and janitorial cooperatives. Employers contact the organizations for referrals, pay the workers directly, and make a donation to the organization for overhead costs.

Beyond the Workplace

Of course the impact of IRCA on undocumented rights also reaches beyond the workplace. For example, even though an estimated 70% of undocumented workers pay taxes, they are not eligible for most federal benefits. Because of IRCA, even access to those benefits and services for which they are eligible is constantly being challenged. For instance, immigrants have been denied access to housing because they were suspected of being undocumented. In some cities, the right of undocumented children to attend public schools has been questioned, even though this right was clearly established by the courts.

IRCA and employer sanctions have caused particular problems for undocumented immigrant women. Like other women, they may remain trapped in abusive relationships because they fear being unable to support themselves (and often their children). But they also fear deportation if they have no papers, or if their legal status is tied to remaining in a valid marriage for a minimum of two years. Advocates have fought for a "battered women waiver" to the 1986 Immigrant Marriage Fraud Act, in order to provide immigrant women in abusive relationships an opportunity to gain legal status if they leave their battering spouses.

Several organizations have sprung up around the country to address the particular needs of undocumented women. Mujeres Unidas y Activas in San Fran-

141

cisco, for example, conducts know-your-rights outreach, offers leadership training, language classes and domestic violence counseling, and serves as a support
network for immigrant women. La Mujer Obrera organizes immigrant women,
including many who are undocumented, in the garment factories in El Paso.
Their hunger strikes and organizing campaigns have gained national attention,
since they target some of the country's leading manufacturers who contract
with local sweatshops at poverty wages.

Unofficial Refugees

Hundreds of thousands of "unofficial" refugees are counted among the undocumented. Largely from Central America and Haiti, these people have escaped
conditions of political turmoil and civil war only to be rejected by the United
States. Central Americans have found some safety from deportation through two
programs. After seeking support for safe-haven measures in Congress for several
years, in 1990 Salvadorans gained "Temporary Protected Status" or TPS. TPS
provided an 18-month period of protection from deportation (and work authorization) for Salvadoran refugees who registered with the INS. President George
Bush announced that TPS participants would continue to enjoy that benefit for at
least another year, although TPS is not being officially extended.

Guatemalans did not receive any deportation protection, but they, along with
Salvadorans, also gained some relief through the settlement of a class action suit
filed by the American Baptist Church in 1985. The "ABC" settlement resulted in
re-adjudication for over 150,000 political asylum cases that had been denied Salvadoran and Guatemalan applicants. In the suit, the plaintiffs claimed that
foreign-policy biases, instead of the merit of individual cases, had resulted in the
overwhelming denial of political-asylum petitions. Ninety-seven percent had been
denied; in contrast, 84% of 1987 asylum claims from anti-Sandinista Nicaraguans
were approved. In the 1990 settlement, plaintiffs gained the right to have their
cases re-examined under revised rules, and could get work authorization while
their cases were pending.

IRCA seems to have given added license to the Border Patrol and to racist
hate groups to commit crimes against
undocumented immigrants. Throughout the U.S.-Mexico border area, harassment and physical violence have
increased dramatically. Community
activists and immigrant and refugee
rights advocates are lobbying for a

> *"IRCA and employer sanctions
> have caused particular
> problems for undocumented
> immigrant women."*

variety of measures to protect basic human rights. These measures include:
local, state and federal investigation, monitoring, and prosecution of anti-
immigrant activity; reform of INS regulations governing the use of deadly force
and instituting some form of civilian review of Border Patrol practices; and an

end to Border Patrol high-speed chases of suspected undocumented immigrants in the border area, which have resulted in numerous fatalities in recent years. They have also created an "Immigrant Rights Urgent Response Network" to coordinate efforts among local and national organizations to press for immediate action on critical issues of abuse.

Some Gains Made

A recent court settlement stipulates that undocumented immigrants in detention should be informed of their legal rights, and should have the opportunity to consult with a lawyer. The settlement stems from a case filed 14 years ago on behalf of a Mexican citizen, Rosa Melchor López, and several other immigrant workers who had been arrested in an INS raid at a Los Angeles shoe factory in 1978. They claimed they were not allowed to talk to a lawyer, were forced to sign a waiver of their rights, and were to be deported.

Expansion of undocumented rights has also been pursued in a number of other areas that are indicative of the integration of the undocumented into broader society. For example, in Takoma Park, Maryland, the "Share-the-Vote"

> *"People have escaped conditions of political turmoil . . . only to be rejected by the United States."*

campaign resulted in a successful non-binding referendum providing non-citizens with the right to vote in local elections, and even to run for office. "This is really a civil rights challenge that's facing the next generation," George Leventhal, who headed the campaign, told the press. "When you broaden the electoral pool, everyone wins." The City Council is to follow up with a binding ordinance.

The issue sparked considerable controversy around the country. The anti-immigrant Federation for American Immigration Reform (FAIR) argued that the proposed ordinance would "undermine the value of U.S. citizenship" and might create another "magnet" for unlawful immigration. Yet others favor the idea, citing numerous examples where non-citizens are permitted to vote in local elections (like New York's community school boards). They note that local voting by non-citizens was a common practice in the nineteenth century and into the twentieth.

Undocumented immigrants have also become part of the environmental movement, joining with other minority community activists to charge that "toxic racism" is responsible for an alarming rate of disabilities and fatalities from exposure to dangerous pesticides, waste dumps and incinerators. Particularly in the Southwest, immigrant communities, including sizeable undocumented populations, have experienced "cancer clusters," babies born without brains or with other deformities, psychological changes, and fertility and reproduction problems which experts say can be largely traced to environmental hazards. Farmworkers are especially vulnerable to pesticides, as are their children, who must often accompany parents in the fields. In the small Latino town of Kettleman City, in south-central California, residents fought one of the country's largest waste disposal and treatment companies, Chemical Waste Management, to block construction of a toxic waste incinerator.

More Efforts Needed

The number of local and national organizing efforts to protect and expand the rights of the undocumented have significantly increased over the last ten years. Nonetheless, community and other immigrant rights advocates feel their efforts have not kept pace with the impact of U.S. economic and foreign policies which continue to spur all types of immigration, and of domestic policies which lead to greater impoverishment and restriction of rights. Perhaps, as many now believe, nothing less than the repeal of employer sanctions will prevent further deterioration of rights.

Employer Sanctions Are Unfair

by National Network for Immigrant and Refugee Rights

About the author: *The National Network for Immigrant and Refugee Rights endeavors to strengthen education, communication, and coordination among immigrant and refugee advocates throughout the United States.*

The issue of employer sanctions was the most debated feature of the proposed Immigration Reform and Control Act of 1986 (IRCA). Years later, sanctions continue to stir an angry debate between supporters and opponents.

At Issue with Employer Sanctions

From the time that employer sanctions was initially introduced, groups such as the National Network argued against the fundamental premise upon which sanctions was based: that undocumented workers are bad for the economy, are taking jobs away from American workers and are draining public welfare, and with former President Ronald Reagan's call to "regain control of the border" from the hordes of "feet people," as he called those crossing the U.S./Mexico border.

As employer sanctions enforcement began, reports of discrimination and other problems lit up local advocate hotlines around the country with complaints from citizens, legal residents, and undocumented.

Not only had sanctions affected the hiring of minority workers, but had begun to affect other workers' rights—wages, overtime pay, working conditions, pregnancy leaves.

In a paper titled, "How Employer Sanctions Undermine the Enforcement of Federal Labor Laws," Equal Rights Advocates and the Coalition for Immigrant and Refugee Rights and Services in San Francisco stated that after employer sanctions became law, many employers have argued that undocumented workers are not covered under federal labor legislation, such as Title VII, the Fair Labor Standards Act (FLSA) or the National Labor Relations Act (NLRA).

From the National Network for Immigrant and Refugee Rights, "Five Years of Criminalizing Immigrant Labor: Battling Employer Sanctions," *Network News*, June/July 1992. Reprinted by permission of the National Network for Immigrant and Refugee Rights, 310 Eighth St., Suite 307, Oakland, CA 94607, (510) 465-1984.

Prior to sanctions, such coverage was generally not challenged. While the courts have usually held that undocumented workers fall within the definition of "employee" and may therefore file administrative complaints and lawsuits for employer violations of federal law, remedies for violations, such as reinstatement and back pay, have been questioned.

Employer Sanctions = Criminalization of Work

The criminalization of work, the effect of employer sanctions, has also become a major concern for labor unions, particularly for those organizing in industries that have become increasingly reliant on immigrant labor, including undocumented workers.

A recent resolution adopted by the Service Employees International Union (SEIU), stated, "Employer sanctions have not helped unions to organize. In fact, the reverse is true. . . . Employers prefer workers who have no rights and are easily intimidated—employer sanctions guarantees them a ready supply. Unions must be free to respond to competition from employers who exploit undocumented workers with our traditional tactic of organizing the competition."

Asian, Latino and women's organizations have all argued that employer sanctions have had a detrimental impact on immigrant communities and on women's rights. In testimony to Congress concerning employer sanctions, the Mexican American Legal Defense and Education Fund (MALDEF), stated, "Unlawful discrimination against the least protected people of our society has resulted in children missing meals, evictions, untold bills not being paid, and other extreme hardships. Instead of preserving jobs for U.S. citizens and employment-authorized immigrants, employer sanctions have paradoxically created a hostile employment market for Latinos and Asians. The price of suffering to the Latino and Asian communities and to society in general is too high to pay for any objective. . . ."

> *"Employer sanctions have had a detrimental impact on immigrant communities and on women's rights."*

Sanctions Linked to Rights Abuses

Many attribute the rise in anti-immigrant violence to employer sanctions. Anti-immigrant "Light Up the Border" protestors near San Diego made clear that their actions were backed by a Congressional mandate to keep out undocumented immigrants. While communities at the U.S./Mexico border have taken the brunt of this violence, no immigrant community has been shielded from harassment and physical violence—rationalized by legislation that has driven further underground millions of undocumented workers and their families.

A number of people and institutions agree that employer sanctions "don't work"—do not stop undocumented immigration. However, those who basically support employer sanctions simply argue that sanctions need to be strengthened in order to "work," rather than address the more complex issue of the causes of migration. On the other hand, immigrant rights advocates have stressed the need to embody strong labor protections and a long range international perspective in immigration policy development.

Repeal Gains Backers

After the issuance of initial reports of discrimination due to employer sanctions, many more voices joined the call for repeal, particularly from the more traditional civil and human rights community. Particularly after the third report of the General Accounting Office (GAO), indicating widespread discrimination due to employer sanctions, and after Congress refused to take expedited action to end sanctions, repeal seemed to gain greater "legitimacy" as the only course of action.

The notion of repeal is no longer just the idealistic demand of a handful of community advocates; it is now considered a substantial political proposal, albeit a controversial one. Among immigrant rights advocates today, few remain uncommitted to repeal. . . .

In April 1992, the Senate Subcommittee on Immigration and Refugee Affairs conducted two days of hearings on the impact of employer sanctions that were largely dominated by Bush Administration and pro-sanctions groups. A few groups opposing sanctions testified, and many more submitted written testimony. . . .

If Not Sanctions—Then What?

Although the problems associated with employer sanctions have grown many times over, advocates expect that the repeal of sanctions will be a protracted campaign. Most members of Congress have stayed away from the debate entirely; there will no doubt have to be a very aggressive Congressional education campaign to help shape employer sanctions opposition. And there will have to be a very cautious examination of what will be proposed in place of sanctions.

If the basic premise remains that undocumented are harmful and should continue to be criminalized, repressive legislation will continue to be proposed. Even some favoring repeal in Congress have simultaneously proposed increases in border personnel and equipment.

> *"A number of people and institutions agree that employer sanctions 'don't work.'"*

Senator Alan Simpson, who continues to support employer sanctions, has zeroed in on the need for a national identification system to strengthen sanctions; he would likely continue to lobby for a national "ID" if repeal gained momentum.

Other similar proposals could be revived: a pilot program "driver's license as work authorization document" was beat back during the consideration of the Immigration Act 1990. The driver's licenses would have required validated social security numbers, a process not much different from the contested proposal for a national ID. Another program now being tested by the INS is the Telephone Verification System (TVS), which would have employers connect with a computerized data base to check on immigrant employees.

Several government agency reports have been critical of some aspects of sanctions. . . . Various agencies have recommended strengthened employer sanctions and border enforcement, continued employer education, expansion of the OSC [Office of Special Council, set up to prosecute IRCA-related discrimination cases], further monitoring by the General Accounting Office, etc. There seems to be some recognition of the need for increased labor law enforcement as well in the context of continuing sanctions. . . .

The April 1992 Senate hearings served to verify long-held assumptions about the limitations of such hearings; additional and diverse platforms are needed for advocacy of repeal. And, the growing volume of various organizational resolutions supporting repeal needs to be translated into broad public knowledge and timely mobilization to build momentum for an aggressive repeal effort.

The INS Violates Immigrants' Human Rights

by Americas Watch

About the author: *Americas Watch, which is a division of Human Rights Watch, was established in 1981 to monitor and promote observance of internationally recognized human rights.*

This viewpoint examines human rights abuses committed by the Immigration and Naturalization Service (INS) and its agents in the enforcement of U.S. immigration laws. The study is limited to the four U.S. states that border Mexico: California, Arizona, New Mexico, and Texas. It also is limited to human rights abuses committed during the arrest and detention of undocumented immigrants. Due process abuses and bureaucratic obstruction during immigration proceedings are not covered.

Even with this limited focus, the findings are appalling. Beatings, rough physical treatment, and racially motivated verbal abuse are routine. Even more serious abuses, including unjustified shootings, torture, and sexual abuse, occur. When they do, investigations are almost invariably perfunctory, and the offending agents escape punishment. The human rights abuses reported here are similar in kind and severity to those about which we have reported in many other countries. Moreover, the response of the U.S. government is as defensive and unyielding as the responses of many of the most abusive governments.

A Lasting Impression

The INS's high tolerance for human rights abuses makes a mockery of the materials that it purports to use to train its agents. According to the Officer Integrity Course for Border Patrol agents (the uniformed enforcement division of the INS):

> The business of the United States Border Patrol is "people." These people come to the United States from all over the world. The Border Patrol Agent

Americas Watch, "Brutality Unchecked: Human Rights Abuses Along the U.S. Border with Mexico." (New York: Human Rights Watch, 1992), pp. 1-5, 11-12, 28-29, 77. Reprinted with permission.

may very well be an alien's first and only contact with an "authority-figure" while in the United States, especially if he/she is apprehended shortly after entry. How these people are treated will leave a lasting impression of, not only the Border Patrol, but the United States in general.

Indeed, the INS leaves a lasting impression on many of the hundreds of thousands of undocumented migrants who are arrested by INS agents each year, not to mention the many U.S. citizens and others lawfully in the United States who happen to get caught in their widely cast nets. Unfortunately, the impression is one of mistreatment.

While there is no justification and often no apparent reason for INS abuse, there are discernible circumstances under which agents are more likely to go beyond apprehending undocumented migrants to "judging" and "punishing" them. Sometimes migrants are brutalized to coerce confessions or to deter them from exercising available legal rights or options. In other cases agents assault migrants when forced to chase them on foot or in vehicles. In detention centers, migrants who are uncooperative or protest poor conditions or the mistreatment of others become targets for abuse.

One reason INS misconduct is so pervasive is that the agency does not adequately train or supervise its agents. In a September 1991 report, the Office of the Inspector General of the Department of Justice lambasted

> *"Investigations are almost invariably perfunctory, and the offending agents escape punishment."*

the INS for the widespread failure of its agents to comply with firearms training and qualification requirements, and for the agency's failure to train agents adequately on the duty to report shootings and other uses of force. Former INS Western Region Director Ben Davidian, in a document condemning an INS reorganization plan, asserted that the training of INS supervisors is "terrible at best."

Low Morale

Another explanation that goes hand in hand with poor agent training and supervision is low agent morale. According to a *Los Angeles Times* report:

> In District offices and Border Patrol stations in the Western Region, rank-and-file staffers . . . talk of general malaise caused by overwork, meager resources and increasing responsibilities. . . . The INS, they say, has lost its focus as it struggles to maintain order and purpose in the face of soaring illegal immigration, a flood of new regulations and increased drug smuggling along the border.

Among Border Patrol agents, low morale also results from the perceived futility of enforcing U.S. immigration laws. The agents know that most of the undocumented migrants they arrest will be sent back to Mexico without charge or punishment and that many will attempt to reenter the United States without authorization another day. Agent frustration may explain some incidents of abuse

... for which no other discernible motive is obvious.

Most outrageous is the INS's willingness to cover up or defend almost any form of egregious conduct by its agents. Among immigrants' rights activists, the prevailing view is that the INS "has a greater interest in the reputation of its officers than in the integrity of a process designed to protect the one-million-plus immigrants it comes into contact with each year.". . . One Border Patrol agent, during a six- or seven-year period, was involved in a theft; two vehicular incidents, one of which resulted in the death of a migrant; two serious assaults on farm workers who were lawfully in the United States; and the violent homicide of an undocumented Mexican minor. Except for a 30-day suspension for the theft incident, the agent was not punished; he continues to serve in the Border Patrol.

Inadequate Complaint Process

One way the INS and its parent, the Justice Department, cover up INS misconduct is by maintaining an unresponsive complaint process that is inadequate to the tasks of exposing and redressing abuses. Prior to 1989, complaints of INS misconduct were handled within the agency by its Office of Professional Responsibility (OPR). In April 1989, Congress established the Office of the Inspector General (OIG) within the Department of Justice, but outside the INS, to strengthen the internal audit and investigative activities of specified federal agencies and departments, including the INS. The OPR and the OIG offices now cooperate.

"Most outrageous is the INS's willingness to cover up or defend almost any form of egregious conduct."

The establishment of the OIG has failed to yield more effective investigations of complaints. According to U.S. Representative Jim Bates, "overlapping jurisdiction [of the OPR and OIG] is used as the excuse for inaction." Many INS personnel who formerly worked for the OPR became investigators with the OIG. In their new capacities they continue to review and investigate complaints of their former INS colleagues' misconduct.

Among the persistent problems with the complaint procedures are:
• the lack of a complaint form.
• the lack of a comprehensive and systematic procedure for informing the public of its right to complain.
• a low ratio of investigators to total employees.
• the failure to notify complainants of the status and disposition of their complaints.
• the lack of an adequate appeals process.
• incomplete complaint statistics and the failure to publish statistics on a regular basis.

Another way that INS misconduct is covered up is through the filing of intimidating criminal misdemeanor or felony charges. It is a federal crime to enter the United States without authorization. If convicted, first offenders face fines of up to 2,000 dollars or six months' imprisonment. Convicted repeat offenders face fines and imprisonment of up to two years. In fact, most undocumented migrants who are arrested by the Border Patrol are never charged under the criminal statutes. Most Mexicans are processed administratively, given "voluntary departure," and bused to the border. Nationals of other countries who can demonstrate that they have the financial means to leave the country are similarly allowed to depart voluntarily. Repeat border crossers and persons seeking asylum in the United States are usually placed in administrative deportation or exclusion proceedings.

> *"Criminal charges . . . [are] used, nefariously, against victims of INS abuse to conceal agent misconduct."*

The Victim Becomes the Accused

Criminal charges for illegal entry are usually reserved for undocumented migrants who are known to be flagrant violators of immigration laws or who are suspected of committing more serious crimes such as alien smuggling or drug-related offenses. But they are also used, nefariously, against victims of INS abuse to conceal agent misconduct. This strategy, in which the victim becomes the accused, is common to police work, but appears particularly pervasive and effective in cases of INS misconduct. INS agents are aware that most abused migrants—because of their unprotected status; unfamiliarity with English, U.S. law, and culture; and fear of deportation—will not defend themselves against trumped up charges and will instead accept deportation or other offered plea bargains, rather than pursue complaints against abusive agents.

Another way that the INS covers up for its agents is by refusing to divulge the names of agents involved in shootings and other serious incidents. As a result, it is difficult for victims of INS abuse to identify those who abused them when filing administrative complaints or civil lawsuits. The agency also takes no steps to remove from active duty officers who have been implicated in shootings or other abuses. By comparison, the policy of the San Diego [California] Sheriff's Department is to place its officers on restrictive duty whenever a serious question of justification is raised about a violent incident. The purpose of the policy is to foster public trust in the department and to give the officer time to recover psychologically from the incident.

The impunity enjoyed by INS agents due to the INS's unwillingness to investigate and punish abuse is reinforced by prosecutors who rarely file criminal charges against abusive agents. Even when prosecutors are willing to file criminal charges, prosecutions of INS agents are difficult because physical evidence of abuse may heal, and because undocumented migrants' transience and fear of arrest impede investigations and the assembly of witnesses.

These same problems plague civil lawsuits against the INS and its agents, as do the cost of obtaining counsel and the slow progress of the proceedings. The INS often settles lawsuits that are brought against it without acknowledging any responsibility for wrongdoing or giving assurance that the offending agent will be disciplined. . . .

A Shooting

Eduardo Zamores: On November 18, 1990, a Border Patrol agent shot 15-year-old Eduardo Zamores as the youth straddled the border fence near the international port of entry in Calexico, California. A 9 mm hollowpoint bullet hit Zamores in the lower left chest and severely damaged his liver, stomach, intestine, and left lung. The shooting, which Marco Antonio Tovar, the Mexican Consul in Calexico, called "the one drop that may overflow the glass," ignited angry protests on both sides of the border. Because the gunshot caused Zamores to fall into Mexico, the incident raised sensitive legal and jurisdictional issues, and produced a sharp diplomatic exchange between the two governments.

As in many previous cases, this shooting occurred before onlookers who were drawn to the fence by the commotion surrounding a Border Patrol arrest. Zamores, who worked on the Mexican side of the border carrying bags for shoppers returning from the U.S., told an AFSC [American Friends Service Committee] investigator that a disturbance caused by an INS agent's attempt to arrest another teenager attracted his attention, and that he scaled the fence to watch. He claims that he was shot for no reason as he perched atop the fence.

INS officials have not publicly disclosed any information about the shooting. Calexico Police Chief Leslie Ginn investigated the case and his conclusion incorporated the shooting agent's version of events. According to the agent, Zamores and two other youths were observed climbing the fence and entering a parking lot on the U.S. side three times in about 90 minutes by agents watching remote, non-recording video monitors. Another agent who approached the boys the first time they entered alleged that he was "pelted by rocks." The third time the boys entered the United States, the agent tried to detain one of them. Another boy already had retreated over the fence and Zamores was on top of the fence facing the U.S. side. The agent alleged that rocks were thrown over the fence, and Zamores had his arm raised as though to throw a rock. A police inspection of the parking lot revealed "rather small rocks" in the vicinity.

> *"He [Eduardo Zamores] . . . claims that he was shot for no reason as he perched atop the fence."*

Despite the fact that his findings relied heavily on the shooting agent's version of events, Chief Ginn announced at a November 29, 1990, press conference that he believed the shooting was unjustified. "During the investigation we conducted, I don't think it was sufficiently revealed that [the agent's] life was in danger." Ginn suggested a range of possible criminal charges, among them assault with a deadly weapon and assault under color of authority, both felonies in California.

Ginn's announcement was intended to reassure Mexican officials and to encourage Mexican police to share the physical evidence that they retained because of Zamores' fall into Mexico. Skeptical about U.S. willingness to prosecute the agent, Mexican police conducted their own investigation of the shooting, and the Mexican government threatened to seek extradition of the agent to stand trial in Mexico. Ginn contended that the refusal of Mexican authorities to turn over physical evidence—including Zamores' clothes and tennis shoes, and the bullet fragments—thwarted his investigation and hampered him from recommending prosecution. Mexican police countered that they had allowed Calexico police to examine all the evidence in Mexico, but would not allow it to leave the country. On December 11, 1990, Calexico police arrested two employees of the Mexican Consulate on bribery charges. It was alleged that they had offered money to a Calexico police employee to learn the shooting agent's name to include in a request for extradition. Charges were dropped because the agents were entitled to diplomatic immunity.

> *"While [Augustine] Pérez [Flores] was on his knees, the agent hit Pérez on the head with his flashlight."*

It is unclear what action, if any, will be taken against the agent. The Mexican government's extradition proceedings are stalled, and while Calexico police have recommended prosecution, the Calexico district attorney has yet to take any action. The results of a separate investigation by the FBI have not been released, although there is no indication that the U.S. government is considering prosecution. The INS, while defending the agent's actions, says that he has been reassigned to desk duties pending the results of federal, state, and local investigations. . . .

Two Beatings

Augustine Pérez Flores: On March 11, 1990, Augustine Pérez Flores was assaulted by a Border Patrol agent during an arrest of a group of people who had crossed the border near San Ysidro, California. When three Border Patrol agents spotted the group, Pérez and four others split off and attempted to hide. When they were discovered, one of the agents approached them and ordered Pérez to kneel. While Pérez was on his knees, the agent hit Pérez on the head with his flashlight. Pérez told an AFSC investigator that the agent asked him if he wanted to file a complaint. But the agent warned him that there would be no witnesses to support his claim, since the others in the group were to be deported to Mexico that night. Another agent threatened potential witnesses with five-year jail terms if they testified against the abusive agent. Pérez abandoned his complaint and accepted voluntary departure. He reported the case only after he reentered the United States. The AFSC forwarded the case to the Office of the Inspector General for investigation.

> *"The INS needs to redirect its mission to emphasize the promotion and protection of human rights."*

Seventeen-year-old Youth: In September 1990, a 17-year-old youth was similarly battered by his arresting officer near San Ysidro. The youth and another person ran when they were illuminated by a Border Patrol vehicle's lights. Two agents pursued them, first on motorcycles and then on foot. The boy twisted an ankle running down a hill and slowed down. The agent chasing him fell on top of him, grabbed him around the neck and began to choke him, then put him face down in the dirt and hit him with a flashlight on the back of the head. The boy was led to a Border Patrol vehicle, where agents examined the wound on his head. The abuse continued; agents pulled his ears, and seized his personal effects and threw them into the bushes. Agents then transported him to the Chula Vista Border Patrol station, and then to a hospital in National City, California.

After being treated, the youth was held in the INS detention center in El Centro. Representatives of Esperanza Para Los Niños, an immigrants rights group that monitors the treatment of minors, told Americas Watch that they learned of the abuse when they visited him in detention. Before they could complete their investigation, the boy was released and could no longer be located. . . .

Basic Human Rights

Many of the problems documented in this viewpoint can be remedied by policy and attitudinal changes on the part of the INS and its agents. Others require regulatory and, in a few cases, statutory changes. Yet remedies are imperative if the basic human rights of undocumented migrants are to be respected. . . .

Undocumented migrants who enter or are living in the United States may be deportable or excludable, but their immigration status does not lessen their entitlement to respect for their basic human rights. As an institution, the INS needs to redirect its mission to emphasize the promotion and protection of human rights in the fulfillment of its responsibility to enforce U.S. immigration laws. This policy must be conveyed, through example and training, to all INS personnel. The INS must make clear to its personnel that failure to respect the legally protected human rights of any person will be punished.

Chapter 4

How Should the Government Respond to Immigration?

Immigration Policy: An Overview

by Thomas E. Muller

About the author: *Thomas E. Muller is an economist and the author of* Immigrants and the American City, *from which the following viewpoint is excerpted.*

Immigration has played a critical role in shaping America, particularly its cities, and will continue to do so in the future. What that role will be, however, depends on the laws we adopt and whether we are willing to rigorously enforce them. Should current policies be maintained? Care must be taken in implementing changes because any sudden shift in course—any drastic opening or closing of the door—would be disruptive and could stir unrest.

A History of Tolerance

Following the passage of what some consider a landmark immigration law in 1990, Congress appeared unlikely to contemplate curtailment of immigration levels. Although the struggle to pass the 1986 Immigration Act had left many legislators weary of tampering with the issue, Congress acted in 1990 to change the immigration statutes in order to increase the number of skilled workers and so-called "independent" immigrants allowed into the country. This resulted in a new annual ceiling of 700,000, which will decline to 675,000 after 1995, and reserved about 140,000 visas for individuals (and their dependents) with special job skills and talent. Remarkably, organized opposition to this considerable increase in legal entry levels was virtually nonexistent. Even the most vocal opponents of immigration did not at the time advocate radical changes in current (pre-1990) policy. For instance, former Colorado governor Richard Lamm, who has warned that a splintering of American society may result from continued large-scale legal and illegal immigration, proposed an annual aggregate limit of 400,000—only 25 percent below the actual level of the late 1980s. The Federation of American Immigration Reform (FAIR) too favored modest reductions but did not actively oppose the 1988 Kennedy-Simpson Senate bill that also sought to raise immigration levels. Seemingly exhausted by its earlier failures, FAIR was unable to mount a serious challenge to the more broadly based groups favoring higher ceilings. Opponents recognized that any proposal for reducing entry levels during the booming 1980s would lack political support. This very much reflected America's history of tolerance. Even during the Great Depression, when nativism reached its peak and the economy its nadir, Congress was reluctant to eliminate the admission of newcomers.

New Opposition to Immigration

Since the 1990 legislation represented the sentiment of both parties in Congress and the executive branch, it is surprising that strong opposition to immigration would arise shortly after its passage. Yet just days before the Los Angeles riot, the conservative *National Review* published an article with the provocative title "Our Disappearing Common Culture: The Forbidden Topic." In a sweeping indictment of American immigration policy, the author argued that, contrary to the position of some leading neoconservatives, the pressure for multiculturalism in schools and elsewhere should be ascribed directly to America's criteria for the admission of aliens. The preponderance of immigrants from the third world was depicted as representing a direct threat to the preservation of Western culture.

In May 1992, shortly after the riot, FAIR suddenly called (for the first time since its formation) for a temporary moratorium on nearly all immigration (only spouses and minor children of U.S. citizens would be exempted). The rationale cited by FAIR for its request was a poll sponsored by the organization showing that more than half (55 percent) of the public supported such a step. The timing of the poll's release, less than three weeks following the Los Angeles riot, gave FAIR considerable media exposure. On the day of the FAIR announcement, an op-ed article written jointly by a historian and a journal editor in the *Los Angeles Times* supported an immigration "respite" (moratorium) on the premise that halting the inflow would help inner-city minorities. At about the same time, Lawrence Harrison, writing in the neoconservative journal *National Interest*, also concluded that "while we study, articulate and legislate such [immigration] reforms and work toward better integration of recent immigrants, we should call for a moratorium on immigration."

> *"Even during the Great Depression . . . Congress was reluctant to eliminate the admission of newcomers."*

Finally, the prestigious *New York Times* added to the clamor two months later by featuring an op-ed piece calling for a five-year freeze on immigration. The rationale given by the writer was to "reduce unfair competition for scarce jobs, give our economy a chance to recover, . . . and, above all, give the millions of immigrants here the opportunity to assimilate." Otherwise, the writer asserts, the United States will create a foreign underclass, thus weakening the nation's ability to compete globally. . . .

The "Open" View

In direct opposition to those calling for a halt to foreigners settling in the United States, several publications still express pro-immigration attitudes, though perhaps with less gusto in the wake of the economic stagnation that engulfed the nation in the early 1990s. Their editors seek to open American borders to anyone that can meet certain health and moral standards and show a willingness to work. This position has been embraced by several business publications and some libertarian newspapers, such as California's *Orange County Register*. Their attitudes are based on a philosophical commitment to an open economy unencumbered by labor or regulatory constraints.

The position of business-oriented *Forbes* is that the nation should admit at least 1.5 million to 1.8 million legal immigrants annually as a means of enriching the United States. This open view is endorsed by other conservative business media. A persistent and very influential voice urging more liberal entry policies has been the *Wall Street Journal*. During the debate on the Immigration Reform and Control Act (IRCA) in 1986, a lead editorial concluded that "if Washington still wants to 'do something' about immigration we propose a five-word constitutional amendment: There shall be open borders." The editorial drew an analogy between the 1986 Immigration Act and the Prohibition (Volstead Act) Amendment to the Constitution. Prohibition could not be enforced, and the amendment was eventually repealed, although 300,000 persons were convicted for drinking. Just as people continued to consume alcohol, the editorial argued, illegal aliens will continue to come and find jobs. When Senator Alan K. Simpson proposed that stronger measures to thwart crossings from Mexico be incorporated into the 1990 immigration bill, the *Wall Street Journal* challenged the move, with editorials charging Simpson with bias toward Mexicans and intent to wreck the bill appearing twice in a span of a few weeks. The *Journal* not only reported the news, but its views became part of the congressional debate. Conservative opposition to liberal American immigration policies was virtually absent until Pat Buchanan challenged President George Bush for the Republican party nomination in 1991. But Buchanan's anti-immigration stance was immediately contested by another well-known conservative, columnist George Will.

The liberal *New Republic* also favors an essentially open-door policy, subject

> *"Several publications still express pro-immigration attitudes."*

159

only to such criteria as proficiency in English (within a few years of entry to the United States) and a willingness to work rather than request welfare. Its position is not based on a commitment to free enterprise but on a desire to overcome the problem of dealing with illegal entrants. The editors believe that such an approach would resolve this issue by eliminating the category of illegal aliens altogether. Concern for the welfare of aliens, seen as scapegoats for economic problems, explains the opposition of the *Nation*, a liberal periodical, to employer sanctions.

> *"A return to the open immigration laws in effect before 1922 does not seem out of the question."*

Following passage of the 1990 Immigration Act, the *Public Interest*, a neoconservative quarterly, included an article by Julian Simon urging substantially greater immigration levels. Virtually unrestricted immigration thus finds support at both ends of the political spectrum.

4 to 5 Million a Year?

How many people would enter under an essentially open-door policy? During the peak immigration period—1910 to 1915—more than a million arrived every year. (Because many of these eventually returned to their native lands, net population transfers were actually much lower.) Immigration during this five-year period turned out to be somewhat less than 6 percent of the national population at the time. If a similar percentage of today's population were immigrants, the total would be about 15 million. Converted to an annual rate of 3 million a year, this would be about three times greater than the current level of combined legal and estimated illegal entry. No doubt, this crude calculation understates the numbers that would come. For one thing, more of today's would-be arrivals have the financial means to pay for the trip. Mass communication disseminates information about the United States unavailable at the turn of the century and encourages immigration, although an open entry policy would also increase the number that would return to their homeland, particularly during periods of slow economic growth. An annual net immigration flow of 4 to 5 million might be a reasonable estimate.

From a narrow economic standpoint, a return to the open immigration laws in effect before 1922 does not seem out of the question. The nation could absorb several million more immigrants a year than are currently admitted and maintain growth; in fact, economic expansion would probably accelerate were new entrants predominantly young and skilled workers. However, such an increase would displace some American workers and have long-term adverse social, distributional, as well as environmental consequences. It seems safe to say that the vast majority of Americans would be unwilling to accept the many millions who would come in the event that most restrictions were lifted. . . .

Congress had hoped that the 1986 Immigration Act would at least slow the flow of illegal aliens to the United States, but this was questionable from the outset. Although the number of illegal aliens who have entered the United States since the mid-1980s and remained is not known, the IRCA-initiated legalization process documents the scope of illegal entry during the previous decade. About 1.8 million persons filed applications for legalization on the basis that they were in the United States illegally prior to 1982. An additional 1.3 million seasonal workers also applied for legalization. In fact, the act has not succeeded in substantially curtailing illegal entry. In 1990, when the American economy began to slow, nearly 1.2 million aliens were apprehended, a rise of more than 23 percent over the previous year, and the rate continued to climb in 1991. Smuggling has, by all accounts, become more sophisticated. Therefore, apprehension levels are not a reliable measure of changes in the size of the illegal population because only a small percentage of those entering illegally are caught at the borders. No statistics are available on the number of visa abusers who come legally and remain after their entry visas expire, but their number is probably growing. . . .

Employers fearing penalties may be less anxious to hire illegal aliens today than they were before 1987, but for many employers reluctance to employ undocumented workers is offset by the prospect of higher profits. The continued willingness to hire aliens is also linked to the knowledge that few employers have been fined or prosecuted for violations such as knowingly accepting fraudulent identity cards.

> *"As long as employers . . . are willing to hire these aliens, . . . [they] will find the means to penetrate the border."*

Within ethnic enclaves, the brisk business in falsified or stolen Social Security cards, driver licenses, and other forms of identification demonstrates that many illegal workers are purchasing needed documents on the street. Undocumented workers who are not part of the amnesty program frequently find jobs with relatives and friends within ethnic enclaves, making them extremely difficult to apprehend. Those who speak some English typically encounter few challenges in using the various forms of documentation to verify their legal status, particularly since employers are not responsible for the authenticity of identity documents. This may explain why only a few thousand illegal aliens from Taiwan, Hong Kong, and Korea applied for legalization, yet apparently substantial numbers are smuggled in and continue to work in large cities. . . .

If There Is Work, They Will Come

The evidence thus far suggests that the 1986 measure is not achieving its primary objective of permanently reducing the number of undocumented workers. The economic self-interest of both employers and workers is often stronger than the bite of the immigration laws. When the European transatlantic migration was constrained in the 1920s, entry was controlled more readily because nearly all immigrants came by ship. Air travel and lengthy national borders that cannot be fully screened for clandestine passage have severely limited the ability to control Western Hemisphere immigration.

Illegal workers came in the 1980s mostly to perform tasks most Americans were unwilling to undertake. Employers gain advantages by hiring such workers, most of whom do not receive benefits enjoyed by others, such as vacation pay or health insurance. Aliens appear more than willing to accept these conditions, for their earnings usually represent a vast improvement over what they could obtain in their country of origin. As long as employers, many of them fellow ethnics, are willing to hire these aliens, the latter will find the means to penetrate the border. . . .

Isolationism vs. Multiculturalism

To what extent economic arguments that favor immigration will once again, as in the 1920s, be overwhelmed by cultural and social concerns is not known. The emerging isolationism promoted by Pat Buchanan and a few archconservatives is manifested in such implicitly anti-immigrant slogans as "America First," last seen during the waning years of the Great Depression. Their reemergence may only be the product of frustration driven by economic woes and racial tensions. But they could also represent suppressed grass roots attitudes, as suggested by public opinion polls. Anti-immigrant sentiment appears also to be rising among some liberals, concerned that black-white tensions will be exacerbated by Hispanics and Asians seeking a stronger political and economic voice. An added worry is that these ethnic groups, less intent on being absorbed into the American mainstream than those in earlier waves, will create separate cultures at odds with cherished notions of American identity. If these views gain wider endorsement and the economy remains sluggish, America will turn inward again, entering a new cycle of isolationism. Ironically, this cycle would begin at the very time when the economy of the United States is almost fully integrated with the world economy and its popular culture a more formidable global force than ever. American immigration policies would mirror political trends, and pressure for restrictive entry measures would rise. These restrictions would be advanced in the forlorn hope that the pre-1960s cultural and demographic patterns could be restored.

> *"Anti-immigrant sentiment appears . . . to be rising among some liberals."*

Whatever the motive for the apparent rise in sentiment against nonwhite immigrants, those concerned with the changing ethnic composition will have to acknowledge that the demographic changes set in motion by the 1965 and 1990 immigration laws and the penetrability of the common border with Mexico are *irreversible*. The attitudes, customs, and political accommodations formed over the course of two centuries by the presence of blacks and whites are already being reshaped to fit a multiracial society. Native and new groups will tend to coalesce, a phenomenon that can be seen in the emerging distinctive culture and language of the Southwest. The sharp growth in the number of Asians in every state during the 1980s is evidence that, unlike earlier times, no area of the nation, large or small, will remain immune to ethnic changes.

The search for a way of measuring economic benefits that accrue from immigration against the costs of liberal entry policies—potential harm to low-income workers, ethnic diversity that can lead to strife, overcrowding, and the fear of losing national identity—has engaged the United States in virtually every decade since its inception. Throughout most of American history, legislators have had to weigh the arguments on behalf of, and in opposition to, liberal immigration. . . .

An Unending Quest for Balance

Much of America's economic and moral strength can be traced to its visionary founders, who wisely encouraged immigration. The response to open its borders was unprecedented, as millions eagerly sought entry. Today the clamor at the nation's gates is ever louder and, to some, more ominous. But the clamor should be a cause of pride, not anxiety; a sign of vigor, not an omen of decline.

The ongoing quest to balance the economic, political, and social consequences of immigration has no end. The United States will certainly remain a magnet to those seeking new opportunities, advancement, or a place of refuge. Immigration laws that tap their youth and ambition without creating internal dissension will harness the human resources America needs to sustain its vitality into the third millennium.

The Government Should Not Allow Open Immigration

by Bruce A. Ramsey

About the author: *Bruce A. Ramsey is an American journalist who has worked in the northwestern United States and the Far East.*

When I moved to Hong Kong in 1989, I thought it was a disgrace that so few Chinese were sympathetic to the Vietnamese boat people. More than 55,000 were penned up in camps, and hundreds more were arriving each week. "The average Hongkonger," I wrote, "would shove them all back out to sea if he had anything to say about it."

From time to time some U.S. congressman comes here and says the same thing. The Vietnamese are running from communism. So are the 60,000 Hong Kong Chinese who emigrate each year, fearing China's domination after 1997. How can the Hong Kong people expect any sympathy if they show none toward people, however poor, who are their moral equivalents?

Immigrants vs. Refugees

The Hong Kong people I knew didn't look at it that way—and I don't either, after living here three years. The Hong Kong people are emigrants, not refugees. They have money. They have professional qualifications. They speak English. And they have played by the American rules. They have filled out pages of forms. They have answered all sorts of questions the U.S. government never asks its own citizens, such as the name of every social, political or community organization they have ever joined. They have certified that they have never been convicted of a felony. They have disclosed their finances, and taken medical exams. And they have waited patiently to get their turn under the hugely oversubscribed U.S. quota. The line for Hong Kong brothers and sisters

From Bruce A. Ramsey (under the pseudonym R.K. Lamb), "The Half-Open Door," *Liberty*, February 1993. Reprinted with permission.

of U.S. citizens is about nine years long.

Refugees are different. They are emergency cases, exceptions to the rules. U.S. policy is to accept only those screened as political—people who can prove they have a "well-founded fear of persecution" if they go back. Most cannot prove this. More than 90% of the Vietnamese boat people are routinely screened out as "economic migrants." The U.S. will not accept them, nor will any other country.

To the Hong Kong Chinese, the Americans have every right to shut their own door on such gate-crashers. When George Bush [sent] Coast Guard cutters to shove the Haitians back into the arms of the *tontons macoutes* he [did] just what Malaysia or the Philippines or Japan does. Shouldn't the U.S. be polite enough not to lecture other countries?

Free Immigration Reconsidered

Some of my readers, I suspect, will argue that America should let them all in: immigrants, refugees, everybody. This is pretty much the most common view among libertarians. Every political question is to be decided by reference to first principles. According to their moral axioms, immigration restrictions are as difficult to justify as apartheid, or a quota on men's shirts.

But free immigration is difficult to argue for in today's world. No rich country allows it. States that have given up quotas on goods retain it on new residents. The European Community is on the verge of allowing free movement of labor. Portuguese and Greeks

> *"Free immigration is difficult to argue for in today's world."*

will be allowed to work in England and Denmark—something not certain to be welcomed by the English and Danes. The proposal does not apply to non-EC peoples such as the Turks, Algerians or Poles. The U.S. and Canada have agreed to free most trade over a 10-year period. They did not free labor, residency or citizenship. They are not even discussing doing these things with Mexico. . . .

When the subject of immigrants and refugees comes up with libertarians, it's usually in an argument with someone who wants to stop them. With gusto, libertarians cite studies that show that immigrants and refugees have been a benefit to America. They argue that America ought to "keep the door open." But the door is *not* open. The status quo is controlled immigration.

Principles vs. Numbers

The real question of immigration is not about principles; it's about numbers. U.S. law allows 700,000 immigrants a year. That's less than three-tenths of 1% of a 252-million population. These slots tend to go to the affluent and educated. They can read the rules, hire the lawyers, fill out the paperwork. A lot of them come over as students and figure out a way to stay on. Some, like a former South African colleague of mine, go through a long rigamarole. He had to find an employer to swear that he had skills not available in the United States. He had to move cross country and change careers to get his green card. An uneducated man never could have done it.

> *"You could have people camped on school playgrounds, in city parks, . . . and in Shantytowns."*

The 700,000 limit allows the U.S. to seem to be a lot choosier about its new citizens than it actually is. It is admitting 74% of them simply because they have a relative in the United States. One person gets in and petitions for his wife and kids, brothers and sisters, and their kids. Only 20% of slots are for people with needed job skills. Canada and Australia are more open than the U.S. in this regard; America could follow their lead and let more people in as investor-immigrants. It could let in only those with money, skills, or PhDs.

But under free immigration it would take everybody.

The flow of refugees has been about 30,000 in most years—a small fraction of the immigrants. How these fare in the U.S. depends mainly on the kind of life they had before. Some, like the middle-class Cubans, have been successful. Others, like the Hmongs, a 16th-century people from Indochina, haven't. In early 1988, of 20,000 Hmongs in the Fresno, California, area, 70% were on welfare. Despite their high-school valedictorians, a higher percentage of Vietnamese are on welfare than of blacks. . . .

Imagine Free Immigration

Under free immigration, there would be . . . no distinction between immigrants and refugees. Anybody who gets in, stays in. What would that be like in a world of mass communications and Boeing 747s? Who knows? Back in the pre-World-War-I days, the United States was a long, hazardous, expensive trip away. There were only so many Irish, Italians and Norwegians who dared try it. People know more now. They are bolder. Tens of millions of people can raise the money to buy the ticket. . . . And the Mexicans, Guatemalans and Salvadorans can just take the bus.

Just imagine it. Shiploads of boat people. Haitians, Dominicans, Jamaicans, Javans, Punjabis, Pathans, Yorubas. You could have people camped on school playgrounds, in city parks, along the streets, and in Shantytowns speaking strange languages. People who believed in executing blasphemers and circumcising women. Men who piss against walls along public avenues. You'd have people selling candy door to door—not to help the Camp Fire Girls, but to feed their families. And not Camp Fire mints, either, but strange, gooey stuff concocted over campfires.

The minimum wage would be swept away, welfare swamped, food stamps shredded. Upper-middle-class salaries wouldn't be affected much, but the going rate for ditch-diggers, lawn mowers and newspaper boys would collapse. White teenagers would vanish from behind the counter at McDonald's. The garment industry would make a comeback, as would leatherwork and toys. Many people would benefit, to be sure—but most of them would be foreigners. Americans at the low end of the wage scale would be hit hard. The "homeless" would go out of business. No one would give 'em a dime.

A big American city would become more like Jakarta or Mexico City—a middle-class world of education, cars and microwave ovens surrounded by struggling people in cardboard shacks.

Survival of the Fittest?

Great, you say. Survival of the fittest! End this apartheid of international frontiers! End this labor protectionism! Let every man compete free and equal—all three billion! No doubt the economists can prove that the gain in utility would be greater than the loss. They'd probably be right. Especially for all those Bengalis and Vietnamese now living on $200 a year.

Well, it *does* fit your principles. But I'm not sure you'll want to live in such a world. In America today, even a lousy job pays $4.25 an hour. Even poor people have TVs and cars. I know libertarians who live in, or have lived in, that world. With free immigration, kiss it goodbye.

Me, I don't want to live in Jakarta. I live in Hong Kong, which is already close enough. Every day I see grown men in the streets selling wind-up panda bears, babies' T-shirts and boiled squid on toothpicks. The television reminds me that less than 10 miles from my home, 55,000 Vietnamese boat people are penned behind barbed wire. There's lots more where they came from: Vietnam is only about as far from here as Seattle is from southern Oregon. Accept the Vietnamese refugees, and another 55,000 would be here quicker'n you could say "Ho, Ho, Ho Chi Minh."

> *"A big American city would become . . . a middle-class world . . . surrounded by struggling people in cardboard shacks."*

Hong Kong won't take them. It's a Chinese city, and the Vietnamese are foreigners. Americans get all indignant over this, but it's the same attitude taken by the Thais, the Malaysians, the Filipinos, the Indonesians, and of course, the Japanese. Nobody here in Asia wants to be somebody else's melting pot.

Immigration Control Essential

This little city-state can't entertain such a thought. It is the most densely populated place in the world. It doesn't even allow citizens of China to live here, except for an elite handful. I've heard arguments that it ought to allow more, but never that it ought to let them all in. Immigration control is supported by Beijing, by London and by the Hong Kong people. There is no other way—because China's GNP per head is $325, and ours is $14,100. (America's is $21,500.)

The boat people knew that they would be put in camps. The camps have been here for years, and have been publicized in Vietnam. The people came here anyway, just for the chance that someone would take them. But nobody will.

In 1989, they had my sympathy. Now I, too, get tired of them and their demonstrations. I begin to think of them as the unwanted cousin who camps out on my doorstep and demands a seat at the dinner table. These people have to go home. They have to be forced to go home so the other 69 million Vietnamese won't come here. Like the Hong Kong Chinese, I begin to get disgusted with the namby-pamby British government, which talks about "mandatory repatriation" but seems to be too genteel to drag screaming refugees onto airplanes.

In the world of the 21st century, America is going to have to do the same thing. You won't have to shut the door on everybody. You're a big country and a rich country, and what's more, a melting pot. You can let in your 700,000 immigrants a year. You can probably let in more, especially if you pick them more carefully. You can let in a few refugees, and pat yourself on the back for being so humanitarian. But don't kid yourself that you have an "open door." Nobody does.

The Government Should Restrict Immigration

by John Vinson

About the author: *John Vinson is president of the American Immigration Control Foundation, an organization that advocates strict immigration controls.*

During the 1990s, Americans will have to make a choice: either reduce our current rate of immigration, which is now greater than at any time in the past, or witness the passing and death of America as waves of foreign people and cultures submerge our land.

Admittedly these are harsh alternatives, but they are also true alternatives. And no appeal to sentiments—such as insisting that we are a nation of immigrants—will change them.

Historical Proof

The proof of this statement is the record of history. It is a history littered with the gravestones of great nations and civilizations which allowed outsiders to overrun them. One outstanding example was the Roman Empire.

The Romans failed to control massive immigration from all parts of their empire because, like some modern Americans, they allowed pride in their national accomplishments to blind them to their national limitations. Overwhelmed by foreigners, the Romans lost the unity and common values they needed to hold their empire together.

Reflecting on this catastrophe, world-acclaimed historian Will Durant noted that:

> If Rome had not been engulfed by so many men of alien blood in so short a time . . . if she had occasionally closed her gates to let assimilation catch up with infiltration, she might have gained new racial and literary vitality from the infusion, and might have remained a Roman Rome, the voice and citadel of the West. The task was too great. The victorious city was doomed by the

From John Vinson, *Immigration Out of Control*. Monterey, VA: American Immigration Control Foundation, 1992. Reprinted with permission.

vastness and diversity of her conquests, her native blood was diluted in the ocean of her subjects. . . .

Though science and technology have changed since the days of Rome, the nature of people and nations has not. If we fail to learn the lesson of Rome, we are doomed to repeat it.

Adapting to the Modern World

This is not to say, however, that we must stop all immigration and abandon our tradition as a haven for refugees. It is to say that we must adapt that worthy tradition to the realities of the modern world. The deep sentiment many of us feel toward our heritage of immigration is proper. But we abuse that sentiment if we use it as an excuse to live in the past. Just as individuals must adapt to change or suffer the consequences, so must nations.

Most Americans already see the need for reasonable limits on immigration, but due to lack of accurate media coverage and public debate, many do not appreciate the extent of the dangers ahead.

An important reason for their lack of full understanding is that powerful commercial, political, and ethnic interests do not want the issue of immigration coming to national attention. They prefer to reap profits and influence from current policies in the short run, even if this means national destruction in the long run.

These interests cloak their self-interest by appealing to our heritage of immigration. But their efforts to stifle debate and subvert majority rule run directly against the most precious American heritage of all—the right of self-governing citizens to decide their future.

A Nation of Americans

If we are a nation of immigrants, how can we limit immigration? But are we first, foremost, and only "a nation of immigrants," to the exclusion of everything else? This is the question that must be answered first.

Quite literally, the answer is no. Most Americans today are not immigrants, though we descend from people who came here. Our primary identity is not where we came from—or that we came from somewhere else. Our identity is what we have become first and foremost: *a nation of Americans.*

As a distinct nationality, we have certain common traits of character and heritage which we can trace back to our earliest days. As a free and self-ruling people, we have the right

> *"Most Americans today are not immigrants."*

to preserve that character and heritage. A nation of Americans can properly control immigration or set any other policies to guide its future and destiny.

This in no way belittles our immigrant ancestors. In fact, it shows respect for them. If we fail to protect our nation's character and identity, we will lose the very thing that attracted immigrants to America and the nationhood to which they contributed in so many ways. . . .

Immigration interests fall into four major categories: Segments of the business community, various ethnic lobbies, promoters of big government, and religious groups.

Their common cause is a revival of the self-serving alliance that the American people defeated with the immigration acts of the 1920s.

For many business interests, massive immigration offers cheap labor. A case in point are agribusinessmen in the Southwest who use legal and illegal immigrants as farm workers. Other large concerns see growing ethnic groups as profitable markets for their products. The Coors beer advertising campaign directed toward Hispanics is only one example.

To most Americans, our border marks our sovereignty and nationhood, but to some companies, profits are more important than patriotism. In their view, borders are just a hindrance to obtaining cheap labor or moving their plants to places where labor is cheap. Easy movement also allows them to escape strict American labor and environmental laws by shifting their operations to countries where these laws are weak and poorly enforced, or even non-existent.

Such movement is a bonanza for the companies, but a raw deal for American workers. They will lose jobs in competition with low-wage countries and the products those countries produce. The wages of

> *"Most Hispanic citizens support steps to control illegal immigration."*

American workers who keep their jobs will tend to move down to the levels of the competing countries.

Sadly, these possibilities for workers sway Congress much less than the wealth and clout of the corporate interests. Nevertheless, these interests are not so powerful that they can ask for favors in terms of pure self-interest. They need respectable-sounding arguments which reflect public interest and concern for society.

A Free Lunch?

Corporate Propagandists. Providing these arguments in abundance are several prominent conservative think tanks, most of which receive ample funding from corporations, including *foreign* interests, and foundations which seek more immigration. One example is the Washington-based Heritage Foundation. Of this organization, columnist Huey D. Johnson of the *San Francisco Examiner* writes, "The Heritage Foundation supports free immigration from Mexico, mainly so its big agribusiness backers can get cheap labor to work in unsafe and degrading conditions few U.S. citizens would tolerate." Another pro-immigration conservative think tank is the American Enterprise Institute (AEI) of Washington, D.C.

These organizations write glowing descriptions of how free movement of workers, products, and plants across borders will benefit everyone. They call this movement "free trade" and drape it with the respectable banner of "free enterprise." They seldom attempt to explain how these radical notions square with preserving national sovereignty or protecting the wages of American workers.

> *"By crying 'racism' at immigration control, . . . Hispanic organizations [are] useful to their corporate sponsors."*

Even the unprecedented levels of immigration we have today draw few complaints from these think tanks. A senior fellow at Heritage is University of Maryland business professor Julian Simon. He has written books and numerous articles claiming that massive immigration "enriches" the United States. Ben Wattenberg, senior fellow at AEI, presents a similar line. . . .

Simon and his cohorts claim that immigration is a cure-all for almost every problem, a "free lunch" for our economy. To ridicule their claims, critics have taken to calling them the "free-lunch lobby." Wattenberg, however, does not object. He likes the term. Once he asked:

> How can you raise revenues without raising taxes . . . ? It sounds like a free-lunch recipe from the funny farm. . . . It is not . . . you can import extra taxpayers. That process is called immigration. . . . Consider each new immigrant. That immigrant, typically skilled these days [sic], gets a job. He/she pays taxes. . . . Is it an economic free lunch? Of course it is. . . .

Admittedly, the idea of something for nothing is attractive. The interests pushing this lobby want the American people to buy it. Unfortunately, some will. But reality will always teach hard lessons to those who ignore her unchanging instruction: There's no such thing as a free lunch.

Using Race

Ethnic Lobbies. "Conservatives" and their think tanks are not the only recipients of funds from special-interest corporations and related foundations. The monied interests supporting massive immigration also make use of "ethnic lobbies" to put pressure on Congress.

Leading examples are three organizations which claim to speak for Americans of Hispanic descent: the National Council of La Raza (NCLR), the League of United Latin American Citizens (LULAC), and the Mexican American Legal Defense and Educational Fund (MALDEF).

They argue forcefully for immigration, and commonly suggest that anyone who opposes their agenda is a "racist." By this definition, however, a majority of Hispanic Americans must be racists because they support limits on immigra-

172

tion. To cite but one example, a 1990 Roper poll found that 74 percent of Hispanics oppose increased immigration. Most Hispanic citizens support steps to control illegal immigration.

One reason is that immigrants from Latin America and other areas often compete with American Hispanics for jobs and services in border areas. But probably the most important reason is that U.S. Hispanics, like other Americans, want to protect the culture and values they share with other citizens.

NCLR, LULAC, and MALDEF don't reflect these views because they do not depend on the Hispanic community to support their work. As syndicated newspaper columnist Georgie Anne Geyer has observed,

> When you look at the Hispanic groups claiming they represent American Hispanics—groups such as the Mexican American Legal Defense and Educational Fund, the League of United Latin American Citizens, and the National Council of La Raza—one finds that most were created artificially from the top down, rather than from the bottom up. Most started with grants from the Rockefeller and Ford Foundations and . . . American corporations. . . . Their leadership is utterly without grassroots support.

According to *Public Interest Profiles* (1988-1989), published by Congressional Quarterly, Inc., foundation grants are 50 percent of the funding sources of LULAC and corporate grants are the remaining 50 percent. For MALDEF, combined corporate and foundation funding is 93 percent of the money it receives. In 1989, a MALDEF official admitted that only *two percent* of his organization's funding came from membership dues. NCLR funding is 45 percent corporate, and 40 percent from foundations.

Crying "Racism"

By crying "racism" at immigration control, these Hispanic organizations can be most useful to their corporate sponsors. With this charge, business interests can divert public attention from their selfish designs and give the campaign for more immigration, legal and illegal, the appearance of a civil rights movement.

A false appeal to civil rights is most evident in the efforts of LULAC, MALDEF, and NCLR to relax control of illegal immigration and extend "rights" to illegal immigrants once they are here. Until recently, everyone understood that illegal immigration is a purely legal issue, having nothing to do with race.

"Liberal politicians want immigrants as voters for their programs."

But these groups are working mightily to twist this proper understanding. They regularly accuse the Border Patrol of "racism" for simply doing its job and enforcing the law. They also apply this smear to citizen groups which simply ask for protection from the social, political, and economic costs of what amounts to a foreign invasion. The smear campaign, dishonest as it is, effectively intimidates many citizens. . . .

The ethnic immigration lobbies have definite goals of their own, in addition to promoting the agendas of their corporate and foundation sponsors. Foremost among these goals is to build political power bases with immigrants, which can be used to demand government programs and other favors.

Big Government and Religious Interests

Big Government Interests. This aim is perfectly in line with the other bloc of interests that want more immigration: liberal groups seeking bigger government. These interests also support the ethnic lobbies. Liberal politicians want immigrants as voters for their programs, and like-minded bureaucrats seek the job opportunities the programs provide. It is no coincidence that one of the Senate's strongest supporters of more government programs, Ted Kennedy, has probably done more than any politician during the past quarter-century to open the floodgates of immigration.

Liberal interests have seen support for more government programs fall off in recent decades. . . . Some liberal Democrats have changed their stands to attract voters. But some have eyed immigration as a way to keep their policies while changing the voters!

Large numbers of poor and poorly assimilated immigrants would be a likely constituency for government programs, especially after being exploited by business as "cheap labor." The social problems caused by massive immigration would not be problems for Big Government boosters, but opportunities to create new programs and spend more money, courtesy of the American taxpayer. . . .

> *"Special interests . . . want the border open to further their own pursuit of profits and power."*

Religious Interests. Other . . . immigrationists are the leaders of various church groups, often those with a "social gospel" orientation, who believe it is their religious duty to side with "underdogs" and build the Kingdom of God on earth. Usually, in their vision, God's Kingdom requires a building fund supplied by taxpayers and administered by social planners and bureaucrats.

More often than not, however, the rank-and-file members of U.S. religious bodies are just as skeptical of massive immigration as everyone else. Typically overtaxed and underrepresented, they are underdogs whose concerns rarely call forth the "compassion" their leaders so generously offer foreigners. . . .

Control the Border

There is no question that the current levels of immigration threaten our country's future. The real question to ask is what practical steps we should take toward reform. . . .

Illegal Immigration

The nation must make an all-out effort to stop illegal immigration. The first requirement is overcoming the self-serving, defeatist attitude of Congress and presidents that "it can't be done." The fact of the matter is that they have scarcely tried. The reason is that the special interests holding sway over Washington want the border open to further their own pursuit of profits and power.

Consequently, the politicians come up with all kinds of absurd excuses as to why we can't control our borders and protect our national sovereignty. Some claim that controlling our Southern frontier might "offend" Mexico. Others say that we lack the resources to secure our borders, even as they spend billions to protect the borders of Germany, South Korea, and other countries.

> *"The government is making no serious effort to stop illegal immigration."*

Occasionally, some of their excuses seem half-believable, such as the claim that we can't adequately police our 2,000-mile southern border. In point of fact, however, we don't have to. At least 90 percent of its length is desert and mountains—difficult terrain for illegal aliens, particularly large groups of them—to cross in a steady stream.

Most illegals come through a handful of easily passable corridors—generally places with urban areas on both sides of the border. At such points, they can cross and then blend into immigrant communities on the American side.

A stretch of border south of San Diego is the most significant of these corridors. Though it stretches only 14 miles inland from the Pacific Ocean, *nearly half of all illegal immigrants enter through it into the United States!* Yet, in this crucial sector, the government deploys less than 200 Border Patrolmen!

Given this situation—and the fact that, at any one time, only 800 Border Patrolmen are on duty on our entire southern border—it becomes obvious that the government is making no serious effort to stop illegal immigration. The Border Patrol is grossly underfunded and understaffed and, year after year, Congress refuses to provide new funds or reinforcements.

A Few Simple Steps

It may be impossible, as immigrationists insist, to seal off the border completely to illegal immigration. But it is quite possible, with just a few simple steps, to reduce sharply the flow of illegal immigration.

A good start would be adoption of the reforms Congressman Elton Gallegly (R-CA) proposed to Congress in 1991. He proposes increasing Border Patrol manpower from 3,800 to 6,600, and steps to reduce the lure of America to illegal aliens. Despite the law against American employers hiring illegals, they make widespread use of fake documents to take jobs here. Gallegly advocates the use of tamper-proof Social Security cards required for employment. Of prime importance, however, is maintaining the law against hiring illegals. Pro-alien groups are working hard to repeal this reasonable provision.

A further step to reduce the appeal of America is cutting off federal assistance benefits to illegal aliens. Gallegly has offered legislation to amend the Constitution so children born to illegal aliens will no longer automatically become American citizens, and therefore eligible for welfare and other assistance.

In addition to Gallegly's reforms, a number of experts have called for erection of sturdy border fences along the corridors where most aliens come in, along with construction of roads parallel to the border to facilitate movement of the Border Patrol. Wall and road construction is already underway in the San Diego corridor.

Another necessary step, advocated by Alan Nelson, former commissioner of the Immigration and Naturalization Service, is sending Mexican illegals back to the interior of their country. The current practice is simply to deposit them on the other side of the border. Often, within hours of being sent over, many aliens will attempt illegal entry again. In the past, the United States practiced interior deportation, notes Nelson, and it worked much more effectively than the present system.

One means suggested to finance border reforms is to charge foreigners a small fee for crossing the Mexican or Canadian borders. This would amount to a user fee. It would be a small imposition on travelers and provide funding without higher taxes.

Deployment of Troops

Possibly a final need, if control of the border is not regained soon, is deployment of state National Guard forces and/or federal troops to reinforce the Border Patrol. Do-nothing congressmen often claim that such a response would be unlawful or impractical, but, once again, their objections are mere excuses.

They commonly maintain that putting troops on the border would violate the Reconstruction-era Posse Comitatus Act, which prohibits the use of troops for police functions. Their argument based on this law has the following weaknesses.

1) The concept of this law is that troops should not have power to charge and arrest civilian *citizens*. This is indeed a safeguard for civilian rule and democratic government. But troops securing the border would not be enforcing laws against American

> "If the present surge of illegal immigration . . . is not an emergency, then the word has no meaning."

citizens. Their efforts would be directed toward foreign nationals—essentially, against an invading army of illegals.

2) Federal statutes, according to the *Yale Law Journal* and other legal sources, give the president authority to deploy troops in emergency situations where federal laws are violated and/or local authorities cannot maintain order. President

Woodrow Wilson, for example, sent Army troops to stop raids across the frontier by Pancho Villa and other Mexican bandits in 1916.

In 1957 and 1962, troops enforced federal integration rulings in two Southern states. During the Detroit riot of 1967, federal troops were dispatched to restore order.

These were emergencies. If the present surge of illegal immigration across our border is not an emergency, then the word has no meaning. Our law is violated on a massive scale, and we are losing the sovereign right to control the direction of our society.

3) To strengthen the legal case for deploying troops on the border, a proviso for this step could be added to the Posse Comitatus Act. In recent years, the act has already been amended to allow for military participation in the war against drugs.

Another excuse used by congressmen to defend their inaction is that troops are not properly trained for patrolling the border. Even ignoring the compatible training of military police and surveillance units, this is one of the weaker excuses. It is similar to saying that the United States could not have declared war on Japan after Pearl Harbor because we didn't have enough men trained in beach landing and jungle fighting.

Troops can learn new jobs. Former San Diego District Attorney Peter Nunez, an advocate of troop deployment, notes that small military units—companies or platoons—could be assigned to work under the direction of Border Patrol officers.

In 1991, Congressmen James Traficant (D-OH) and Clarence Miller (R-OH) introduced legislation to deploy troops on the border. Respectively, they proposed use of up to 10,000 and 12,000 troops.

A Serious Statement

Putting troops on the border, at least as a temporary emergency measure, would make a statement that the United States is serious about protecting its laws and sovereignty. It is a factor that potential illegal immigrants would consider before planning to cross the border.

Stopping illegal immigration has strong public support. A 1990 Roper poll (the same one that found that 77 percent of the people opposed increasing legal immigration) found that *91 percent* of the people wanted "strong measures" to control illegal immigration. Eighty percent agreed with deploying troops on the border.

In summary, the issue is not whether limiting legal and illegal immigration is feasible. It can be done. Nor is the question one of public support for reasonable limits. Most Americans want secure borders and controls on legal immigration.

The real issue is whether the majority of Americans, who seek these moderate and sensible goals, can prevail against the extremism of powers and interests who put self-interest before country.

The Government Should Impose a Moratorium on Immigration

by Dan Stein

About the author: *Dan Stein is the executive director of the Federation for American Immigration Reform (FAIR), a Washington, D.C., organization that favors greater restrictions on both legal and illegal immigration.*

Recent public opinion polls show that Americans are becoming more concerned about immigration. According to a 1992 Roper poll, 55 percent of the respondents support a temporary moratorium on all legal immigration, except for spouses and minor children of U.S. citizens.

A moratorium—a temporary freeze in immigration—may sound like a radical proposal. Given their support for the idea, most Americans apparently accept the concept. Many ideas that seemed radical previously are suddenly finding new acceptance at a time when many Americans believe the political process is spinning out of control. From the concept of a balanced budget amendment, to term limitations for members of Congress, . . . Americans are voicing their dissatisfaction with a political process that has lost touch with the people.

Influx Takes Its Toll

Census data from 1990 reveal that immigration is a major contributor to U.S. population growth, reshaping the culture and character of our nation, and is a partial factor in the growing gap between rich and poor. As a result of an unprecedented wave of immigration since the mid-1960s, the United States now has the greatest foreign-born population in our history. And there is no end in sight. Changes made in the immigration laws in 1990 mean that today's foreign-born population of 20 million will grow to at least 30 million by the year 2000.

The stress of this unending influx is beginning to take its toll. The riots in Los

Dan Stein, "Why America Needs a Moratorium on Immigration," *The Social Contract*, Fall 1992. Reprinted with permission.

Angeles, and growth projections for California as a whole, present a compelling case that, right now, America is unprepared for more people. Our schools, housing, employment, living standards and deteriorating infrastructure demand a short pause in immigration.

The idea is not new. In the 18th and 19th centuries, immigration waves were short and modest. They often corresponded to acute, short-term situations. But in the 20th century, the situation is different. The huge wave that began in 1890 started with cheap steamer fares and recruitment by labor contractors. It ended in 1921 only because Congress finally imposed limits that curtailed immigration substantially.

Breathing Space

As noted immigration historian John Higham and Sloan Foundation expert Michael Teitelbaum have observed, the lull in immigration beginning with 1920 and continuing through the mid-1960s provided the breathing space that enabled the newcomers in that large wave to assimilate and prosper.

An immigration moratorium would provide an opportunity to examine what has happened to this society in the recent decades of massive, unprecedented legal and illegal immigration. We must then move toward establishing immigration policies which will allow us to stabilize our population, halt the decline in American living

"An immigration moratorium would provide an opportunity to examine what has happened to this society."

standards, and reduce the increasingly divisive cultural fragmentation and ethnic tension.

Immigration to the United States in all forms now surpasses 1 million annually. Nearly 3 million are on waiting lists abroad for visas to enter permanently. A study by the Census Bureau found that there are 20 million immediate relatives of American citizens and resident aliens who are potentially eligible for entry with an immigration preference. A 1989 *Los Angeles Times* poll in Mexico found that 4.7 million Mexicans—about 6 percent of their population of 85 million—intended to emigrate to the United States.

A Trickle Becomes a Flood

All indicators show that the U.S. migrant intake system is overloaded, and is easily manipulated by fraud and deceit. Using phony documents and false claims, immigrants routinely are able to create delays and outwit overburdened hearing examiners. False claims of U.S. citizenship are nearly impossible to detect, while those who overstay visas can easily remain in the U.S. indefinitely.

Worldwide demand for settlement in the United States will escalate in the 1990s. The Third World's labor force will expand by half-a-billion job seekers in the next decade, and will look beyond the borders of their economically underdeveloped countries for economic hope. Millions of earlier immigrants will bring in family members, and political and social unrest abroad will generate millions more refugees worldwide. Like a chain letter, an initial trickle turns into a stream that becomes a river and then a flood. Like shoveling snow in a blizzard, the more rapidly immigrants are admitted by a beleaguered INS, the faster grows the backlog of relatives waiting to enter.

Because all efforts by Congress to solve these problems have quickly collapsed under intense special interest pressure, America needs a three-year moratorium to:

- reduce illegal immigration;
- implement and improve a national documents protocol to verify work eligibility;
- revise immigration laws to reduce substantially overall numbers (to around 300,000 annually); and
- complete a comprehensive analysis of the long-term effects of future immigration and population growth on the demography, the environment, and the cultural and employment/economic resources of our country.

Ultimately, we need to answer this question: what should be the purpose of immigration, now and in the future?

Until we answer that basic question, a moratorium on immigration may be the only option we have left.

The Government Should Use Foreign Aid to Reduce Immigration

by Sergio Díaz-Briquets and Sidney Weintraub

About the authors: *Sergio Díaz-Briquets is the author of* The Health Revolution in Cuba, *the coauthor of* Social Change and Internal Migration, *and the editor of* Cuban Internationalism in Sub-Saharan Africa. *Sidney Weintraub is Dean Rusk Professor at the Lyndon B. Johnson School of Public Affairs at the University of Texas in Austin. Both authors formerly served on the U.S. congressional Commission for the Study of International Migration and Cooperative Economic Development.*

The 1970s and 1980s witnessed unprecedented levels of global migration—much of it unauthorized—from developing to developed countries. Unexpected movements of people created regional tensions, exacerbated economic and social problems in host countries, taxed international humanitarian support systems, and created what some refer to as compassion fatigue in many receiving countries.

Provide Jobs at Home

The bipartisan Commission for the Study of International Migration and Cooperative Economic Development was created to address the push factors that motivate unauthorized immigration to the United States from western hemisphere countries. Extensive consultations abroad, domestic hearings, and research confirmed two fundamental conclusions:

(1) Although there are other important factors, the search for economic opportunity is the primary motivation for most unauthorized migration to the United States; and

(2) Even though job-creating economic growth is the ultimate solution to reducing these migratory pressures, the economic development process itself tends in the short to medium term to stimulate migration by raising expecta-

Reprinted from: *The Effects of Receiving Country Policies on Migration Flows*, edited by Sergio Díaz-Briquets and Sidney Weintraub, 1991, by permission of Westview Press, Boulder, Colorado.

tions and enhancing people's ability to migrate. Development and the availability of new and better jobs at home, however, is the only way to diminish migratory pressures over time.

These conclusions led the Commission to focus on measures that the United States and sending countries might take cooperatively to provide jobs in their home countries for increasing numbers of potential unauthorized immigrants. This summary offers recommendations to both the United States and sending countries that, when taken together, would contribute to mutually beneficial economic growth, thereby easing the undocumented migratory flow over time. . . .

U.S. Trade Policy and Foreign Development

World Bank research confirms that countries with industries capable of meeting foreign competition at home and abroad fare better than countries with industries protected by import barriers and where development strategy focuses primarily inward. The sooner the migrant-sending countries can improve their economies, the shorter will be the duration of pressures to emigrate to the United States.

There has been a dramatic transformation in Latin American development policies from protectionism and state control to reliance on market forces, competition, and maximum participation in the world economy. Exports have now become a major factor in the economies of the region with the United States being their dominant foreign market.

But increased exports require access to international markets. Export policies of migrant-sending countries can succeed only to the extent that economic policies in the industrial countries complement them. If efforts at export promotion are frustrated by trade restrictions, entire development programs may falter.

U.S. actions that frustrate the development of the economies of migrant-sending countries in the western hemisphere will ultimately encourage emigration. The Commission recognizes that the U.S. market is one of the most open in the world to foreign products and investment, and that trade issues are socially sensitive when imports from low-wage countries compete head-on with U.S. production. The United States, under these circumstances, has the dual role of protecting the jobs and living standards of its citizens and of fostering economic conditions that discourage unauthorized immigration. U.S. economic policy should therefore promote an open trading system.

"Job-creating economic growth is the ultimate solution to reducing . . . migratory pressures."

Improved access to U.S. and other developed country markets is the key to the economic future of the area. The United States recognized this in 1983, when the Caribbean Basin Initiative (CBI) was enacted; in 1987, when the

U.S.-Mexico Framework Agreement on Trade and Investment was negotiated; and again—on a grander scale—in 1989, when the U.S.-Canada Free Trade Agreement (FTA) came into effect.

Mexico is an important competitor in the world marketplace. The smaller economies of the Central American and Caribbean countries do not have that potential. The Commission strongly advocates their integration—and Mexico's—into larger trading areas. . . .

Targeting Migrant-Sending Regions for Economic Growth

The pattern of concentrated migratory flows from specific regions within countries suggests it may be possible to reduce undocumented immigration to the United States by targeting economic development in those areas.

For regional development programs to succeed, it is essential that development policies be sustained, sectoral policies be coordinated, and resources be allocated carefully. Regional development efforts should not be targeted to resource-poor areas with meager development prospects. They should instead be oriented to nearby regions with greater development potential that may offer improved economic alternatives to prospective migrants.

"U.S. economic policy should . . . promote an open trading system."

Regional development is particularly appropriate for Mexico, where considerable numbers of undocumented migrants are known to originate from specific areas in a few states. Mexico should itself take the initiative by improving the physical infrastructure of regions containing migrant-sending communities and by providing incentives for domestic and foreign investors to locate there.

• International financial institutions should give priority to development projects that focus on decentralized growth in Mexico's poorer regions.

Developing Small Business

Small businesses in the formal and informal sectors are a major force in the economies of Mexico, Central America, and the Caribbean. The small enterprise sector provides employment for about one-third of the region's economically active population. Small businesses tend to be family owned and operated, hire few employees, and are generally undercapitalized and technologically disadvantaged. Their access to credit is limited, as is their choice of managerial, marketing, and production techniques.

Bureaucratic requirements often constrain entry into the formal sector and pose major problems for small firms already within it. The informal sector thus often serves as a refuge for the urban poor, and it provides employment to an increasing number of women. However, remaining outside the legal framework

183

increases risks and vulnerability to exploitation.

In recognition of their income and employment potential, credit and technical assistance to small businesses are the focus of many development organizations, including AID [Agency for International Development], the World Bank, and the Inter-American Development Bank. These agencies work in cooperation with local, nongovernmental groups at the grass-roots level. The programs are intended to generate additional income and employment, but are precarious because of high default rates.

> *"Improved access to U.S. . . . markets is the key to the economic future of the area."*

- National and international development agencies should work with sending-country governments to reduce legal and bureaucratic impediments to small business development.
- Local and foreign private business sectors should increase support for small business assistance programs. Ways should be sought for greater participation of private commercial banks in financing small businesses, including those owned by migrant households. . . .

Structural Adjustment Process

The guiding development strategy in Latin America and the Caribbean in the decades following World War II was to create domestic industries whose output could substitute for imports. Because many domestic markets were too small to support an efficient industrial base, especially in the Caribbean and Central America, regional integration schemes developed to widen the scope for import substitution. These organizations stressed protected regional markets.

The programs had mixed results. Imports did not generally decline; instead, they shifted from final consumer products to intermediate goods needed in the new industries created. Because the programs were financed at the expense of agriculture, its output usually suffered. In most areas, the concentration on overall economic growth translated into increasingly unequal income distribution. Although Mexico, the Dominican Republic, Trinidad and Tobago, and some Central American countries achieved high rates of economic growth, they were not prepared for the shift from producing simple consumer goods to more complex products requiring higher levels of technology.

From Protectionism to Competition

Development strategies have now shifted emphasis from protectionism to competition. Most migrant-sending countries in the western hemisphere—with Mexico in the forefront—are restructuring their economies. Private initiative is increasing. Private foreign direct investment is avidly sought. Export promotion is taking its place alongside the production of goods for the domestic market.

The process of structural adjustment involves the transition of an economy from a state-dominated model to one in which the market plays the major role, where prices rather than administrative decisions determine the allocation of most resources, and where regulation is designed primarily to foster rather than stifle competition. Undertaking the steps needed to decrease price distortions and allocate resources to the most efficient areas of a country's economy is always a painful process. It entails such actions as devaluing the currency, eliminating subsidies, and increasing interest rates. Imports usually become more expensive and the cost of borrowing increases.

- The United States should condition bilateral aid to sending countries on their taking the necessary steps toward structural adjustment. Similarly, U.S. support for non-project lending by the international financial institutions should be based on the implementation of satisfactory adjustment programs. Efforts should be made to ease transitional costs in human suffering.
- U.S. policies should complement and not frustrate adjustment mechanisms in migrant-sending countries. In practical terms this means, for example, that a move toward export promotion should not be negated by U.S. import barriers. . . .

Rapid Population and Labor Force Growth

Most of the world's developing regions experienced a phenomenal acceleration in population growth rates following World War II. Immunizations through modern public health programs, large-scale sanitation measures, and the introduction of chemical insecticides and antibiotics dramatically reduced mortality, particularly of infants and young children. In the absence of offsetting declines in births, the rate of natural increase soared.

Mexico's population more than tripled between 1940 and 1980, from 20 to 67 million people. An additional 21 million added during the 1980s brings the total to 88 million. This pattern was much the same in Central America, whose population (including Panama) increased from about 9 million in 1950 to over 28 million in 1990. With minor variations, these trends were repeated elsewhere in the western hemisphere.

"Regional development is particularly appropriate for Mexico."

With a delay of one to two decades, such growth in population produces equally rapid growth in the labor force. One million persons enter Mexico's labor market each year, compared with 2 million new job seekers in the United States, which has almost three times Mexico's population. In the entire Caribbean Basin region and Mexico, the number of people in the labor market will have almost quadrupled from 24 million in 1950 to 92 million by the year 2000.

In response, almost all migrant-sending countries have fostered voluntary family-planning programs. A secondary but equally important objective of these programs is to promote maternal and child health.

- The Commission endorses the continued financing of voluntary family planning efforts, including those which promote natural family planning. If they are to be effective, such efforts to foster responsible parenthood must take into account the Latin American moral and cultural atmosphere in which they are implemented.

Education Is Key

Raising educational levels is essential to socioeconomic development and reduction of migratory pressures. An educated population is key to raising productivity. Increasing education is correlated to declining fertility and improved nutritional standards. Vocational education is a prime necessity. Better-paid, skilled manual workers—badly needed in migrant-sending economies—are not as prone to emigrate as less trained workers earning lower wages.

Educational programs in localities with high migration rates could emphasize development of skills, vocational and white collar, for which there is a relatively high demand in the broader economic region. This would entail assessing prospective labor demands by skill levels and gearing regional school systems to provide students with appropriate training. This goal is attainable in a large country such as Mexico, which has a well-developed system of rapidly growing secondary cities.

> *"An educated population is key to raising productivity."*

One way to overcome the shortcomings of the limited resources and relatively small populations of the smaller Central American and Caribbean countries is to create or strengthen existing regional training institutions to serve the needs of more than one country. These training centers have already been effective in helping reduce shortages of highly educated workers.

- Congress and AID should program assistance funds for increased vocational education in migrant-sending countries.

Following the 1984 recommendations of the National Bipartisan Commission on Central America (Kissinger Commission), the United States funded programs to provide educational opportunities in the United States for disadvantaged persons from Central American and Caribbean countries. Such programs not only enhance educational opportunities and employment potential when students return to their home countries, but expose them to the culture and democratic ideals of the United States as well.

- The Congress should continue to fund such programs, include Mexico as a participant, and expand the scope of scholarship programs in the United States. . . .

186

Sending countries are generally unconcerned about the impact their migrants may be having on receiving countries. They often view emigration as a necessary escape valve. The United States has not made this issue a high priority and has

been reluctant to raise it in bilateral discussions with sending countries. Neither the United Nations nor the international community as a whole has paid much attention to the issue of international migration, except in the context of refugee or refugee-like movements. In many cases, migration has been viewed by both sending and receiving countries as a foreign policy irritant. In others, it is not considered important enough to be on bilateral agendas.

> *"The United States should give higher priority to the issue of unauthorized migration."*

- The International Organization for Migration (IOM) should play a larger role in western hemisphere migration discussions by convening meetings and seminars with high-level participation from the United States and Latin American member governments.
- The United States should give higher priority to the issue of unauthorized migration and seek greater cooperation on the part of sending countries regarding certain enforcement measures (for example, to curtail smuggling rings or fraudulent document activities). . . .

Creating an Agency for Migration Affairs

Migration responsibilities are currently diffused among several different cabinet departments and agencies. No mechanism exists within the U.S. government to assess the impact of U.S. policies and actions on migration, to rank migration against other priorities, or to bring it to the attention of decision makers. Failure to pay sufficient attention to the effects of U.S. policies and actions on migratory flows has over many years contributed to a large influx of unauthorized immigrants.

The Commission believes that a reorganization of the current structure within the executive branch for handling migration is urgently needed to ensure that migration be given a high priority on the U.S. domestic and foreign policy agendas, and that migration consequences be carefully considered by policy makers involved in trade, development, and international economic matters.

- Immigration and refugee matters should be centralized and streamlined into a new agency for migration affairs.
- Relevant federal agencies should be required to prepare and disseminate immigration impact statements (similar to environmental impact statements) to accompany major U.S. government decisions regarding development assistance and trade with migrant-sending countries. . . .

In sum, the Commission is convinced that expanded sending-country access to U.S. and other markets through increasingly free trade is the most promising stimulus to their future economic growth. The more able the migrant-sending countries are to sell their products abroad, the less their people will feel the need to seek economic opportunity away from home.

The Commission has found, however, that the development process itself tends to stimulate migration in the short to medium term by raising expectations and enhancing people's ability to migrate. Thus, the effects of the development solution on unauthorized migration will be observable only decades or generations hence. Any serious cooperative effort to reduce migratory pressures at their source must stay the course in the face of contradictory short-term results.

Primary responsibility for their own development rests with the sending countries themselves. But if the United States is to cooperate in a long-term search for a mutually beneficial outcome, it must recognize that achieving it requires steadfastness of purpose over many years.

The Government Should Allow Open Immigration

by Dan Lacey

About the author: *Dan Lacey, who died in 1993, was an author on employ-ment-related subjects. His books include* The Paycheck Disruption, Work in the 21st Century, *and* The Essential Immigrant, *from which the following viewpoint is excerpted.*

What if you looked at the front page of your morning newspaper and encoun-tered a huge headline that said: "Immigrants don't consume prosperity, they create it?"

To most Americans, that headline could be true only in a fantasy world; but in truth, . . . those who study the American economy scientifically know that both consumption and immigration add to America's affluence, rather than subtract from it. In a consumption-based economy such as America's, ever-rising con-sumption has always been the seemingly magical force that makes wonderful things rise from the bare earth.

Never Too Many

There are mountains of evidence that there will never be too many people seated around the table, as most American adherents to the religion of jobilism [a dogmatic protection of jobs for the sake of the protection of jobs] believe would be the case if America's borders were opened. All the attempts at legislat-ing immigration restrictions have been unnecessary exercises in political pander-ing. There is no need to maintain an ever-growing immigration bureaucracy.

With a new dose of mass immigration flowing through the country's veins, the decline of the average American's standard of living could be reversed. America needn't forsake its immigrant heritage to survive; it is not necessary for people of less fortunate lands to suffer and die along America's borders so that Americans can prosper. The discussion of immigration need not be a mat-

From Dan Lacey, *The Essential Immigrant*, published by Hippocrene Books, Inc., 1990. Reprinted with permission.

ter of shameful racist emotions disguised in pompous rhetoric; a politician with enough guts could champion open immigration and survive proudly to take credit for the results.

Despite overwhelming evidence that prosperity follows where immigrants go, one generation after another of Americans has come to believe that each arriving wave of immigrant labor somehow diminishes the material wealth of those already situated within the country.

> *"It is not necessary for people of less fortunate lands to suffer and die along America's borders."*

Politicians have continually exploited that fallacy by passing one irrational, disjointed, insincere immigration law after another. Equipped with virtually no understanding of economics, the majority of Americans have reacted favorably to the emotion-based immigration restrictions those politicians effected. To do otherwise would seem as foolish as an attempt to reverse the laws of gravity.

The idea that open immigration is the key to a resurgence of America's economy—and, consequently, a resumption of the material improvement of the America lifestyle—seems radical to most Americans. But it's not at all radical to those familiar with the forces that drove America to its world dominance of the 1950s and '60s. Indeed, even the very mainstream *Wall Street Journal*, hardly a voice of economic iconoclasm, promotes open immigration as the keystone of a new era of economic success.

"There Shall Be Open Borders"

To celebrate Independence Day 1989, for example, the *Journal*'s "Review & Outlook" section reprinted Emma Lazarus's Statue of Liberty poem about immigrants in full, lamented the fact that immigrants were being hounded at work, then commented, in part:

> Three years ago today, we offered an alternative. We wrote, "If Washington still wants to 'do something' about immigration, we propose a five-word constitutional amendment: There shall be open borders.

> We added, "Perhaps this policy is overly ambitious in today's world, but the U.S. became the world's envy by trumpeting precisely this kind of heresy." A policy of liberal borders is no more or less radical than the notion that a democracy founded in a new, wild world could become the envy of all nations. . . .

> This nation needs the rejuvenation that recurrent waves of new Americans bring. Latins, Vietnamese and West Indians are the new Irish, Italians and Poles. We must guard against slipping into the self-satisfied view that we are good enough as is, no more need apply or trespass on the American experiment.

Such advocacy occurs rarely, if ever, in America's nonbusiness news media.

Indeed, with the exception of the *Wall Street Journal* and a few other relatively sophisticated business periodicals, America's news media have served as loyal disciples of the jobilism that supports most contemporary resistance to immigration. And many people who consider themselves to be business leaders, and can therefore be presumed to be somewhat familiar with the economics of work, exacerbate the fear of immigration by holding jobs as public relations hostages: They routinely threaten to eradicate jobs if the government doesn't provide the subsidies their businesses demand, and the news media routinely echo those threats.

To at least some extent, the level of misunderstanding of economic cause-and-effect has become worse now that television news has become Americans' dominant source of information: Economists have never been good at simple explanations, and when it comes to explaining the advantage of immigration to the U.S. economy, they just can't come up with the essential short, succinct, declarative sentences—the "soundbytes"—by which television journalism lives.

The Most Important Commodity

One of the most frustrated of such economists is William B. Johnston, vice-president of special projects at the Hudson Institute and project director for the writing of *Workforce 2000*, the most highly regarded and frequently quoted study of the future of the American labor force produced in the 1980s. Although *Workforce 2000* originally was conceived merely as an academic study funded by the U.S. Department of Labor, more than 50,000 copies of it have been sold to American business owners, managers and others concerned about the future availability of workers. *Workforce 2000* reminded corporate America that in the contemporary world of business, people are the most important commodity. . . .

In an attempt to explain his findings on immigration to interviewers trained at the "School of Jobilism," Johnston has developed one illustration of economic subtleties that makes his point quite well. He calls it his "Tale of Two Cities."

"Look at Detroit and then look at Los Angeles," he suggests. "There are a lot of different things going on in those cities, but one aspect of the bottom line is that there are very few immigrants in Detroit and overwhelming numbers of immigrants in Los Angeles. And yet Los Angeles is a much better place to find a job, and it has a much faster growing economy than that of Detroit.

"Immigration has not swamped Los Angeles. It has made Los Angeles a bigger, more vibrant place than it has ever been before—on its way to be-

> *"Open immigration is the key to a resurgence of America's economy."*

coming the capital of the Pacific. The lack of immigration, on the other hand, hasn't saved Detroit from the problems it has because of the ups and downs of the automobile industry.". . .

One of the most commonly raised points in discussions of America's contemporary immigration policies is that many immigrants to America arrive illegally, skirting American law in attempts to find a better life. Whenever that point is raised, it adds an implication of criminality to the concept of an immigrant. It tends to steer the discussion away from economic considerations and toward the effectiveness and appropriateness of police activities directed at the immigrants ominously labeled "illegal aliens."

> *"We must guard against slipping into the self-satisfied view that we are good enough as is."*

But Johnston's advocacy attacks even that well-entrenched concept. Immigrants who enter America illegally, he points out, often energize the American economy even more than their colleagues who arrived within the parameters of American immigration law.

"As evidenced by the border closing efforts, America doesn't like illegal immigration," he says. "But from the viewpoint of an economist, illegal immigration is the best kind of immigration in certain respects because those people have to leap a high hurdle: they have to break the law and leave everything behind in order to find work.

"That automatically gets you a self-selected group of people who are very highly motivated. Illegal immigrants have always been the motivated, the most chance-seeking people, and that's what this country's always been about.". . .

The Danger of Restriction

In addition to all the evidence that mass immigration could invigorate the American economy, there is empirical evidence that cutting off the flow of hungry-to-work immigrants would be dangerous: It could accelerate the gradual decline of the American economy.

Dr. Thomas Muller, an economist who is highly regarded for his research on the effects of immigration while with The Urban Institute, points out that the Immigration Act of 1924 was one of the factors that caused the depression of the 1930s to be historically a bad one.

"The depression started after immigration was curtailed," Muller points out. "There's no direct cause-and-effect relationship, but one of the causes of the depression was a sharp reduction in demand for housing and consumer goods beginning in about 1926-27. That happened to have coincided with a couple of other things going in that direction.

"Had we maintained immigration at the levels of the early 1920s, which would have been the case had it not been for the Immigration Act of 1924, consumption would have been substantially higher. It would not have prevented the depression, but it would have made it more shallow." Some other countries, such as Canada, didn't legislate against immigration until they were several years into the depression, he points out, and in those countries the effects of the depression were not nearly as severe as in the United States.

Muller's research demonstrates that immigrants generally do not compete with Americans for jobs. Indeed, the entry of low-skilled, hungry-to-work immigrants has often pushed exiting Americans up the employment ladder and improved the quality of life in America.

"When the Chinese came into California, the very unskilled Irish who worked on the railroads—most of whom could neither read nor write—became the crew leaders. The Chinese accepted the bottom level of the work, and the Irish were promoted," Muller points out. . . .

Immigration Benefits Minorities

Muller, who is the author of a study of immigration policy underwritten by the prestigious Twentieth Century Fund, has focused much of his research on the effects of immigration on racial and ethnic minorities in America.

"Basically, what we've found," Muller says, "is that there has been no relationship between black unemployment and the flow of Hispanic immigrants. Hispanics tend to be at the lower end of the [economic] spectrum. But if you look at Hispanics, you find no measurable adverse effect [on blacks]." Perhaps that explains why Senator Edward M. Kennedy's immigration policy staff experiences little pressure from the black community on immigration issues: Although the plight of urban blacks is used as evidence by anti-immigration activists, the blacks themselves perceive no threat from recent immigrants.

In fact, Muller points out, American blacks could benefit from high levels of immigration by low-skill, low-wage groups. "They'd benefit because of their occupational preference," he explains. "Blacks are disproportionately employed in government. If you look at any large city in America, black public-sector employment is very high and it's increasing. Virtually all the net gain in municipal employment in recent years represents black employment."

Most aging urban areas would be declining more rapidly in terms of population if it were not for the flow of low-income immigrants, who tend to move into urban areas as those areas are abandoned by native-born Americans moving to the suburbs and beyond.

> *"In the contemporary world of business, people are the most important commodity."*

"What you have [because of immigration] is an expansion of population, which creates demand in the public sector, which then expands black employment opportunities," Muller says, adding that there is also an emotional element to the relationship between low-wage immigrants and blacks: To most contemporary blacks, working as a cleaning person is a stigmatized remnant of the times when blacks were held down even more than today, so becoming a cleaning woman is the last thing they are willing to do. Many of the new immigrants now fill the cleaning jobs, allowing black women to move up, much as the Chinese did for the Irish in the 19th century. . . .

In addition to the fact that higher immigration results in higher consumption and consequently fuels the economy, one of the most easy-to-understand explanations of why mass immigration causes economic growth exists within the basic economic formula for business expansion. It is a very

> *"Illegal immigrants have always been the motivated, the most chance-seeking people."*

simple formula that economists typically express in arcane mathematical symbols, thereby boring, confusing and/or alienating noneconomists who need to receive information in conversational terms.

In simple language, the formula for expansion is this: A prudent company will expand as long as the amount of money it gets for producing one more unit of its product is greater than the amount of money that it has to spend to produce that one additional unit. (For those with incurably technical minds, economists express the expansion-encouraging situation as MR>MC, marginal revenue is greater than marginal cost.) Companies that go bankrupt often seem to be unaware of this formula: By selling a few additional units of their products without regard to the cost of adding an entire second shift of workers or a new line of production machinery, for example, those *unprudent* companies expand into oblivion.

Apply the formula for prudent expansion to contemporary America and it's easy to see why having employers bid higher and higher wages to attract a shrinking number of available workers isn't the boon to the economy that it seems to be from a paycheck viewpoint. Although wage bidding may seem to create an economic windfall, it quickly brings expansion to a halt: The point at which the cost of one more unit exceeds the money brought in by one more unit is reached more quickly than it would be in a situation where labor was plentiful.

Then a negative chain reaction develops. There is less work for people who build the commercial buildings that expansion would have demanded, for example; building contractors therefore buy fewer trucks, truck manufacturers buy fewer parts and less steel, and so on.

Nashville or Detroit?

This interaction between the cost of labor and the rate of business expansion has helped create America's largest, most prosperous cities: New York, Chicago and, most recently, Los Angeles. Because immigration has at some point filled those cities with ambitious, inexpensive workers, many companies were established there. Eventually, groups of companies became industries, the products they produced became more sophisticated, and wage scales moved up.

In many parts of contemporary America that same type of interaction continues to be an essential economic force. While the American auto companies based in Detroit—a heavily unionized city where workers are conditioned to high hourly rates and extensive benefit packages—continue to skid down toward obsolescence, the Japanese-owned auto companies gathering in Tennessee—where labor is relatively cheap, the workers have rejected the unions and there has always been a shortage of economic opportunities—are booming and expanding.

Labor unions and other jobilists argue that the Japanese automakers are achieving success at the expense of the working person. But take a look at Detroit, and then at Nashville, and it's easy to see which is the better place to be. Then consider the fact that dozens of American and Japanese companies have decided to build their future plants just south of the Mexican border. The positive effect that the availability of low-wage labor has on economic expansion is irrefutable. . . .

From Commodity to Revered Leader

Do the arguments in favor of mass immigration treat people as a commodity . . . ? Maybe so, but discussing immigrants as a commodity is the candid and honest way to discuss the role that immigrants truly play in the success of the American economy. Romanticism aside, neither the science of economics nor the people who own and manage businesses can calculate the people factor in any way other than as a commodity; indeed, modern economists and managers regard people as the most *essential* commodity.

That fact clashes with the romantic notions with which America's paycheck [employer-dependent] class regards itself. Just as most people would cringe at the seemingly cold terms physicians and clergymen use to discuss their patients and parishioners when talking with colleagues behind closed doors, paycheck-class Americans would be shocked to see that they are represented as mathematical digits and dollars signs on corporate management reports.

> *"Immigrants generally do not compete with Americans for jobs."*

It is, however, very important to note that although the Irish who were herded into the steerage of ships bound for America to serve as ballast were most definitely regarded as a commodity, that fact didn't prevent one of their progeny [John F. Kennedy] from becoming the most revered American president of the 20th century.

The Government Should Legalize Illegal Immigrant Residents

by Jorge G. Castaneda

About the author: *Jorge G. Castaneda is a graduate professor of political science at the National University of Mexico.*

In the most unexpected and tragicomic way, immigration without papers, rights or status has returned to the center stage of American politics. The Clinton Administration's problems with nannies and nominees shifted an errant spotlight onto an issue generally ignored in Middle America: the mass presence of undocumented immigrants in its midst. It is, in fact, one of the central problems facing the United States as a whole, not just California, Texas and the barrios of Chicago.

Growing Dramatically

Every study concurs. The latest, [from] the Commission on Agricultural Workers . . . , states that the 1986 Immigration Reform and Control Act did not resolve the "problem." Undocumented immigration from Latin America and the Caribbean has not stopped. It has grown dramatically since 1988, and will continue to do so. It has become far more diverse geographically, originating in countries where it never occurred previously, and in its economic, gender and social composition—now often urban, literate, lower middle-class and, increasingly, female. It has extended into areas of the United States heretofore untouched by the trend, from New York, where Mexicans, for example, had never dared to venture, to Seattle, from North Carolina to New Haven. And it has penetrated areas of the U.S. job market that until a decade ago were largely unknown to men and women from Mexico, El Salvador, Guatemala and Peru: domestic work, restaurants and parking lots.

Jorge G. Castaneda, "What's Necessary Should Be Legal," *Los Angeles Times*, February 12, 1993. Reprinted with permission.

As U.S. society changes—as women join the work force, and as more of the middle class has money for what used to be luxuries—and as the restructuring of the American economy goes forward, new needs arise. So do new ways of satisfying them: help at home with the laundry and the lawn, fast-food employees willing to flip hamburgers for pennies, a human touch to care for the very young and the elderly. Mexicans, Salvadorans, Peruvians and Colombians (among others) will do it, kindly and efficiently. And Americans who employ them are ever grateful for their presence and their cost; what would life be without them?

> *"Keeping the process in the twilight zone of tolerated illegality is the worst of all possible worlds."*

As anyone who has witnessed how the old and new migration networks operate throughout Latin America will affirm, the chances are slim for any significant let-up in the flow in the near future. The silver-bullet theory of immigration control, free trade and more Border Patrol agents will prove to be as irrelevant as all the earlier quick fixes proved to be. The lack of opportunities south of the Rio Grande and the abundance of "high-paying" jobs in the United States, which is what $4.75 an hour sweeping factory floors or $15 an hour doing housework represents for millions of Latin Americans, ensure that the flow of people north will persist. The communications revolution, domestic and international—from CNN to bargain air travel—ensures that. And the job networks and contacts that each newcomer finds make it likely that those who try to follow will succeed.

The Pernicious Possibilities

No country, if given the choice, would prefer to allow mass, illegal immigration rather than staunch it. Being a country where a unified, accepted and even glorified rule of law plays a key role in bringing cohesion to a perennially fragmented society, the United States in particular would obviously hope to frame its options neatly: allow and legalize the immigration it needs, and nothing more than that; stop the rest.

To choose between allowing illegal immigration and banning it is not exactly a difficult task. It is, unfortunately for the democratic fabric of this nation, an impossible one. The choice is not between an easy course and an unacceptable one, but rather between two pernicious possibilities: accepting mass immigration legally because it is inevitable, necessary and highly desirable, or doing the same illegally because the country cannot face the facts of what it is doing. This dichotomy is a tougher one to swallow, but it is the one that must be dealt with.

There is such a strong case against undocumented immigration that the one in favor of legalization seems hardly worth arguing. But keeping the process in the twilight zone of tolerated illegality is the worst of all possible worlds: It makes criminals of all those who hire undocumented foreigners, and of the foreigners themselves. It forces wages down, strips millions of individuals of the rights and dignity that most Americans take, quite rightly, for granted, and creates a huge "black hole" in American democracy. Millions work, pay taxes, use and provide services, but are denied any of the rights enjoyed by citizens and other legal residents: the right to have a say in government, the right to organize and petition and complain, the right to due process, the right to say no. Transforming the undocumented into legal workers, and the legal into individuals with some of the attributes of citizenry, even if devoid of nationality, is the best remedy among various objectionable or unworkable solutions to this intractable problem.

There are obstacles, undoubtedly. Legalizing current undocumented immigrants would encourage more to come; there is a virtually unlimited supply ready to move and it will last until the jobs run out. The cultural resistance in the United States to the type of immigration involved—poor, brown, Catholic—is, to say the least, powerful; so is its political expression, from Pat Buchanan to part of what's left of the labor movement.

It would take great leadership and much daring to swing the American public behind immigration reform and legalization. That only makes the effort to change all the more worthwhile, for the consequences of letting bad enough alone can, with time and misfortune, tear a nation apart.

The Government Should Allow More Legal Immigration

by Julian L. Simon

About the author: *Julian L. Simon is a teacher of business administration at the University of Maryland, College Park, and the author of* The Economic Consequences of Immigration.

By increasing somewhat the flow of immigrants—from about 600,000 to about 750,000 admissions per year—the immigration legislation passed by Congress late in 1990 will improve the standard of living of native-born Americans. The bill represents a sea change in public attitude toward immigration; it demonstrates that substantially increasing immigration is politically possible. That's all good news, and we should celebrate it.

The bad news is that the legislation does not *greatly* increase immigration. The new rate is still quite low by historical standards. A much larger increase in numbers—even to, say, only half the rate relative to population size that the United States accepted around the turn of the century—would surely increase our standard of living even more.

Immigration Benefits the Nation

The political problem for advocates of immigration is to avoid the letdown to be expected after the passage of this first major legal-immigration bill in a quarter-century. And since the law contemplate[d] additional legislation (by providing for a commission to collect information on immigration), it is important to educate the public about how immigration benefits the nation as well as the immigrants.

Increased immigration presents the United States with an opportunity to realize many national goals with a single stroke. It is a safe and sure path—open to

From Julian L. Simon, "The Case for Greatly Increased Immigration." Reprinted from: *The Public Interest*, No. 106 (Winter 1991), pp. 89-103, © 1991 by National Affairs, Inc.

Chapter 4

no other nation—to achieve all of these benefits: 1) a sharply increased rate of technological advance, spurred by the addition of top scientific talent from all over the world; 2) satisfaction of business's demand for the labor that the baby-bust generation makes scarce; 3) reduction of the burden that retirees impose upon the ever-shrinking cohort of citizens of labor-force age, who must support the Social Security System; 4) rising tax revenues—resulting from the increase in the proportion of workers to retirees—that will provide the only painless way of shrinking and perhaps even eliminating the federal deficit; 5) improvement in our competitive position vis-á-vis Japan, Europe, and the rest of the world; 6) a boost to our image abroad, stemming from immigrants' connections with their relatives back home, and from the remittances that they send back to them; and 7) not least, the opportunity given to additional people to enjoy the blessings of life in the United States.

All the U.S. need do to achieve these benefits is further to relax its barriers against skilled immigrants. Talented and energetic people want to come here. Yet we do not greatly avail ourselves of this golden opportunity, barring the door to many of the most economically productive workers in the world. . . .

The most important issue is the total number of immigrants allowed into the United States. It is important to keep our eyes fixed on this issue, because it tends to get obscured in emotional discussions of the desirability of reuniting families, the plight of refugees, the geographic origin and racial composition of our immigrant population, the needs of particular industries, the illegality of some immigration, and so on.

The Federation for American Immigration Reform (FAIR)— whose rhetoric I shall use as illustration—says that "[i]mmigration to the United States is at record levels." This claim is simply false. The recent inflow clearly is far below the inflow around the turn of the century. Even the inclusion of illegal immigrants does not alter the fact that there is less immigration now than in the past.

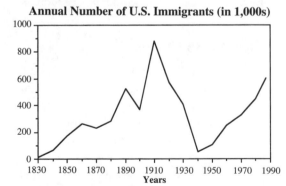

Annual Number of U.S. Immigrants (in 1,000s)

Economically speaking, more relevant than absolute numbers is the volume of immigration as a proportion of the native population. Between 1901 and 1910 immigrants arrived at the yearly rate of 10.4 per thousand U.S. population, whereas between 1981 and 1987 the rate was only 2.5 per thousand of the population. So the recent flow is less than a fourth as heavy as it was in that earlier period. Australia and Canada admit three times that many immigrants as a proportion of their populations.

200

Illegal Immigration

Another way to think about the matter: in 1910, 14.6 percent of the population was born abroad, but in 1980 less than 6 percent of us were. Not only is the

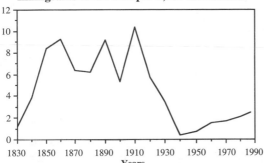

Immigrants to the U.S. per 1,000 Inhabitants

present stock of immigrants much smaller proportionally than it was earlier, but it also is a small proportion considered by itself. We tend to think of ourselves as a "nation of immigrants," but less than one out of fifteen people now in the U.S. was born abroad, including those who arrived many years ago. Who would guess that the U.S. has a smaller share of foreign-born residents than many countries that we tend to think have closed homogeneous populations—including Great Britain, Switzerland, France, and Germany? We are a nation not of immigrants, but rather of the descendants of immigrants.

Furthermore, the absorption of immigrants is much easier now than it was in earlier times. One has only to read the history of the Pilgrims in Plymouth Colony to realize the enormity of the immediate burden that each new load of immigrants represented. But it is the essence of an advanced society that it can more easily handle material problems than can technically primitive societies. With every year it becomes easier for us to make the material adjustments that an increase in population requires. That is, immigrant assimilation becomes ever less of an economic problem—all the more reason that the proportion of immigrants now seems relatively small, compared with what it was in the past. . . .

For years, phony inflated estimates of the stocks and flows of illegal immigrants were bandied about by opponents of immigration in order to muddy the waters. Since the 1986 Simpson-Mazzoli law's amnesty we know that the numbers are actually quite modest, much lower than even the "mainstream" estimates cited in the press. So that scare no longer serves as an effective red herring for opponents of immigration.

Now let us consider the costs and benefits of immigration—even though economic issues may not be the real heart of the matter, often serving only as a smoke screen to conceal the true motives for opposition. Only thus can one explain why the benefits of immigration do not produce more open policies. Because opponents of immigration wield economic arguments to justify their positions, however, we must consider their assertions. . . .

The main real cost that immigration imposes on natives is the extra capital needed for additional schools and hospitals. But this cost turns out to be small relative to benefits, in considerable part because we finance such construction with bond issues, so that we operate largely on a pay-as-you-go basis. Immigrants therefore pay much of their share.

The supposed cost that most captures the public's imagination, of course, is welfare payments. According to popular belief, no sooner do immigrants arrive than they become public charges, draining welfare money from the American taxpayers, and paying no taxes.

Not True

Solid evidence gives the lie to this charge. In an analysis of Census Bureau data I found that, aside from Social Security and Medicare, about as much money is spent on welfare services and schooling for immigrant families as for citizens. When programs for the elderly are included, immigrant families receive far *less* in public services than natives. During the first five years in the U.S., the average immigrant family receives $1,400 in welfare and schooling (in 1975 dollars), compared with the $2,300 received by the average native family. The receipts gradually become equal over several decades. Arthur Akhbari of St. Mary's College in Canada has shown that recent Canadian data produce almost identical results. And Harriet Duleep's finding that the economic results of Canadian and U.S. immigration are quite similar, despite the different admissions systems, adds weight to the conclusion that U.S. immigrants pay much more in taxes than they receive in benefits. . . .

As to illegal immigrants and welfare, FAIR typically says that "[t]axpayers are hurt by having to pay more for social services." Ironically, several surveys—for example, one by Sidney Weintraub and Gilberto Cardenas of the University of Texas—show that illegals are even heavier net contributors to the public coffers than legal immigrants; many illegals are in the U.S. only temporarily and are therefore without families, and they are often afraid to apply for services for fear of being apprehended. Illegals do, however, pay taxes. . . .

The Non-Threat of Displaced Native Workers

The most dramatic argument against immigration—the bogeyman in the mind of organized labor, which has been its most powerful political opponent since the nineteenth century—has been that foreigners take jobs held by natives and thereby increase native unemployment. The logic is simple: if the number of jobs is fixed, and immigrants occupy some jobs, there must be fewer available jobs for natives.

In the shortest run, the demand for any particular sort of worker is indeed inflexible. Therefore, additional immigrants in a given occupation must to some degree lower wages

> *"We are a nation not of immigrants, but rather of the descendants of immigrants."*

and/or increase unemployment in that occupation. For example, the large recent influx of foreign physicians increases the competition that U.S. physicians face, lowering their earnings. But because immigrants come with a variety of skills, workers in most occupations feel little impact. And in the longer run, workers in most occupations are not injured at all.

A good-sized body of competent recent research shows that immigration does not exacerbate unemployment, even among directly competing groups; in California, for instance, immigrants have not increased unemployment among blacks and women. And the research, done by several independent scholars from a variety of angles, uses several kinds of data. For example, Stephen Moore and I systematically studied immigration's effects upon overall unemployment, by looking at the changes in unemployment in various U.S. cities that have experienced different levels of unemployment. We found that if there is displacement, it is too little to be observable.

> *"Illegals are even heavier net contributors to the public coffers than legal immigrants."*

The explanation is that immigrants not only take jobs, but also create them. Their purchases increase the demand for labor, leading to new hires roughly equal in number to the immigrant workers. . . .

Tax Payments

If immigrants paid relatively little in taxes they might still burden natives, despite using fewer welfare services. But data on family earnings, which allow us to estimate tax payments, show that this is not at all the case.

Immigrants pay more than their share of taxes. Within three to five years, immigrant-family earnings reach and pass those of the average American family. The tax and welfare data together indicate that, on balance, an immigrant family enriches natives by contributing an average of $1,300 or more per year (in 1975 dollars) to the public coffers during its stay in the U.S. Evaluating the future stream of these contributions as one would a dam or harbor, the present value of an immigrant family—discounted at the risk-free interest rate of 3 percent—adds up to almost two years' earnings for a native family head. This means that the economic activities of an average immigrant family reduce the taxes of a native head of household enough to advance his or her possible date of retirement by two years.

Curiously, contemporary welfare-state policies render immigration more beneficial to natives than it was in earlier times when welfare was mainly voluntary. There are two main reason why today's immigrants make net contributions to the public coffers. First, far from being tired, huddled masses, immigrants tend to come when they are young, strong, and vibrant, at the start of their work lives. For example, perhaps 46 percent of immigrants are in the prime labor-force ages of twenty to thirty-nine, compared with perhaps 26 percent of natives. And only 4 percent of immigrants are aged sixty or over, compared with about 15 percent of natives. Second, many immigrants are well educated and have well-paying skills that produce hefty tax contributions. . . .

Most important in the long run is the boost that immigrants give to productivity. Though hard to pin down statistically, the beneficial impact of immigration upon productivity is likely to dwarf all other effects after these additional workers and consumers have been in the country a few years. Some of the productivity increase comes from immigrants working in industries and laboratories that are at the forefront of world technology. We benefit along with others from the contribution to world productivity in, say, genetic engineering that immigrants could not make in their home countries. More immigrants mean more workers, who will think up productivity-enhancing ideas. As Soichiro Honda (of motorcycle and auto fame) said: "Where 100 people think, there are 100 powers; if 1,000 people think, there are 1,000 powers."

It is well to remember that the development of the atomic bomb hinged on the participation of such immigrants as Enrico Fermi, John von Neumann, and Stan Ulam, among many others. Contemporary newspaper stories continue this historical saga, noting the disproportionate numbers of Vietnamese and other Asian immigrant youths who achieve distinction in competitions such as the Westinghouse Science Talent Search. Ben Wattenberg and Karl Zinsmeister of the American Enterprise Institute write that among the forty 1988 finalists, "22 were foreign-born or children of foreign-born parents: from Taiwan, China, Korea, India, Guyana, Poland, Trinidad, Canada, Peru, Iran, Vietnam and Honduras." They also note that one-fourth of recent valedictorians and salutatorians in San Diego have been

> *"Immigrants not only take jobs, but also create them."*

Vietnamese, and that thirteen of the seventeen public high school valedictorians in Boston in 1989 were foreign born. Sometimes it seems as if such names as Wang Computers and Steve Chen dominate our most vigorous industry.

The Bottom Line

An economist always owes the reader a cost-benefit assessment for policy analysis. So I combined the most important elements pertaining to legal immigrants with a simple macroeconomic model, making reasonable assumptions where necessary. The net effect is slightly negative for the early years, but four or five years later the net effect turns positive and large. And when we tote up future costs and benefits, the rate of "investment" return from immigrants to the citizen public is about 20 percent per annum—a good return for any portfolio.

Does all this seem to be a far-out minority view? In 1990 the American Immigration Institute surveyed prominent economists—all the ex-presidents of the American Economic Association, and then-members of the Council of Economic Advisers—about immigration. Economists ought to understand the economic effects of immigration better than others, so their views are of special interest. More than four-fifths of the respondents said that immigration has a very favorable impact on economic growth; none said that its impact is unfavorable. Almost three-fourths said that illegals have a positive economic impact. And almost all agree that recent immigrants have had the same kind of impact as immigrants in the past.

The Real Reasons for Opposition

I began by citing various reasons for our failure to take in more immigrants, despite the clear-cut benefits of doing so. The first is ignorance of the benefits described above. Second is the opposition by special interests, such as organized labor (which wants to restrict competition for jobs) and ethnic groups (whose members often fear that immigration will cause their proportion of the population to decrease). The third reason is well-organized opposition to immigration and a total lack of organized support for it.

FAIR, for example, has a large budget—it amassed $2,000,000 in revenues in 1989—and a large staff. It supports letter-writing campaigns to newspapers and legislators, gets its representatives onto television and radio, and is in the rolodex of every journalist who writes on the subject. Several other organizations play a similar role. On the other side, until recently no organization advocated more immigration generally. Now at least there is the fledgling American Immigration Institute; and the de Tocqueville Institute did excellent work on immigration in 1989 and 1990, before taking on other issues.

The fourth check to immigration is nativism or racism, a motive that often lies beneath the surface of the opposition's arguments.

Rita Simon of American University, who has studied the history of public opinion toward immigrants, has found that the arguments against immigration have remained eerily identical. In the first half of the nineteenth century, Irish immigrants in New York and Boston were seen as the unassimilable possessors of all bad qualities. One newspaper wrote: "America has become the sewer into which the pollutions of European jails are emptied." Another asked: "Have we not a right to protect ourselves against the ravenous dregs of anarchy and crime, the tainted swarms of pauperism and vice Europe shakes on our shores from her diseased robes?"

"Immigrants pay more than their share of taxes."

The 1884 platform of the Democratic party stated its opposition to the "importation of foreign labor or the admission of servile races unfitted by habit, training, religion or kindred for absorption into the great body of our people or for the citizenship which our laws confer."

Francis Walker, Commissioner General of the Immigration Service, wrote in 1896:

The question today is . . . protecting the American rate of wages, the American standard of living, and the quality of American citizenship from degradation through the tumultuous access of vast throngs of ignorant and brutalized peasantry from the countries of Eastern and Southern Europe.

In the 1920s the *Saturday Evening Post* also directed fear and hatred at the "new immigrants" from Southern and Eastern Europe: "More than a third of them cannot read and write; generally speaking they have been very difficult to assimilate. . . . They

> *"The beneficial impact of immigration upon productivity is likely to dwarf all other effects."*

have been hot beds of dissent, unrest, sedition and anarchy."

Although statements like these are no longer acceptable in public, many people still privately sympathize with such views. One can see the traces in nativist codewords that accuse immigrants of "disturbing national homogeneity" and "changing our national culture.". . .

Simply Take More In

Political power and economic well-being are intimately related; a nation's international standing is heavily influenced by its economic situation. And today the future of any country—especially of a major country that is in the vanguard with respect to production and living standards—depends entirely on its progress in knowledge, skill, and productivity. This is more true now than in the past, because technology changes more rapidly than in earlier times. Even a single invention can speedily alter a country's economic or military future—consider, for example, the atom bomb or the computer—as no invention could in the past, even the invention of the gun. That's why immigration safely, cheaply, and surely provides the U.S. with perhaps the greatest opportunity that a country has ever had to surpass its political rivals.

And the best way for the U.S. to boost its rate of technological advance, and to raise its standard of living, is simply to take in more immigrants. To that end, I would suggest that the number of visas be increased by half a million per year for three years. If no major problems arise with that total (and there is no reason to expect a problem, since even another one or two million immigrants a year would still give us an admissions rate lower than we successfully coped with in earlier times, when assimilation was more difficult), then we should boost the number by another half-million, and so on, until unexpected problems arise.

Immigration policy presents the U.S. with an opportunity like the one that faced the Brooklyn Dodgers in 1947, before blacks played baseball on any major-league team. Signing Jackie Robinson and then Roy Campanella, at the price of antagonizing some players and club owners, put the Dodgers way ahead of the pack. In the case of immigration, unlike baseball, no other "team" can duplicate our feat, because immigrants mainly want to come here. All we need is the vision, guts, and ambition of Dodger general manager Branch Rickey. (A bit of his religious zeal mixed in would do no harm.)

Can we see our national interest clearly enough to reject unfounded beliefs that some groups will lose jobs to immigrants, and to surmount the racism that remains in our society? Or will we pay a heavy price in slower growth and lessened efficiency for maintaining our prejudices and pandering to the supposed interests of groups—organized labor, environmentalists, and others—whose misguided wishes will not benefit even them in the long run?

Bibliography

Books

Lawrence Auster   *The Path to National Suicide: An Essay on Immigration and Multiculturalism.* Monterey, VA: American Immigration Control Foundation, 1990.

Frank D. Bean, George Vernez, and Charles B. Keely   *Opening and Closing the Doors: Evaluating Immigration Reform and Control.* Lanham, MD: University Press of America, 1989.

George J. Borjas   *Friends or Strangers: The Impact of Immigration on the U.S. Economy.* New York: Basic Books, 1990.

Leon Bouvier   *Peaceful Invasions: Immigration and Changing America.* Lanham, MD: University Press of America, 1992.

Vernon M. Briggs Jr.   *Mass Immigration and the National Interest.* Armonk, NY: M.E. Sharpe, 1992.

David Carliner et al.   *The Rights of Aliens and Refugees.* 2d ed. Carbondale: Southern Illinois University Press, 1990.

Leo R. Chavez   *Shadowed Lives: Undocumented Immigrants in American Society.* Orlando, FL: Harcourt Brace Jovanovich, 1992.

Linda Chavez   *Out of the Barrio: Toward a New Politics of Hispanic Assimilation.* New York: Basic Books, 1991.

Ted Conover   *Coyotes: A Journey Through the Secret World of America's Illegal Aliens.* New York: Vintage Books, 1987.

Wayne A. Cornelius, ed.   *The Changing Role of Mexican Labor in the U.S. Economy.* La Jolla, CA: Center for U.S.-Mexican Studies, 1989.

Sergio Díaz-Briquets and Sidney Weintraub, eds.   *The Effects of Receiving Country Policies on Migration Flows.* Boulder, CO: Westview Press, 1991.

Robert W. Fox and Ira H. Mehlman   *Crowding Out the Future: World Population Growth, U.S. Immigration, and Pressures on Natural Resources.* Washington, DC: Federation for American Immigration Reform, 1992.

Lindsey Grant   *Elephants in the Volkswagen: Facing the Tough Questions About Our Overcrowded Country.* New York: W.H. Freeman and Company, 1992.

David M. Heer   *Undocumented Mexicans in the United States.* New York: Cambridge University Press, 1990.

208

Daniel James	*Illegal Immigration: An Unfolding Crisis*. Lanham, MD: University Press of America, 1991.
Dan Lacey	*The Essential Immigrant*. New York: Hippocrene Books, 1990.
Eugene McCarthy	*A Colony of the World: The United States Today*. New York: Hippocrene Books, 1992.
Thomas Muller	*Immigrants and the American City*. New York: New York University Press, 1993.
Carole Nagengast, Rodolfo Stavenhagen, and Michael Kearney	*Human Rights and Indigenous Workers: The Mixtecs in Mexico and the United States*. La Jolla, CA: Center for U.S.-Mexican Studies, 1992.
Francisco L. Rivera-Batiz, Selig L. Sechzer, and Ira N. Gang, eds.	*U.S. Immigration Policy Reform in the 1980s: A Preliminary Assessment*. New York: Praeger, 1991.
Julian L. Simon	*The Economic Consequences of Immigration*. Cambridge, MA: Basil Blackwell, 1989.
Dan Stein, ed.	*Immigration 2000: The Century of the New American Sweatshop*. Washington, DC: Federation for American Immigration Control, 1992.
John Vinson	*Immigration Out of Control: The Interests Against America*. Monterey, VA: American Immigration Control Foundation, 1992.
Ben J. Wattenberg	*The First Universal Nation*. New York: Maxwell Macmillan International, 1991.
Daniel Wolf	*Undocumented Aliens and Crime*. La Jolla, CA: Center for U.S.-Mexican Studies, 1988.

Periodicals

Charlotte Allen	"America: Restricted Territory," *Insight*, March 16, 1992.
American Friends Service Committee	*Sealing Our Borders: The Human Toll*. Third Report of the Immigration Law Enforcement Monitoring Project, February 1992. Available from 1501 Cherry St., Philadelphia, PA 19102.
Gary S. Becker	"An Open Door for Immigrants—the Auction," *The Wall Street Journal*, October 14, 1992.
Leon F. Bouvier and John L. Martin	"Four Hundred Million Americans! The Latest Census Bureau Projections," *Center for Immigration Studies Backgrounder*, January 1993. Available from 1815 H St. NW, Suite 1010, Washington, DC 20006-3604.
Peter Brimelow	"Time to Rethink Immigration?" *National Review*, June 22, 1992.
Patrick Buchanan	"America Has a Right to Preserve Its Identity," *Conservative Chronicle*, August 28, 1991. Available from PO Box 29, Hampton, IA 50441.

Bibliography

Linda Chavez	"Just Say Latino," *The New Republic*, March 22, 1993.
Nick Ervin	"Facing the Immigration Issue," *Hi Sierran*, October 1992. Available from the Sierra Club, 3820 Ray St., San Diego, CA 92104-3623.
Richard Estrada	"The Impact of Immigration on Hispanic-Americans," *Chronicles*, July 1991. Available from PO Box 800, Mount Morris, IL 61054.
David Gergen	"A Dreadful Mess at the INS," *U.S. News & World Report*, March 22, 1993.
Paul Glastris	"Immigration Crackdown," *U.S. News & World Report*, June 21, 1993.
Beatriz Johnston Hernandez	"Running the Gauntlet," *The New Internationalist*, September 1991.
Donald L. Huddle	"Immigration, Jobs, and Wages: The Misuses of Econometrics," *The NPG Forum*, April 1992. Available from Negative Population Growth, Inc., PO Box 1206, Teaneck, NJ 07666-1206.
Daniel James	"Bar the Door," *The New York Times*, July 25, 1992.
Michael Kinsley	"Gatecrashers," *The New Republic*, December 28, 1992.
Weston Kosova	"The INS Mess," *The New Republic*, April 13, 1992.
Richard Lacayo	"Give Me Your Rich, Your Lucky . . . ," *Time*, October 14, 1991.
Melinda Liu et al.	"The New Slave Trade," *Newsweek*, June 21, 1993.
Michael J. Mandel et al.	"The Immigrants: How They're Helping to Revitalize the U.S. Economy," *Business Week*, July 13, 1992.
Elizabeth Martinez	"When No Dogs or Mexicans Are Allowed . . . ," *Z Magazine*, January 1991.
Jack Miles	"Blacks vs. Browns," *The Atlantic*, October 1992.
Stephen Moore	"Immigration Policy: Open Minds on Open Borders," *Business and Society Review*, Spring 1991.
Cecilia Muñoz	"Immigration Policy: A Tricky Business," *NACLA Report on the Americas*, May 1993.
NACLA Report on the Americas	"Coming North," July 1992. Special issue on immigration.
Debbie Nathan	"A Death on the Border," *The Progressive*, March 1993.
Jeffrey Rosen	"Good Help," *The New Republic*, February 15, 1993.
Steve Salerno	"We Call Them Trabajos," *The World & I*, March 1991. Available from 2800 New York Ave., NE, Washington, DC 20002.
Peter H. Schuck and Rogers M. Smith	"Consensual Citizenship," *Chronicles*, July 1992.

David Simcox   "Effective Enforcement of Employer Sanctions." Testimony before the Senate Committee on the Judiciary, Subcommittee on Immigration and Refugee Affairs, April 10, 1992. Available from the Center for Immigration Studies, 1815 H St. NW, Suite 1010, Washington, DC 20006-3604.

David Simcox   "The Environmental Risks of Mass Immigration," *Scope*, Fall 1992. Available from the Center for Immigration Studies.

Julian L. Simon et al.   "Why Control the Borders?" *National Review*, February 1, 1993. (Several contributors debate the pros and cons of immigration.)

Trisha Smith   "Tired of Waiting: Day Laborers Organize Against Drive-By Jobs," *Third Force*, March/April 1993. Available from Center for Third World Organizing, 1218 E. 21st St., Oakland, CA 94606.

Deborah Sontag   "Rudeness Goes Public: Calls to Restrict Immigration Come from Many Quarters," *The New York Times*, December 13, 1992.

Dan Stein   "Making Sense of America's Refugee Policy," *USA Today*, September 1992.

George Sunderland   "Invasion USA: The Sequel," *Conservative Review*, April 1992. Available from 1307 Dolley Madison Blvd., Suite 4A, McLean, VA 22101.

Cathi Tactaquin   "'Nannygate' or 'Sanctionsgate?'" *Crossroads*, March 1993.

John Tanton and Wayne Lutton   "Welfare Costs for Immigrants," *The Social Contract*, Fall 1992.

United States General Accounting Office   "IRCA-Related Discrimination." Testimony before the Senate Committee on the Judiciary, Subcommittee on Immigration and Refugee Affairs, April 3, 1992. Available from PO Box 6015, Gaithersburg, MD 20877.

The Village Voice   "Alien Nation," February 2, 1993. Available from 36 Cooper Square, New York, NY 10003.

Tim Weiner   "Pleas for Asylum Inundate System for Immigration," *The New York Times*, April 25, 1993.

Martin Morse Wooster   "Coming to America," *Reason*, November 1991.

Organizations to Contact

The editors have compiled the following list of organizations that are concerned with the issues debated in this book. All of them have publications or information available for interested readers. The descriptions are derived from materials provided by the organizations. This list was compiled at the date of publication. Names, addresses, and phone numbers of organizations are subject to change.

American Civil Liberties Union (ACLU)
132 W. 43d St.
New York, NY 10036
(212) 944-9800
(212) 921-7916 (fax)

The ACLU is a national organization that champions the rights found in the Declaration of Independence and the U.S. Constitution. The ACLU Immigrants' Rights Project works with refugees and immigrants facing deportation, and with immigrants in the workplace. It has published reports, position papers, and a book, *The Rights of Aliens and Refugees*, that details what freedoms immigrants and refugees have under the U.S. Constitution.

American Friends Service Committee (AFSC)
1501 Cherry St.
Philadelphia, PA 19102
(215) 241-7000

The AFSC is a Quaker organization that attempts to relieve human suffering and find new approaches to world peace and social justice through nonviolence. It lobbies against what it believes to be unfair immigration laws, especially sanctions criminalizing the employment of illegal immigrants. It has published *Sealing Our Borders: The Human Toll*, a report documenting human rights violations committed by law enforcement agents against immigrants.

American Immigration Control Foundation (AICF)
PO Box 525
Monterey, VA 24465
(703) 468-2022
(703) 468-2024 (fax)

AICF is an independent research and education organization that believes massive immigration, especially illegal immigration, is harming America. It calls for an end to illegal immigration and for stricter controls on legal immigration. The foundation publishes the monthly newsletter *Border Watch* and two pamphlets: John Vinson's *Immigration Out of Control*, and Lawrence Auster's *The Path to National Suicide: An Essay on Immigration and Multiculturalism*.

American Immigration Lawyers Association (AILA)
1400 I St. NW
Washington, DC 20005
(202) 371-9377

AILA is a professional association of lawyers who work in the field of immigration and nationality law. It publishes the *AILA Immigration Journal* and compiles and distributes a continuously updated bibliography of government and private documents on immigration laws and regulations.

Americans for Immigration Control (AIC)
717 Second St. NE, Suite 307
Washington, DC 20002
(202) 543-3719

AIC is a lobbying organization that works to influence Congress to adopt legal reforms that would reduce U.S. immigration. It calls for increased funding for the U.S. Border Patrol and the deployment of military forces to prevent illegal immigration. It also supports sanctions against employers who hire illegal immigrants and opposes amnesty for such immigrants. AIC offers articles and brochures stating its position on immigration.

Americas Watch (AW)
485 Fifth Ave.
New York, NY 10017
(212) 972-8400
(212) 972-0905 (fax)

AW, a division of Human Rights Watch, is an organization that promotes human rights, especially for Latin Americans. It publicizes human rights violations and encourages international protests against governments responsible for them. AW has published *Brutality Unchecked: Human Rights Abuses Along the U.S. Border with Mexico*.

The Brookings Institution
1775 Massachusetts Ave. NW
Washington, DC 20036
(202) 797-6000
(202) 797-6004 (fax)

The institution, founded in 1927, is a liberal research and education organization that publishes material on economics, government, and foreign policy. It publishes analyses of immigration issues in its quarterly journal, *Brookings Review*, and in various books and reports.

Cato Institute
1000 Massachusetts Ave. NW
Washington, DC 20001
(202) 546-0200
(202) 546-0728 (fax)

The institute is a libertarian public policy research foundation dedicated to stimulating policy debate. It believes immigration is good for the U.S. economy and favors easing immigration restrictions. As well as various articles on immigration, the institute has published Julian L. Simon's book *The Economic Consequences of Immigration*.

Center for Immigrants Rights (CIR)
48 St. Mark's Pl., 4th Fl.
New York, NY 10003
(212) 505-6890

The center offers immigrants information concerning their rights. It provides legal support, advocacy, and assistance to immigrants and strives to influence immigration policy. The center publishes fact sheets on immigrant rights and immigration law and the quarterly newsletter *CIR Report*.

Center for Immigration Studies
1815 H St. NW, Suite 101
Washington, DC 20006-3604
(202) 466-8185

The center studies the effects of immigration on the economic, social, demographic, and environmental conditions in the United States. It believes that the large number of recent immigrants has become a burden on America and favors reforming immigration laws to make them consistent with U.S. interests. The center publishes reports, position papers, and the quarterly journal *Scope*.

El Rescate
2675 W. Olympic Blvd.
Los Angeles, CA 90006
(213) 387-3284

El Rescate provides free legal and social services to Central American refugees. It is involved in federal litigation to uphold the constitutional rights of refugees and illegal immigrants. It compiles and distributes articles and information and publishes the newsletter *El Rescate*.

Federation for American Immigration Reform (FAIR)
1666 Connecticut Ave. NW, Suite 400
Washington, DC 20009
(202) 328-7004
(202) 387-3447 (fax)

FAIR works to stop illegal immigration and to limit legal immigration. It believes that the growing flood of immigrants into the United States causes higher unemployment and taxes social services. FAIR has published many reports and position papers, including *Ten Steps to Securing America's Borders* and *Immigration 2000: The Century of the New American Sweatshop*.

Foundation for Economic Education, Inc. (FEE)
30 S. Broadway
Irvington, NY 10533
(914) 591-7230
(914) 591-8910 (fax)

FEE publishes information and research in support of capitalism, free trade, and limited government. It occasionally publishes articles opposing government restrictions on immigration in its monthly magazine the *Freeman*.

214

The Heritage Foundation
214 Massachusetts Ave. NE
Washington, DC 20002
(202) 546-4400

The foundation is a conservative public policy research institute. It has published articles pertaining to immigration in its *Backgrounder* series and in its quarterly journal, *Policy Review*.

National Alliance Against Racist and Political Repression (NAARPR)
11 John St., Rm. 702
New York, NY 10038
(212) 406-3330
(212) 406-3542 (fax)

NAARPR is a coalition of political, labor, church, civic, student, and community organizations that oppose the many forms of human rights repression in the United States. It seeks to end the harassment and deportation of illegal immigrant workers. The alliance publishes pamphlets and a quarterly newsletter, *The Organizer*.

National Coalition of Advocates for Students (NCAS)
100 Boylston St., Suite 737
Boston, MA 02116-4610
(617) 357-8507
(617) 357-9549 (fax)

NCAS is a national network of child advocacy organizations that work on public school issues. Through its Immigrant Student Program it works to ensure that immigrants are given sufficient and appropriate education. The coalition has published two book-length reports: *New Voices: Immigrant Students in U.S. Public Schools* and *Immigrant Students: Their Legal Right of Access to Public Schools*.

National Council of La Raza (NCLR)
810 First St. NW, Suite 300
Washington, DC 20002
(202) 289-1380
(202) 289-8173 (fax)

NCLR is a national organization that seeks to improve opportunities for Americans of Hispanic descent. It conducts research on many issues, including immigration, and opposes restrictive immigration laws. The council publishes and distributes congressional testimony and reports, including *Unfinished Business: The Immigration Control and Reform Act of 1986* and *Unlocking the Golden Door: Hispanics and the Citizenship Process*.

The National Network for Immigrant and Refugee Rights
310 Eighth St., Ste. 307
Oakland, CA 94607
(510) 465-1984
(510) 465-7548 (fax)

The network includes community, church, labor, and legal groups committed to the cause of equal rights for all immigrants. These groups work to end discrimination and unfair treatment of illegal immigrants and refugees. The network aims to strengthen and coordinate educational efforts among immigration advocates nationwide. It publishes a monthly newsletter, *Network News*.

Negative Population Growth, Inc. (NPG)
PO Box 1206
Teaneck, NJ 07666-1206
(201) 837-3555
(201) 837-0270 (fax)

NPG believes that world population must be reduced and that the United States is already overpopulated. It calls for an end to illegal immigration and an annual cap on legal immigration of 200,000 people. This would achieve "zero net migration" because 200,000 people exit the country each year, according to NPG. NPG frequently publishes position papers on population and immigration in its *NPG Forum*.

The Rockford Institute
934 N. Main St.
Rockford, IL 61103-7061
(815) 964-5053
(815) 965-1827 (fax)

The institute is a conservative research center that studies capitalism, religion, and liberty. It has published numerous articles questioning immigration and legalization policies in its monthly magazine *Chronicles*.

United States General Accounting Office (GAO)
441 G St. NW
Washington, DC 20548
(202) 275-2812

The GAO is the investigative arm of the U.S. Congress and is charged with examining all matters related to the receipt and disbursement of public funds. It frequently publishes reports evaluating the effectiveness of U.S. immigration policies.

Index

Chinese, 20
Chin Wing, 18, 45
Chiswick, Barry, 86, 124
Chronicles, 101
Clinton, Bill, 55, 89
Coalition for Freedom, 25
Coalition for Immigration and Refugee Rights
  and Services, 103, 145
Coalition for Immigration Law Enforcement
  (C-FILE), 100
Coffey, Ruth, 100
colonias, 27
Commission for the Study of International
  Migration and Cooperative Economic
  Development, 181
Commission on Agricultural Workers, 196
communities
  black, 50
  border, 26-27, 146
  East Asian, 20
  Mexican-American, 22
Confucianism, 20, 23
Congressional Budget Office, 117
Conlan, Mark Gabrish, 67
Connor, Roger, 113
Conservative Review, 101
Council of Economic Advisers, 204-205
crime, 30, 48, 75-76
  see also organized crime
Customs Service, 25-26

Dalton, Humphrey, 72
Davidian, Ben, 150
Declaration of Independence, 49
DeConcini, Dennis, 28-29
democracy, 48-49
Democratic party, 87, 89, 205
Department of Commerce, 88
Department of Education, 21, 76, 95
Department of Justice, 26, 77, 151
Department of Labor, 30
de Tocqueville Institute, 205
Detroit, 191
Diamond, Sara, 97
Diaz, Randy, 136
Díaz-Briquets, Sergio, 181
Dixon, Richard P., 83
Doe v. Plyler, 82, 93-97
Donnell, William C., 41
Drug Enforcement Administration, 26
Duke, David, 62, 65
Duleep, Harriet, 202
Dunn, Robert N., Jr., 87
Durant, Will, 169

East Wood, 41, 43, 45
Economic Consequences of Immigration, The,
  19, 60
economic development, 194-195
  education and, 186-187

immigration and, 19, 181-195, 204-206
education, 76-77, 93-97
  bilingual, 22-23
  cost of, 95-97
  school registration documents and, 94-95
Egypt, 91
Ehrlich, Anne, 102
Ehrlich, Paul E., 72-73, 102
Emergency Immigrant Education Program, 95
employment, 107-112
  employer sanctions, 28-29, 47, 126, 128-131,
    139-140, 145-148, 161
  wages and, 87-88, 111-112, 125
Equal Rights Advocates, 145
Espenshade, Thomas J., 84, 115
Esperanza Para Los Niños, 155
Estrada, Gilbert, 135

Fair Labor Standards Act (FLSA), 145
Falasco, Dee, 118-119
family structure, 49-51
  Asian, 51
  Hispanic, 51-52
Farrell, Christopher, 69
Fauntroy, Walter, 47
FBI (Federal Bureau of Investigation), 90-91,
  154
Federal Civil Rights Commission, 98
Federation for American Immigration Reform
  (FAIR), 47, 64, 67, 70, 102, 115, 117-119, 143,
  157-158, 200, 205
female-headed households, 52
Fermi, Enrico, 204
Ferro, Benedict, 92
fertility rate, 17
Fields, Joe, 100
Flores, Augustine Pérez, 154-155
Foda, Forag, 91
food stamps, 81, 116
Forbes, 47, 159
Forked Tongue, 23
Fourteenth Amendment, 94
Franklin, Benjamin, 55
Free School Lunch Program, 95
Fuchs, Jonathon, 37
Fukuyama, Francis, 46

Gallegly, Elton, 78, 100, 175-176
Garcia, Arnoldo, 63
Garcia, Richard, 62
Gates, Daryl, 99
General Accounting Office, 129-130, 147-148
Geyer, Georgie Anne, 173
Gigot, Paul, 47
Gilmartin, Kevin M., 134
Ginn, Leslie, 153-154
global competitiveness, 19
Golini, Antonia, 73
Gonzalez, Roland, 132
Graham, Otis, 19, 74

Index